THE
ESSENTIAL

RUSSELL MARTIN

 SAY YES QUICKLY BOOKS

7715 East Highland Avenue

Scottsdale, Arizona 85251 USA

The excerpts of novels and narrative nonfiction books included in this anthology were first published in hardcover by Stewart, Tabori & Chang; Henry Holt & Company; The Linden Press at Simon & Schuster; Dutton and Broadway Books, both imprints of Penguin Random House, and the University of New Mexico Press. Subsequent paperback editions were released by numerous publishers. "Driving My Father Home" was first published in Denver's *5280 Magazine,* "The End of Days" was first published in the *San Juan Mountain Journal*, and three other short pieces were first published at Substack.

Cover photograph by Sher Novak.

ISBN: 979-8-9898660-3-8

First paperback edition.

ALSO BY RUSSELL MARTIN

Cowboy
Matters Gray and White
The Color Orange
Beautiful Islands, a novel
A Story That Stands Like a Dam
Out of Silence
Beethoven's Hair
Picasso's War
The Sorrow of Archaeology, a novel
Daily Bread, a novella

THE
ESSENTIAL
RUSSELL
MARTIN

≋

Excerpts from Award-
Winning Novels, Narrative
Nonfiction Books, and
Short-Form Pieces that
Span Forty Years

≋

for Sher, with love

We are the storytelling species, Homo once-upon-a-tempus, our brains built for seeking out relationships among things, for creating cerebral sorts of order, and for sensing the rudiments of narrative structure: how it was in the beginning, the middle, and at the end. — Russell Martin

Contents

INTRODUCTION

S ome time ago, during the run of years when several
of my books were first published by Henry Holt &
Company, I was blessed to be edited by the legendary Marian
Wood. It was Marian, now deceased, who first raised the
possibility of publishing a collection of my work someday, a
Russell Martin reader, so to speak. She believed such a book
could find readers, and I was flattered that she thought I
could write enough good stuff over time to be worthy one
day of the publishing equivalent of a greatest hits album.

But then Marian made the move from Chelsea to Soho,
from Holt to Putnam and the larger Penguin empire, and I
moved to Salt Lake City, Denver, Los Angeles, Ojai, Ventu-
ra, and finally to Scottsdale, where I will remain. These days
I'm getting old and wrinkled in the desert heat, and it's from
this place that I have greatly enjoyed curating this collection
of book excerpts, novel excerpts, and articles. They aren't
"hits" so much as simple examples of the kind of work I've
done since I first wrote professionally for weekly newspapers
in Telluride, Colorado, half a century ago, back when both
Telluride and I were filled with uncertainty and excitement
about what the future would hold.

I was writing for regional and national magazines in the early 1980s when a then-unknown caterer named Martha Stewart read an article of mine in the *New York Times Magazine* one Sunday and suggested to her then-husband Andy Stewart that I might be a good choice to write the book he wanted to publish about the mystique and mythology of the American cowboy. Andy called me; I did my best to remain calm as I said, sure, I'd be pleased to meet and talk with him, and I've mostly written books during the forty years since.

I've made a few documentary films—collaborative ventures I've loved—and I have ghostwritten books for others, but books of my own have been my stock in trade. Without question, the ghostwriting connected me to people and places I otherwise wouldn't have encountered, and it has engendered some lasting friendships. But ghostwriting—like kissing your sister, as they say—kind of doesn't count. I've written books for astronauts, politicians, businesspeople, surgeons, actors, and film directors, and I'm grateful to have had the opportunities and the employment. But writing for me has always been *hard*, and writing for others has proven the hardest of all. I've always enjoyed pretending I was someone else for a bit, but in the end, the subjects *I* have chosen and the words with which *I* wrote about them have always been the most rewarding work I've done at my desk.

Collected here are three excerpts from novels and a novella, five articles, and excerpts from seven narrative nonfiction books—all of them published between the years 1983 and 2022. As I try to determine if they contain common threads—similar subjects or themes or styles—I'm struck that I have typed a good bit about the work people choose to do and how they go about it. I've written about people with disabilities a number of times, and I've been lured by the inspired work of artists—painters, musicians, writers—who have achieved extraordinary creative heights. Both Europe and the New World have captured my attention, and I've been as interested in history as in the present moment, I know. I've written about death a few times, and once I wrote about the young men, most of them actually still boys, who forged a football team that had a transcendent season.

It was Marian Wood, I remember, who first cautioned me that in choosing an entirely new subject virtually every time I began a new book, I ran the risk of never building a legion of readers. I thought about that, and I knew she was right, but for some reason—likely because the world in all its varieties and complexities simply seemed so enticing—I didn't heed her warning.

So, this collection roams widely. I'm proud of that, even though perhaps I shouldn't be, grateful for the range and reach of what's here. But most of all, I feel lucky—fortunate to have been able to listen, watch, and pay some attention, and then to sit down to try to find words with which to spin these stories.

I've been awfully lucky, yes.

Russell Martin
Scottsdale, Arizona, USA
March 2024

DRIVING MY FATHER HOME

It was the early autumn of 1968, that year in which so much of the world seemed to have come unmoored from its moral shore, and I was en route to Barcelona—a sixteen-year-old bound for a school-year year abroad saying goodbye to his family at Denver's old Stapleton airport. While we waited for my flight, we stood for a time in the warm September sun on a rooftop observation deck, all of us finding those moments a little awkward, I remember, watching a succession of propellered airplanes arrive and depart among the jets and saying only a little. My father—tall, self-possessed, his hair worn in a flat-top in those days—was particularly quiet, which was his lifelong way, and many years later I was surprised when my mother told me that after he rather stiffly had shaken my hand and watched me recede from sight down a jetway, he had begun to cry. Perhaps they simply were tears mixed of pride and hope, but I suspect he also observed how very frightened I was to be heading alone out into a world where he would not be by my side.

It's certain that my father cried a few more times in his life—on the day his mother died, on the day when a grandson was stillborn—but as far as I know, he cried only once more in a context that had something to do with me. Within days of that second and final occasion, in the spring of this year, by chance I was scheduled to fly to Barcelona again—this time to spend two months at work in a city I still love decades later—but my father clearly was living his last days, and the question of whether it was the right time to leave for Europe was one I necessarily attended to constantly.

My father had been ill for a number of years—a lifetime of smoking had made the essential act of breathing a difficult and always-anxious struggle for him—and in the five months since Thanksgiving he had been hospitalized seven times in Lake Havasu City, Arizona, the town on the California border where London Bridge has been reborn in an unlikely desert setting and where he and my mother spent each winter. I had seen him twice during that time, and his doctors repeatedly had made it clear to him and to all of us that although his life could not endure too long, it was impossible to predict when his last breath would come. His own deep hope was to be able to return to Cortez, the town in southwestern Colorado that had been his home throughout his life—to the house he had built and lived in for fifty years—before he died, but by now his condition had worsened enough that it was difficult to imagine him surviving an eight-hour journey in a car, and his continuous need for augmented oxygen and the myriad complexities of flying him home made that option unthinkable. A further complication was the fact that he had been hospitalized yet again, and his physicians—although mindful of his desire to return to Colorado—argued that he was far too ill to attempt the trip, implying without being brave enough to tell him directly that he might well die en route.

As do so many spouses in similar circumstances, my mother struggled to find a way to attend to both the needs of my father's body and those of his still-strong spirit until one morning the way simply was clear to her, and she reached me by telephone in Denver with a resolve that had hugely brightened her outlook. Could Lydia, my life-mate, and I fly to Arizona; could we get there soon and drive my father to Cortez? Could we help her negotiate a path through a labyrinthine medical bureaucracy that would allow him to leave the hospital against his doctors' orders?

When Lydia and I arrived the following morning and my mother met us at the airport, she reported—as if to collectively assure us that we *were* doing the right thing—that when she had told my father, lying still and wordlessly in his hospital bed, that I was on my way and that *somehow* we would get him home, he had cried again. This time, however, I suspect the tears came from his own fears—rather than out of a parental concern for mine—and this time the journey at hand was simply a final trip to an old man's truest and safest home.

We arrived at the hospital at ten o'clock that morning, but it was three in the afternoon before we had met with and assured a succession of nurses, therapists, physicians, and administrators that we knew we were acting against their recommendations, and my father had signed documents attesting to that fact, relieving the hospital of any liability, should his condition worsen. At last I pulled my parents' car up to the door where a none-too-acquiescent nurse had delivered him in a wheelchair, dressed in pajamas now instead of a hospital gown. He appeared particularly fragile as he squinted against the bright desert sun; he had grown terribly thin except that both his belly and his feet now were shockingly swollen, and his once-thick hair had begun to fall out in distressing clumps.

Getting him transferred and comfortably seated in the car took long and worry-filled minutes, then I drove slowly the few blocks to the condominium where he would spend a final night in Arizona. He was hugely unsteady on his feet, and from behind I wrapped my arms around his chest and lifted him up each step that led to the second-floor condo, then he collapsed into his leather easy chair—his depression at his helplessness and his dying waxing over him like a pall—until it was time to eat the supper of barbecued ribs he had requested, which, together with a stiff scotch, markedly lifted his spirits.

We rented a small U-Haul trailer and filled it with my parents' winter belongings, careful not to let my father observe that our packing of all of his things proved the likelihood that he would not return to a place he had grown very fond of over the preceding decade. Then, shortly after dawn the following morning, three of us worked quickly to close up the condo, load a substantial supply of oxygen bottles, and ready my father for the long day ahead before we descended the stairs—slowly, laboriously, his breathing and what little strength he had terribly taxed by the effort—then we drove out of town with the quietest kind of ceremony, the desert air sweet and still cool, the craggy summits of the *picachos* glowing orange in the early light.

It was a measure of the way in which my father planned each day of his life as meticulously as he could that shortly before our departure he asked my mother to call a lifelong friend and retired mortician to ask what, in fact, we should do if he were to die during the drive. The advice we received, and which my father responded to without emotion, was for us to do nothing other than continue on to Colorado—certainly not to stop or alert any authorities—and the friend went so far as to suggest that anyone inquiring might be told that my father was simply, and very soundly, asleep.

And he did sleep during much of the drive, his gentle snoring a kind of assurance to the three of us that all was temporarily well, and I realized as I drove through the encircling desert that in half a century of living I'd never really been able to do anything for my father before. I'd never truly come to his aid in the way it seemed certain that I was now—doing a very small thing aimed at allowing him to be in the place where he chose to be on the day his difficult breaths and his eighty-one years were done. Well into my middle age, the tables had turned at last, and my deep sadness at his demise was mitigated by a satisfying kind of pleasure I took in being needed at that moment by this often-silent man.

C laude Vincent Martin, my father, had grown up on a dryland farm at the far western edge of the bowl-shaped valley surrounding Cortez, his own parents poor enough that none of the early photographs of him show him wearing shoes. But somehow—and in a way that was echoed by so many men of his generation—he was able over the span of his years to dramatically alter those early circumstances and to make a life for himself and his family that was nothing less than a remarkable achievement. It was his lifelong focus on planning the thing that would happen next that surely helped him survive the Allied forces' march across France in 1945, and it was his understanding that he ultimately could offer his children nothing more important than opportunities to grow that allowed him to readily accept significant economic sacrifices in order to send me to Spain and give all three of his children the best possible experiences in college. From early jobs shining shoes, candling eggs, and stacking feed sacks, he eventually made his way to the ownership of an insurance business that bore his name, one with branches in several neighboring towns, as well as a position as a director of a local bank he valued highly enough that he faithfully attended meetings by conference call during his winter sojourns in Arizona.

Yet for eighty-one years there was something in his quiet nature, in his lifelong employment of very few words, that made him essentially enigmatic, that made people want to know more of him, and for me, his only son, always there was a desire for deeper connection, for a way to *feel* a direct link between his life and mine, for proof that he loved this boy whom he had wrought, this man who was so different from him in so many ways. But we get the lives—and the parents—that are given to us, and my father always had proven to me that I could accomplish anything I chose to, even if it remained a bit of a struggle for him to give me an all-embracing hug. I know I thanked him for a mountain of gifts to me, and I wanted to believe that even in my most interior place there was nothing I held against him.

And the wonder at the end of his days was that in a way I cannot yet entirely comprehend, there *was* emotional linkage at last, a connection that quietly accompanied us in that final spring of his life as I did what I could to get him home. At those times when I would wrap my arms around a chest stripped of all its muscle to lift him from a chair; when he would hold my hand tightly with his own to steady himself as he took a few uncertain steps; when he would turn to me repeatedly from the passenger seat of the car on the day of our long drive to ask in a raspy whisper, "How're we doing?" and I would nod that all was well, I know I felt closer to him than ever before in my life—not because he was dying, but because he was alive, and he was vulnerable, and I'm vulnerable so often as well, and at last we seemed made of the same stuff.

D riving east on Interstate 40, we wound through the sprawling town of Kingman then climbed up out of the Sonoran desert. Blooming ocotillos gave way to twist-ed juniper trees, and as we crested the Mogollon Rim, tall ponderosas commanded the view, yet we were shocked to see how many of them—hundreds across the sweep of a single hillside—were dying, their needles a tawny brown instead of deep green, the trees weakened first by drought and then killed by an infestation of beetles. No one mentioned the metaphor, yet neither was it lost on any of us, my father least of all, as we looked out at the devastation, at how death stood starkly in the foreground that morning, how much it commanded the day.

But my father's appetite continued to attest to his ongoing life, and he was eager on the northern outskirts of Flagstaff to stop at a roadhouse called Mary's Café that he and my mother made a regular stopping point, the kind of place where men with their names tooled onto their belts nurse cups of black coffee all morning, where waitresses who've led hard lives call each of their customers "Hon." It took some time to get my father inside and securely settled in a booth, and my mother was very distressed when she checked to see how low his blood-oxygen level had dropped in the effort for him to hobble just thirty feet. But he was hungry nonetheless, and at eleven o'clock he was cheered that we still could order breakfast, and he heartily ate eggs and bacon and biscuits and gravy and then, in response to something our waitress said, utterly astonished us by offering a few bars of an old folk tune called "I Was Born About Ten Thousand Years Ago"—"and there's nothin' in this world that I don't know"—in the deep base voice with which he very seldom sang. Perhaps it was the tempting smell of the cigarette smoke that clouded the café's air; perhaps it was the clatter of plates and cups and its convivial country cadences, but whatever it was, Mary's Café was a remarkable tonic for my father that morning. Although his hand trembled wildly as he lifted each bite of food to his mouth, he also laughed from his belly a couple of times before we departed, and Lydia, my mother, and I exchanged furtive glances as we slowly made our way to the car, agreeing with our hopeful expressions that we just might pull this project off.

An hour later, however, as we crossed the bald-rock and blowsand sweep of the Navajo reservation—at about the spot where the hoodoo rocks rise out of the earth west of Tuba City—my father's breathing grew so quiet and so infrequent that I took my foot off the accelerator and let the car slow, then eased it to the side of the road before the changes in noise and motion roused him and he wanted to know why we were stopping. I had to pee, I told him, which wasn't an entirely manufactured answer, and he decided he would join me outside rather than use the plastic urinal we carried with us, and I remember grinning broadly in the bright sun and insistent wind at the sight we were offering passing cars—an old man in pajamas and his long-haired and barefoot sidekick unabashedly at work watering the Navajo desert.

A spring dust storm blew up as the road wound out of Tsegi Canyon, and by Kayenta it was almost impossible to see, but we pressed on and finally the wind subsided and at last I could point out in the far distance the summit of Ute Mountain—the peak that had been a high and constant touchstone for him, and for me, since each of us was born—and which was landmark evidence that April afternoon that my father was almost home. I tried not to make too much of the accomplishment, but as we descended a small hill and crossed the San Juan River and highway signs announced what otherwise was the subtlest sort of border, I said nonchalantly, "Well, it looks like we've made it to Colorado." A hoarsely spoken "good" was all my father could offer in reply, but there seemed to be unmistakable appreciation in that single word as well.

Driving into Cortez has been a complex thing for me to do for most of my adult life, likely because it's a place I love and am aggrieved by in nearly equal parts, but on that day, I can attest, our arrival was nothing more than a simple satisfaction for me, evidence that we had accomplished what two days before we'd rather quixotically set out to do. The oilfield yards on the south end of town, the used-car lots and the Sonic Drive-In, the snow-clad La Plata mountains hanging high above Main Street in the east, the "Martin Agency" sign on the narrow building near the corner where we turned and drove the final eight blocks to my parents' brick and shingle-roofed house—everything I saw and felt was wonderfully welcome, I suspect, because this time *my* arrival wasn't at issue. This time, my father's return was all there was to consider and be grateful for, and I think I saw Cortez through his eyes that afternoon in ways I never could have before.

Once more it took long and difficult minutes for him to negotiate the short distance from the garage to the chair where he could surrender the day. We exchanged portable oxygen canisters for the "concentrator" whose distinctive hum had filled my parents' house for nearly a decade by now, then began to unpack. My father was deeply tired, and he napped while the three of us scurried around him, but before long he was awake again and alert and obviously more at ease than he'd been in some days. He studied the maple cabinetry and the fireplace he had built back when he remained a robust and constantly creative man, and I was pleased when he said something aloud and with obvious pride about how well they appeared to be aging.

Neighbors kindly supplied us with supper and once more my father ate like someone who had lots of living to do, but he was utterly exhausted soon thereafter and my mother took him to bed. Moments later, I rushed into their bedroom in response to her call for help and found him lying naked on the carpet beside the bed. He had fallen as she tried to dress him in clean pajamas for the night. She was terrified that he had injured himself, but he weakly said he thought he was fine, and I bent down on a knee to pick him up. He had lost so much weight over the course of the winter that I simply cradled all that was left of him in my arms, then got to my feet and lowered him to his bed. My mother was quick to cover him, then he whispered a thank you that sounded both defeated and very sad, and something in tucking him in seemed to speak of the fundamental circularity of things.

I had been a very colicky baby, or so the family folklore goes, and my mother says my father walked miles through that same house with me in his arms on hundreds of repeated nights before at last I would grow comfortable and calm and he finally could lower me to my bed. I don't remember those nights, of course, but I know the recent night when I laid my helpless father in his bed is one whose memory will be clear to me—and important—for a very long time. The turning of tables, the doing—quite literally—for him what he had done countless times for me was sacramental, I think, a simple physical act whose meaning somehow arcs outward and grows large. I know that picking him up and putting him in bed offered as much help to me as it did to him—offering, in my case, the kind of insight all of us depend on to make some sense of our complex lives. And I like to think that half a century ago I played a role that presented a similar kind of meaning-making to him, a man who kept so much inside himself and who seldom used words to sort things out.

My father was deeply depressed on the day Lydia and I said farewell to him, and the words the three of us mustered were brief and simple ones. For him now, the days alternated very predictably between good and bad, between a bit of optimism and a kind of exhausted despair, and it was impossible to know how long into the spring or summer he would live. Still the planner he always had been, he repeatedly asked by telephone about our preparations for the trip to Barcelona, and in part because it didn't feel fair to simply wait for him to die before we departed, we finally made the decision to go as planned, and were very excited. But as we waited for our first flight at Denver International Airport at midday on Monday, May 12, suddenly I grew inexplicably tired. Moments before, I had been full of adrenaline and the lively juice of anticipation, but now I was completely exhausted, my energy spent, and I didn't have a hint of the reason why until two hours later when we reached O'Hare airport in Chicago, where news was waiting for us that my father had died.

His death was quiet, and he was spared the fighting for his final breaths that I know he long had feared, and his family and friends mourned his death and celebrated his life throughout the following week. Then eight days after my father's death, we resumed our trip, and Barcelona was the right place for me to begin to grieve his loss. That visually captivating and wonderfully unconventional city was the first place I lived without him—a city in which I began to move from the paralyzing fear of the unknown toward true delight in the wonderfully unpredictable world at large—and the year I spent there as a sixteen-year old was, without question, the most formative gift he ever gave me. I don't suspect that my father would have become enchanted by Barcelona in the way I long ago was and am once more, but we were rather different, my father and me. Yet I discovered as we drove across Arizona on a wind-swept April day something I wasn't otherwise wise enough to understand.

What a gift of strange and mysterious magnitude it was to learn at last how much he loved me only through *my* efforts to be of assistance to him—helping him struggle to climb inside a car, holding him upright as he so unsteadily made his way to one last smoky café breakfast, simply driving him home, then laying him down for the night that single time before all his nights divinely fused into one.

CONCERTO

P ablo Casals was born thirteen years before the invention of the automobile and died four years after spacecraft first took men to the moon. At twenty-two,
he performed selections from Fauré and Saint-Saëns for
Queen Victoria, and at eighty-five he performed pieces by
Mendelssohn and Schumann for John F. Kennedy. His
ninety-seven years spanned one of the bloodiest eras in human history, and for virtually all his life he remained dedicat-
ed to the freedom of artistic expression and the impassioned
pursuit of justice and peace.

Casals was a man of extraordinary sensitivity and supreme
conviction, a physically unassuming man who utterly captivated people with his presence. He was deeply patriotic
and loved his Spanish homeland of Catalunya more than he
cared for perhaps anything else, but he also believed that love
of country also often tragically blinds people to the true humanity of us all. Throughout his long life, Casals employed
music as a means of urging people everywhere to work toward the highest ideals of humanity, and for fully thirteen
years following the end of World War II—during a time in
which he remained one of the world's most renowned vir-

tuosos—he refused to perform publicly, believing his stark and stubborn silence could speak more eloquently in opposition to war and injustice than could his sonorous and always moving music. His life was deeply emblematic of the joys and sorrows of the twentieth century, and his enduring dedication to peace and justice make him a vital and compelling figure for us to remember once more as a new century see wars and brutal violence swelling ever more menacingly around the world.

C asals had become a world-renowned cellist by the time he returned to his native Catalunya in 1919, determined to slow the pace of his travels, to make a stable home once more, and to pursue the "playing" of the instrument that intrigued him most—the orchestra. But although the city of Barcelona had a wonderful musical tradition, its two orchestras were at best mediocre at the moment; neither had a regular concert schedule, neither rehearsed frequently, and neither was interested in Casals's offer of help.

Despite huge hurdles, more than a little ridicule, and at great cost, Casals patiently created his own orchestra during the ensuing years, the Orquestra Pau Casals, one comprised, he made certain, of musicians who possessed his own passion, indefatigable energy, and the belief that virtually nothing vitally important was impossible to achieve. By the mid-1920s, Casals's orchestra—with him serving as both director and principal conductor—had achieved great renown throughout Europe and, in addition to the demands of the orchestra's regular season, tours, and recording schedule, Casals personally had initiated a series of Sunday morning concerts in which the orchestra, often joined by soloists of international repute, performed free of charge for low-income workers and their families.

In February 1931, Casals's Barcelona orchestra celebrated the formation of the Spanish Republic with a concert that drew 20,000 Barcelonans to hear Beethoven's Ninth Symphony and its concluding hymn of brotherhood, the Ode to Joy. Already a deeply political man, one convinced that democracy and freedom could prevail in Spain and throughout the world, Casals believed the creation of the Republic represented the best hope for true progress in Spain, despite the often-bitter struggles for power of dozens of political parties, labor unions, and associations of anarchists.

For five years, the Republic was both fragile and terribly fractious, and, as it happened, Casals and his orchestra were preparing for another performance of Beethoven's Ninth—this one part of the Barcelona Olympiad that Spaniards were staging in opposition to Hitler's Olympic games in Berlin—when, on July 18, 1936, their rehearsal was interrupted by a messenger who brought Casals an urgent note from the Catalan minister of culture, informing him that the Republic was under attack.

A military insurrection led by General Francisco Franco had spread from Spanish Morocco onto the Spanish mainland, and rebel military officers in collusion with Franco were expected to begin an armed revolt in Barcelona at any moment, the minister of culture's note explained. It urged the musicians to flee for their safety at once, but at Casals suggestion, the assembled musicians completed their rehearsal of the symphony's final movement and performed the Ode to Joy as both a prayer for peace throughout Spain and as a symbol of the certainty that—although some time likely would pass—one day they would be reunited.

More than 75,000 civilians were murdered throughout Catalunya and the rest of Spain in only the first month of a war that endured for three full years, a war in which the fabric of the nation was torn to shreds, and during which the insurgent generals led by Francisco Franco succeeded in taking control of most of the nation's land-mass, but only with the help of tanks, munitions, and the air forces of fascist Germany and Italy. In April 1937, Hitler's Luftwaffe experimented for the first time with the brutal new form of air-warfare it called blitzkrieg, destroying the Basque town of Gernika and killing thousands of innocent townspeople in three hours of unrelenting bombing. Cities throughout Spain—Barcelona among them—were massively damaged by air strikes, and the death toll rose to half a million citizens and soldiers. Casals's life was constantly threatened, and he repeatedly was targeted for assassination by both pro-fascist insurgents on the political right and rabid anarchists and communists on the left.

Nonetheless, Casals refused to go into hiding or to be silent in opposition to the mortal blow the Germans, Italians, and insurgents were attempting to deal to the Republic.

At the end of the radio broadcast of a Barcelona concert in the summer of 1938, Casals pleaded first in English, then in French to the people of Europe's two strongest democracies, as well as the United States: "Do not commit the crime of letting the Spanish Republic be murdered. If you allow Hitler to win in Spain, you will be the next victims of his madness. The war will spread to all Europe, to the whole world! Come to the aid of our people!" But the cellist and conductor's prophetic plea went unheeded, of course. Barcelona fell to the fascists in January 1939, and the dream of Spanish democracy ended soon thereafter. As Franco's tanks rolled into the outskirts of the city, University of Barcelona administrators rushed to bestow an honorary doctorate on much-beloved Pablo Casals—by now as important in his role as a moral leader of his nation as he was as a musician—as their final act before dismantling the university and fleeing for their lives.

Casals was one of hundreds of thousands of Spaniards who made their way by train, automobile, and on foot to the French border, which they hoped to cross in search of asylum. The French government at first refused them, then relented only after the victorious Franco had dismissed out of hand the notion of creating a neutral zone for refugees on the Spanish side of the border. Casals traveled first to Paris, where he presumed he would slowly reestablish himself as both a performer and conductor—although it seemed clearer than ever to him that France also would soon feel the weight of Nazi oppression. But in Paris, he fell into a deep and paralyzing despair: he had spent the fortune he had amassed as a performer on his orchestra and in aid the Republican government; he had exhausted himself in his long and diligent efforts to see both thrive; for three years he had lived in hiding as a hunted man, moving constantly from one friend's house to another, and now his beloved homeland, much of it demolished by war, was in the grasp of a madman. Casals told friends he hoped he could succeed in willing his own death.

At last, those friends persuaded him to leave Paris and travel to Prades, a town at the foot of the Pyrenees in the Catalan-speaking region of far-southern France. Living in a small hotel, Casals began to regain his energy, but his recovery was fueled in largest part by his shocking discovery of the conditions in which his countrymen were forced to live in dozens of concentration camps that lined the Spanish border. In its attempts to appease the Nazis, the French government of Edouard Daladier treated the Spanish refugees as hated communists to which it would never give aid, and Casals was appalled by what he observed at the camps. "The scenes I witnessed might have been from Dante's Inferno," he wrote. "Tens of thousands of men and women and children were herded together like animals, penned in by barbed wire, housed—if one can call it that—in tents and crumbling shacks. There were no sanitation facilities or provisions for medical care. There was little water and barely enough food to keep the inmates from starvation. Though it was winter, they had been provided with no shelter whatsoever—many had burrowed holes in the wet sand to protect themselves from the pelting rains and bitter winds. Scores had perished from exposure, hunger, and disease."

Immediately, Casals initiated a massive relief effort, one spurred by the letters he wrote day and night to individuals, foundations, and news organizations around the world describing the plight of the Spanish Republicans and pleading for funds and supplies to assist them. Although he suffered from terrible headaches and recurring vertigo, Casals made constant trips to the camps himself, ferrying supplies, serving food, and offering what encouragement he could. But soon, living conditions for Casals himself and for the townspeople of Prades became almost as difficult as they were for the inmates of the camps.

Hitler had invaded Poland in September 1939, and by the following summer virtually all of mainland Europe, including France, had fallen to the Nazis. As a known and renowned anti-fascist, Casals was placed under close surveillance at the Prades house he and his friend Joan Alavedra, a Catalan poet, and Avavedra's family shared. Together, they survived on turnips, dried beans, and wild greens, and Casals, in his mid-sixties now, became so weak and slowed by rheumatism that his lifelong habit of playing a Bach suite on his cello at dawn each day became all but impossible, and friends in England and the United States urged Casals to seek safety and medical attention in their countries.

In turn, German army officers regularly pressed Casals to travel to the German fatherland—the birthplace of Bach, Beethoven, Mozart, they reminded him—where, he was assured, he would live in luxury as an honored artist and friend of the Third Reich. But Casals declined repeatedly to move either east or west. He continued to write daily in support of the Spanish refugees, and—at a time when he was physically weakest and the war effort against the Nazis seemed to have terribly stalled—he nonetheless found the will to compose El Pessebre, "The Manger," an oratorio that set to music Alavedra's long poem about the nativity of Jesus. "If the suffering of man was part of that tale," he wrote, "it also spoke of a time when man's long ordeal would be ended and happiness would be his at last."

On the day in September 1944 when the Nazis who now occupied Prades plotted to arrest Casals and "teach him a lesson," he was saved, as he had been repeatedly during the past decade, by the implorations of someone who knew and loved his playing—this time a young German who convinced his superiors that Casals's renown was so great worldwide that his death never would be forgiven. Eight months later, Casals's own ordeal and that of all of Europe seemed to come to an end with the Nazi surrender.

Although he remained very weak, his rheumatism abated as his diet improved in the months after the end of the war in Europe, and slowly he was able to begin playing the cello again. In June 1945, Casals traveled to London to perform with an orchestra for the first time since 1939. The Albert Hall was packed for Casals's single appearance with the London Philharmonic, and outside a crowd estimated at 50,000 people chanted "Viva Casals" as he left the building, his international stature undiminished during the years of the war. At a BBC studio following the concert, he recorded a message in Catalan, greeting his countrymen and assuring them that following the defeat of Hitler and Mussolini, soon the valiant Allied forces would enter Spain to rid Europe of its final fascist dictator.

But the Allies, who had had all they wanted of war, soon expressed no interest in ensuring that last defeat, and by the fall of 1945, Casals's great happiness and his hope for Spain and all the world had terribly paled. Atomic bombs had, in a flash, annihilated hundreds of thousands of citizens in the Japanese cities of Hiroshima and Nagasaki, and neither France, Britain, nor the United States was moving toward mobilizing troops for an invasion of Spain. Casals returned to Britain to plead with government officials for help in the liberation of Spain but was met with disinterest and condescension. The situation in Spain was complex, he was informed, and while, yes, there were bad things about the Franco regime, there were good things as well. Surely over time diplomatic pressure would persuade Franco to loosen his iron grip, Casals was told to his outrage and bitter sense of abandonment.

"Was it conceivable, I asked myself, that the Spanish people—the very people who had first taken up arms against fascism—were doomed to continue living under fascist rule? And the hundreds of thousands of refugees who had believed an Allied victory would mean the return of democracy to Spain—including those who had fought alongside the Allies—were they to be condemned to permanent exile?"

The answers to his questions were yes, it became shockingly clear. And the musician who always had found ways to express through performing his hope for humankind, and whose letters, speeches, and volunteer efforts had literally saved hundreds, if not thousands of lives, now struggled to imagine what he might do to persuade the western democracies not to forget Spain as a new and democratic era in Europe began to unfold. In his deep depression and sense of defeat, Casals declined to accept honorary degrees offered him both by Oxford and Cambridge universities, and in the moments before he began to perform at a November 1945 solo concert in Liverpool, Casals announced that the evening's concert would be his final performance in Britain or anywhere else in the world until democracy was restored in Spain and the country's refugees were free to return to their homes. Already exiled from Spain for seven years, Casals now also vowed to exile himself from the sublime pleasure he always had taken in performance. "But how else could I act," he repeatedly asked as friends and colleagues implored the seventy-year old musician to reconsider his solitary act of protest. "One has to live with himself."

For fully thirteen years, Casals did not appear on any stage, either as a cellist or conductor. For thirteen years—a time during which Franco's Spain was admitted to the United Nations and the United States offered the dictator massive foreign aid in return for the establishment of air bases on Spanish soil—Casals did not make any recordings. He remained in Prades, heartsick and stubbornly certain that his simple act of protest and conscience mattered more than income or acclaim. When his close friend Albert Schweitzer attempted to persuade him to begin performing again, Schweitzer argued that surely "it is better to create than to protest."

"Why not do both?" Casals replied. "Why not create and protest both?"

In the summer of 1958 Casals joined Schweitzer in a written appeal to the U.S. and Soviet governments to end the arms race and ban future nuclear testing. And, at last, Casals surrendered to his friend's implorations, agreeing to perform at the United Nations in a concert for peace that would be broadcast to seventy-four nations around the world. Casals, now 82, performed Bach's Sonata No. 2 in D Major inside the General Assembly Hall at the U.N.'s headquarters in New York. The program then continued from Paris, where violinists Yehudi Menuhin and David Oistrakh and sitar player Ravi Shankar performed. The concert concluded with the Orchestre de la Suisse Romande's performance in Geneva of the final movement of Beethoven's Ninth Symphony. As Casals listened—rather miraculously, it seemed to him—to the Geneva performance from New York City, he marveled that such technological miracles were possible in the modern world. He could not help but wonder whether human ethics and aspirations had kept pace with those advances, and he wondered, too, whether he would ever again step onto a podium in Barcelona to conduct Beethoven's ode to freedom and to joy.

P ablo Casals died prior to his 97th birthday at his home in Puerto Rico in 1973. General Francisco Franco died in 1975, and his successor, King Juan Carlos, immediately, remarkably, and without violence democratized Spain. In November 1979, Casals's wife Marta, whom he had married in 1957, returned his remains to Spain where there were interred in the cemetery of the village of Vendrell, south of Barcelona, where he was born. Among the thousands of messages from around the world that Senyora Casals received in honor of the reburial was this one from fellow cellist Mstislav Rostropovich, who had fled the Soviet Union four years before:

> "This is one of the most stirring moments of my life, when the body of the greatest artist of the twentieth century finally finds peace in the land which he so loved and which brought him so much suffering during his lifetime. . . . This humane and symbolic act is especially close to my heart as I perhaps better than others know well what it means to be deprived of one's country."

Forty years after he had fled for his life from Catalunya and Spain, the extraordinary artist who was born Pau Casals i Defilló had come home, his country freed from fascist rule at last.

ACCIDENTS

An excerpt from MATTERS GRAY AND WHITE

The summer was ending all too soon, and I was flying back to spend more time with Ferrier. New snow clung to the summits of the peaks, and from the air, the yellow leaves of aspen trees covered the mountains' shoulders like smooth and gleaming blankets.

Ferrier had had to drive to the city earlier in the day. He met my plane at the gate, and we rushed to get to his car, parked illegally at the curb of the airport's departure deck—the doctor tempting both fate and the circling tow truck by leaving it unattended. But the Saab had escaped impoundment, and we drove away—two desperadoes galloping ahead of a posse.

Cool air whipped at the car's open windows as Ferrier wove his way through traffic, trying to negotiate the forty miles between the airport and the suburban town where he lived and worked in a breakneck thirty minutes. He had come into the city that Monday to testify at a personal injury trial—one of his patients was suing the insurer of the man who, two years before, had smashed his car into hers, sending the patient's skull crashing into the windshield, her injuries resulting in temporal lobe epilepsy and what now seemed to be a permanent impairment of memory and intellect. Ferrier had been a crucial witness. The patient's lawyers had hoped that he could convince the jury that Barbara Bishop's disabilities were indeed major and that they would limit her throughout her life. But his testimony had taken an hour longer than he had expected it to, my plane was a half hour late, and Ferrier still had four patients to see at his office—the first one due in forty minutes—and he had wanted to make a stop to check on a young woman in County Hospital's intensive care unit who, two nights before, had suffered a massive hemorrhage. I buckled my seat belt and braced my feet against the floor, for some reason reticent to remind Ferrier that it was a speeding automobile that had begun Barbara Bishop's problems.

"Part of me actually enjoys the legal work," he said as he downshifted, boxed in for a moment by two trucks. "It's a huge headache, and I sure as hell would never become one of those forensic-medicine characters, but when it's for my own patients, it can be interesting. Maybe just because it's different. This thing with Barbara Bishop, I bet she actually gets a pretty big award. The attorney for the insurance company seemed like a total dolt—unprepared, seemingly uninterested. You'd think those companies would have some very big guns representing them, but . . ."

"So you tried to make it sound like her life was totally ruined by the accident?"

"Have you met Barbara?"

"A couple of times."

"Well, then you have a sense of what has happened to her. The epilepsy is real, and there's no question that it was caused by the accident, but millions of people have epilepsy and function very normally. Barbara was an incredibly intelligent person, extremely bright, and now she doesn't remember how to get to the grocery store or the fact that she invited a friend over for lunch. It's possible that she could work again someday, but she probably won't. Her kids have begun to have problems, partly because their mother, who used to be terrific with them, now does all these goofy things. And all of it stems from the trauma she suffered when the guy ran the red light."

"But you surely made it sound as grim as you could on the witness stand."

"Well, I didn't lie, if that's what you mean. Everything I said is totally documented in her records. But sure, I was testifying to try to help her get some compensation and I tried to make the best case I could—which was a good one, I think, since the other side's lawyer didn't challenge a word I said. I don't see a doctor's role as being neutral in that kind of situation. She's my patient, so I'm on her side, and I wanted to do the best job I could of explaining just what that accident did to her."

Barbara Bishop, thirty-nine at the time, thin, lithe, and witty, was driving across town on an afternoon two Septembers before when her Japanese station wagon was sideswiped by a drunken man in a pickup truck. She did not remember the accident, nor could she now recall the events that had taken place in the weeks before she was hit or in the first three months following the accident. According to the medical reports made at the time, Barbara was unconscious for only a few minutes, and she was not hospitalized until a week after the accident, complaining of the onset of severe headaches, neck pain, nausea, dizziness, and loss of memory. Her hospital stay was short; the symptoms began to subside, and she had no more medical attention until the following April, when she reported to David Vincent, her family physician, that the headaches seldom bothered her now, and the dizziness was no more than a minor nuisance. But she was, nonetheless, still lethargic, depressed, and her sharp memory had never returned. "I'll walk into the kitchen for something, then I'll have to go back to the living room to ask my husband what it was I was going to get," she told Dr. Vincent. And there was something new: At least once a day she would experience a strange "nauseating sensation" that would soon include an unpleasant taste and smell, which Barbara described as eating melted Styrofoam, followed immediately by a period in which she seemed to "miss time," as though she had suddenly vanished. But it was only the experience of "coming back" at the end of each episode that made her aware of what had just happened. Dr. Vincent subsequently ordered an EEG, which revealed intermittent abnormal "slow" electrical activity in the region of her left temporal lobe. He then prescribed Dilantin, but Barbara took it for only three days before stopping it because, she later said, she was just too depressed to be on medication.

At the urging of the lawyer she had retained in her case against the drunk driver, and with the concurrence of David Vincent, Barbara did agree to begin seeing a psychiatrist. At the close of a series of sessions with Barbara during the summer months, the psychiatrist, Leon Bennett, wrote to Dr. Vincent that his diagnostic findings followed three "axes" or areas of progressive concern": "Axis I: Bereavement, complicated by ongoing loss and by the ongoing demands of litigation. Acute and atypical depression is present and a major depressive episode may at times be diagnosable." In simpler terms, Barbara, he believed, was grieving over the loss of her mental faculties much as someone would grieve over the loss of a loved one, and the grief would be hard to put to rest until the suit was settled. "Axis II: The possibility of a preexisting, nondisabling personality disorder. But it is not diagnosable at this time, given the acute psychopathology present." In other words, Barbara might have been psychologically disturbed before the accident, but he could not be sure because of her current mental disabilities. "Axis III: Postconcussion syndrome. Rule out epilepsy"—meaning he believed she certainly suffered the common posttraumatic symptoms that follow blows to the head—sleeplessness, headache, dizziness, lethargy, depression— and that the possibility of epilepsy had to be investigated. Were the bad tastes and smells and the periods of missing time evidence of temporal lobe epilepsy? It was Leon Bennett who sent Barbara to Ferrier for an evaluation of the question of seizures.

Ferrier first saw Barbara Bishop in September, a year before the trial. I had just begun following Ferrier and I remember that Barbara was lighthearted, animated, seemingly full of energy when she walked into his office, brimming with conversation and intrigued by the objects on his desk and the pictures on his walls. She tucked her feet under her when she sat in the chair opposite his desk and she immediately reached for a wooden letter opener, caressing it in her hands, staring at it, focusing so much attention on it that she had to ask Ferrier to repeat what he had said.

Her story took a long time to tell. She had no personal memory of the accident and it was hard for her to remember what she had been told about it. She remembered her childhood medical history, as well as the births of her children, but each recollection tended to spark a tangential train of thought and her comments would often run far afield before Ferrier, via a subsequent question, would bring her back to the subject she had abandoned. Barbara described herself as once having been very self-confident, certain of her own intellect, boldly dependent on it in her interactions with others. "I knew I could do anything I wanted to," she said. "I had a good head on my shoulders, and I used it. I loved school. I did graduate work in architecture, community development, and water resources. I was interested in all kinds of things. I probably kept changing disciplines because it was only the academics that seemed really challenging. I didn't want to have to get a job."

When Ferrier focused on Barbara's mental status during the year since the accident, she grew sullen, suddenly quiet, tearful. She seemed at once to be both ashamed of her current self and sympathetic to her plight. Her voice now devoid of its energy, she listed a catalog of changes. "I get lost going places; I forget what I'm saying half the time. I have this weird tendency to say cruel or tactless things, which was never the case before. I'm irritable, irrational; I can't do simple math—balancing a checkbook is impossible. Socially, I've become a hermit. I can't concentrate. In a roomful of people I can't hear a single conversation; I hear them all, all at once, and it drives me crazy. I was an extrovert; I loved people, but now I'm just afraid."

Barbara began to sob when she described the battery of neuropsychological tests that Leon Bennett had performed. "I knew the accident had screwed me up, but I had never confronted the extent of the change in me. Those tests were a terrible shock. I finally had to confront the fact that I had become basically stupid."

When the subject shifted to the issue of possible epilepsy, Barbara's descriptions of the strange gastric sensations, the bad tastes and smells, and her sense of "coming back" from an unsettling kind of absence—together with the abnormal EEG report contained in her records—quickly convinced Ferrier that an ongoing seizure disorder was a very strong possibility. When Barbara admitted in response to his further questions that on a few occasions she had fallen to the floor before she "came back"—that she had also bitten her tongue and become incontinent—Ferrier had to assume that a seizure focus in her left temporal lobe was also occasionally prone to generalize into a grand mal attack.

Following his examination of her, Ferrier told Barbara he was certain that the accident had sufficiently damaged her left temporal lobe to have caused an ongoing seizure disorder, one that was probably permanent, but that medication would very likely control. She was still reluctant to begin a regular drug regimen— and the notion of having to take Dilantin or some other seizure medication *forever* sounded hideous—but Ferrier told her she simply had no choice. When he added that successfully interrupting the seizure activity could possibly improve her memory, Barbara acquiesced.

During the succeeding months, four hundred milligrams of Dilantin each day made a marked difference. The periods of "missing time" that had occurred at least once a day now were as infrequent as once a week. The Dilantin seemed to erase what Barbara described as a cloud that had muddled her thinking, and amitriptyline, an antidepressant prescribed by Dr. Bennett, seemed to ease her depression. But through that winter and into the following spring, her memory and mentation did not improve. She still could not stand to be in a group of people, she still could not do simple math, and the realization of her loss still caused a kind of desperation. Barbara had to begin to keep a detailed appointment book, making entries to remind herself when her kids would be home from school, reminding her to check to see if the stove was off and to take her medication, reminding her of the days and times when a deposition was scheduled, or a strategy session with her lawyer was planned, or when she was due for yet another evaluation by a psychologist, a psychiatrist, or a neurologist—the seemingly endless series of examinations supposedly leading toward a settlement or a trial.

But there was no settlement. The drunk driver's insurance company would not agree that the epilepsy was caused by the accident, and it held out the opinion of a forensic psychiatrist that Barbara's disabilities were psychological rather than organic as proof that it should not settle. Richard Arkin, Barbara's lawyer, sent Ferrier a letter late in the summer. He apologized for the inconvenience, but the trial was now scheduled for late September, he said, and Ferrier would have to be subpoenaed.

"When I have to do depositions in the office," Ferrier said as we sped along the freeway, "I charge the same as if it's an evaluation of a new patient, $100 an hour. The lawyer has to wait until there's an opening; I certainly don't go out of my way for them. But when I actually have to go to court—and you either show up or they throw you in jail—I charge the hell out of the insurance companies that the lawyers work for—200 big ones an hour from the time I leave the office—partly because it's such a huge pain in the ass. We have to cancel a half day's or whole day's patients and figure out some way to reschedule them, squeeze them in at lunch, or whatever. And partly because I sort of think it's fair. They *always* ought to figure out a way to settle, for God's sake, or there ought to be other ways to judge what kind of compensation somebody deserves. This system where the insurance companies squeal like hell when they have to pay a claim and where the ambulance chasers live off the misfortunes of people who've been injured, using their dramatic skills to make the jury members cry, seems crazy. Of course, I'm making money from people's injuries, too, aren't I? Maybe there really isn't much difference, but it seems like there is. I can definitely feel guilty for charging what I do, but dammit, it serves them right for taking two whole years to settle this thing."

I t was three o'clock. Ferrier's first patient was surely waiting for him, but he pulled into the doctors' parking area at the rear of the hospital instead of turning into his office. "This'll be quick," he said. "I need to keep close tabs on this woman for the next day or two." I followed him through the door and down a dark corridor. "She had a massive intracranial hemorrhage on Friday night— very interesting story—and Burns had to go in and clamp off her right carotid on Saturday, but it doesn't look like she's going to make it. Her EEG is virtually flat-line. No gag reflex. No response to pain since early yesterday. I've already talked a bit with her family about ending the life support. If we don't see any improvement before long, we'll hope they can make a decision. They want to—" He stopped in midsentence as we passed the waiting room near the intensive care unit. A man in his thirties, wearing jeans and a cotton sweater, his face full of the exhaustion that comes from endless waiting, leaned against the jamb of the open door. Beyond him, seated on a couch, were two older people, certainly husband and wife, the husband smoking a cigarette, the wife simply sitting. Ferrier slowed enough to smile and say hello. "I'll stop back after I've seen her," he added before he pushed through the swinging doors.

A few months before, I had watched Ferrier examine a braindead three-year-old boy, his fragile cerebrum also destroyed by a spill of blood, the child's face bespeaking the peace and permanence of death while his heart still beat and his lungs, assisted by a respirator, still heaved with the ebb and flow of air. And I had seen Ferrier perform the same confirmatory tests on four other people whose ages made their deaths seem less unkind—their skin pale and wrinkled, almost hairless, their eyes fixed and open, as if they were asking when the end could come. In each case, I had watched the patient's final minutes with a sense of being present in the midst of something profound. The deaths seemed to me, spared as I was from the overwhelming sense of loss that a friend or family member would feel, less sad or tragic than transcendent. Something elemental was in process, something that, despite the web of tubes and hoses, seemed simple and direct, and that demanded reverent attention.

But watching Jayne Welty die was very different. She was thirty-three, dark and beautiful. Her hair had been combed recently, her brown eyes were open, and a clear tube was inserted into each nostril and held in place by a strip of white tape. A bandage covered the surgical incision on her neck, the skin at her throat was freckled, her hospital gown hugged her breasts. She reminded me of my wife, Karen; she reminded me of all the women I had ever thrilled to observe in secret, and I was shocked that my first reaction to this woman at the edge of death was to be attracted to her.

My second reaction was to think that she must not die. She was too young, too lovely, somehow her motionless body still suggesting so much life. I saw no resignation in Jayne Welty's face, no final understanding in her open eyes. This was simply sleep, wasn't it? Couldn't Ferrier wake her up and tell her she would be all right? Surely something could be done.

An intensive care nurse named Beverly had walked into the room with us. She stood by the bank of monitors that circled the head of the bed and spoke to Ferrier in a controlled yet compassionate voice that suggested Jayne was a special patient. "I've been checking for a pain response every hour or so. Still nothing. Her urine output has slowed a lot, less than 150 cc's since six this morning. But she's still tripping the respirator on her own. Pulse is steady."

"How much fluid is she getting?"

"Sixty cc's an hour."

Ferrier took a pen from his shirt pocket, picked up Jayne's hand, and pressed the shaft of the pen against her thumbnail, its paint scraped away by repeated testing. Ferrier squeezed her nail until he grimaced, but Jayne's arm did not withdraw. She remained motionless; her expression did not change. Next Ferrier lifted the bedcovers and similarly squeezed the nail of her large toe. He sighed when he finally released the pressure, when it was clear he could not elicit a response. "I'm going to need some ice water and a large syringe," he told Beverly.

"Sure," she said, and she left the room.

Bending over the bed, Ferrier tapped Jayne's cheeks, calling her name, telling her who he was, asking her to close her eyes. He blew into each eye, then touched each cornea with the tip of a cotton swab, but still there was no response. He laid his palm across her forehead and briskly turned her head from side to side—a test of the oculocephalic or "doll's eyes" reflex. Instead of moving in the direction opposite of her head rotation, as would have been normal, Jayne's eyes remained fixed and moved with her head. When Beverly returned, Ferrier filled the syringe with water and injected it into Jayne's left ear. A patient with intact brain-stem function would have turned her eyes to the left, toward the cold stimulus, in this test of the caloric reflex, but Jayne's eyes did not move. When he injected water into her right ear, still her eyes were fixed.

Ferrier sat on the edge of the bed, his hand on Jayne's forearm. "Jayne, are you going to come back to us?" he asked, as though she might actually offer him a response, but one was not forthcoming. Ferrier looked down, tapped his feet on the floor, and waited.

"I'm going to push to take her off," he said after a long silence, turning to look at Beverly. "What do you think?"

"There isn't much to pin our hopes to, is there?"

"How often is the family coming in?"

"Her husband's in for a bit every hour. Her parents not quite so often."

"I'll tell them they can stay in as much as they want now, if you don't mind. We'll try to arrange a family conference for this evening, and maybe we can reach a decision," he said as he stood. "Thanks, Bev."

"Sure, Doctor," she said, combing Jayne's hair away from her forehead with her fingers.

I stood outside the waiting room, but I could hear Ferrier explaining to Jayne's husband and parents that he had seen no change for the better. He told them that the slowed output of urine added to Jayne's poor prognosis, and he said he would like to meet with them and the rest of the family later. "We don't have to make any decisions this evening—and any decision will be yours to make—but I'm afraid it's time we all discussed taking her off the life support in a little more detail—what would be best for Jayne and best for you all."

"If she came off the machine, how long would she live?" asked a voice that must have been her mother's.

"Well, if we do decide to take her off, we'll only do so when we're certain that her brain is no longer functioning, that her brain is dead. So my opinion would be that she would already *be* dead at that point. In most situations like this, patient's hearts can keep pumping anywhere from a few minutes to several days. It's hard to be any more definite than that. But—"

"She wouldn't want to live on a machine," said the voice that belonged to her husband. "But you're sure? I mean that . . . that she can't. "

"I want to wait a bit longer—till this evening, or even tomorrow morning. But yes, I'm basically as sure as I ever am." Ferrier's voice was faint from the place where I stood in the empty corridor. "But you need time to think about this, to talk about it. I can come back at about six o'clock and we'll all sit down together, if that's a good time for you."

"Her sisters will be here by then," her mother said.

"Good. I'll see you then."

"Thank you," someone said.

Ferrier caught my eyes as he left the room, pursing his lips as if to say there was nothing that could be said.

Jayne Welty lived outside San Francisco. She was a sales representative for a book publishing company and came to town frequently on business. For almost a year, she had been having an affair with a man who worked in a local bookstore. On Friday evening, they had had dinner together, then had gone to her hotel. According to what Stan Singleton, her lover, later told Ferrier, Jayne had drunk only a glass or two of wine; she seemed to feel fine and was in good spirits. They went to bed sometime after midnight. Then, in the midst of making love, just as Jayne was reaching an orgasm, she suddenly went unconscious. Stan tried to rouse her but could not. Ten minutes later, Jayne regained a groggy kind of consciousness, moaning, complaining that the light in the room hurt her eyes, vomiting, her limbs convulsing slightly before she became comatose again. Stan was worried, afraid, confused. What on earth could have happened? Could her exertion simply have knocked her out? Had she failed to tell him she had seizures? But by now, Jayne was breathing normally; the convulsing had stopped and she seemed to be in a deep and quiet sleep. Stan watched her sleep and worried for four more hours.

It was beginning to grow light when Stan became convinced that Jayne was not sleeping. He could not wake her, her limbs had begun to shake again, and she had wet the bed. He called for an ambulance. Ferrier got a call from County Hospital's emergency room at a quarter after six.

When Ferrier first examined Jayne, she was responsive to pain stimulus—she successfully pulled her hands and feet away from pressure on her nails—but her eyes were dilated, her neck stiff, reflexes virtually absent, and she had a temperature of 102°. Wanting to rule out the possibility of meningitis and in order to investigate the possibility of stroke, Ferrier performed a lumbar puncture and a CAT scan. The fluid he pulled from the tap needle was dark red, so bloody he almost hoped he had hit a vein, but a second puncture confirmed his fears—he had indeed extracted cerebrospinal fluid, the normally clear fluid now contaminated by a huge bleed in the subarachnoid space surrounding Jayne's brain and possibly in her brain itself. The CAT scan had shown that there likely was bleeding in the right frontal area of her cerebrum, and a subsequent angiogram pinpointed an aneurysm—a saccular weakness in the wall of a blood vessel—in her right internal carotid artery, just beyond the junction of the ophthalmic artery.

The hemorrhage had stopped, at least for the time being, but a second bleed was very possible and had to be prevented. The location of the aneurysm, however, made it impossible for a surgeon to be able to open her skull and directly approach and seal the artery near the source of the bleed. The only surgical option was to open Jayne's right common carotid artery as it rose through her neck, to insert a clamp around it, and to *slowly* close the clamp, maintaining the supply of blood to her right hemisphere primarily through her left carotid system and its network of interconnecting arteries at the so-called circle of Willis at the base of her brain.

Roger Burns was ready to operate by eight o'clock that morning, joined by Dwayne Steidel, the EEG technician, and by Ferrier, who closely monitored the electrical activity in Jayne's right hemisphere as Burns began to close the valve. Closing it too quickly could effectively infarct her whole right hemisphere; waiting too long to plug the artery's flow would allow the aneurysm the opportunity to rehemorrhage and do more damage. As the operation began, Jayne had been hyperventilated to decrease the pressure inside her skull and lessen the possibility of a fatal herniation—the tendency of a swollen brain to press the vital brain stem through the hole at the base of the skull. She had been given massive dosages of mannitol, a chemical that effectively draws fluids into blood vessels, also in hopes of reducing the pressure inside her skull. She had been given steroids to minimize tissue swelling, and she had been put deeper into coma with pentobarbital, a barbiturate that would slow the metabolic action in her brain, producing less lactic acid and other by-products of the oxidation of glucose that tend to retain fluids inside brain tissues.

With the valve in place in Jayne's common carotid artery, and the EEG electrodes in place on her scalp—the machine's needles tracing the frantic, rhythmic squiggle of her brain waves—Roger Burns began the slow process of shutting the artery's flow. Listening to Ferrier call out what evidence of right-sided slowing he saw on the tracing paper, Burns at last completely closed the plastic valve, the blood in her left carotid system successfully circulating into her right hemisphere, the right-side electrodes never indicating a dangerous amount of slowing.

Virtually all that could be done for Jayne had now been done. The hemorrhage was controlled as best it could be, brain fluids lessened, swelling minimized. But her cerebrum had suffered a massive injury, and as well, the huge hemorrhage had caused dangerous, perhaps irreversible damage to other parts of her brain. Five hours after the surgery, Jayne had not regained consciousness, and a new EEG showed serious slowing in both cerebral hemispheres. Jayne's husband and her parents arrived at the hospital at eight o'clock that evening, while Dwayne and Ferrier were performing still another electroencephalogram, this one evidencing more deterioration, signaling a poorer prognosis.

Ferrier met Jayne's family outside the doors of the intensive care unit in a quiet corridor bathed in bright fluorescent light. He had spoken with her husband on the phone early that morning— Stan Singleton had placed the call from the emergency room. Singleton had said he was a friend and, before Ferrier got on the phone, explained that there had been an accident. Singleton had stayed at the hospital throughout the day, imagining, while he waited, the conversation he would surely have to have with the husband he had never met. As he was about to leave that evening, he told Ferrier he would be back early the following day. Thirty minutes after he had gone, Bill Welty and Jayne's parents arrived in a rented car.

Standing with them in the deserted hallway, Ferrier explained to Jayne's family what had transpired during the course of the long day. Ferrier was tired, relaxed now that there was little left for him to do, apprehensive about Jayne's chances, but hopeful as he offered his detailed account.

"What can cause something like this?" Jayne's father wanted to know.

"Well, the hemorrhage was almost certainly caused by an aneurysm, a weakness in the wall of that artery. Aneurysms are very prone to hemorrhage, but beforehand, you don't know they're there and they can rupture very suddenly. When patients are fortunate, the rupture is small and they get what we call a warning bleed, one that is small enough to do minimal damage but still show us that a weak artery has to be clipped. Unfortunately, in Jayne's case, the first bleed was a major one."

Bill Welty hardly spoke during that first meeting with Ferrier. He stood with his hands in the pockets of his pants, his lips parted, his eyes showing more shock than sadness. "Would it have helped if her friend had found her sooner)" he asked at last, his question finally bringing tears.

"Well . . . it, well no. Almost certainly not."

The word *stroke* derives from the Anglo-Saxon word *strican,* meaning to strike. It is synonymous with *apoplexy,* a word all but abandoned nowadays, one derived from the

Greek word *apoplexia,* which means to strike down. Both words refer, of course, to the suddenness with which many strokes or apoplexies strike, often doing their foul damage in little more than an instant. In the medical parlance, the several types of stroke are known as *cerebrovascular* a66idents—calamities caused not by invading viruses or by mysterious degenerative processes within the brain itself, but by abnormalities of the blood vessels that supply the brain. Brains affected by stroke are not diseased, but rather damaged— injured, sometimes destroyed, by hemorrhage or by occlusion, the blockage of a vessel's blood supply. Most stroke patients do suffer disease—hypertension and atherosclerosis (narrowing of arterial walls) are the diseases that account for the majority of strokes, but they are diseases of the cardiovascular system, not of the brain. The brain is a victim only because it is intricately laced with arteries, veins, and capillaries; because it receives so much of the body's blood supply; and because it is so fragile. Even a minor hemorrhage or a temporary occlusion can result in the permanent loss of function of a limb, of sight, or speech.

Aneurysms, ballooning weaknesses in vascular walls, are the principal causes of hemorrhage. Vessel walls in the brain that are congenitally weak or that have been stressed by disease, and that very often have been pounded from within for decades by high blood pressure, are very prone to rupture. Sudden exertions sometimes precipitate the ruptures, but they can occur at any time, without warning. Ruptured arteries are doubly destructive; the rupture drains much or all of the blood the artery normally carries, cutting off the part of the brain that is dependent on it, as well as creating a hematoma—a clot, an often enlarging pool of effused blood whose pressure destroys or inhibits normal neuronal activity. Whether lodged in the subarachnoid space beneath the layers of meninges, or within the brain itself, pressure from a hematoma can, depending on its size, cause temporary loss of localized function or complete brain failure, resulting in coma, permanent impairment, or death.

Occlusions of veins and arteries, caused either by a "thrombus" or an "embolus," precipitate the destruction of brain tissue by causing the "infarction" or death of neurons that normally receive essential oxygen and glucose via the blocked blood vessel. A thrombus is a blood clot formed at a site where blood flow is slowed by the roughening of a vessel wall or by the narrowing caused by the buildup of fatty deposits and other material. Thrombi can occur in the large carotid arteries that supply the head—causing, when they do, loss of function throughout much of one cerebral hemisphere—as well as in the many thousands of threadlike vessels that supply every fold in the gray-matter cortex, the brain stem, or cerebellum, their effects major or minor, or even asymptomatic, depending on their location.

An embolus, in contrast, is a plug of material—clotted blood, cholesterol, fat, air, bacteria, tumor tissue—circulating in the bloodstream that lodges between the walls of an artery it is too large to pass through, limiting or blocking the flow of blood to the arterial system that lies beyond the blockage. One of the most frequent causes of cerebral emboli are clots formed in the heart, most of them the result of chronic cardiac diseases, and about half of all circulating emboli thrown off by the heart travel to the cerebral arteries. A speck of embolic material that may cause no damage at all if it lodges in an artery that supplies other internal organs or the extremities, can result in severe and permanent neurological deficits if it lodges in a vessel that supplies the brain. The pathological processes responsible for arterial hemorrhage and occlusion are obviously very different, as are the ways in which they do damage—one destroying areas of the brain or limiting their function by spilling blood, the other by damming the blood supply. And there are more distinctions: Occlusions from emboli tend to be peripheral, causing infarcts of the cerebral cortex. So-called berry aneurysms tend to form on the major arteries at the base of the brain, their hemorrhages flooding over the cortex or within deep brain structures.

Thrombi within blood vessels tend to occur slowly, often when patients are sedentary, relaxing or sleeping, their effects crescendoing over hours or even days. Hemorrhages and emboli, on the other hand, tend to cause sudden symptoms and to strike without warning. Hemorrhages strike during periods of stress or activity.

On first examination, patients who have suffered an infarct— either from a thrombus or an embolus—usually complain of weakness on one side of their bodies; they often suffer "hornonymous hemianopsia"—the loss of the left or right field of vision in both eyes—speech is slurred or absent; many are dazed or confused, but few complain of pain. Patients who have just suffered a subarachnoid hemorrhage or a major hemorrhage inside their brains, in contrast, are usually in much more serious condition when they first receive medical attention; they are often comatose or semiconscious, their examinations tend to reveal a generalized neurological deficit more often than a localized loss of function. Those patients who can communicate often complain of head pain.

In most cases of infarct, the maximum degree of impairment is evident within three days following the accident, and most of the recovery that is possible usually will have occurred within three to six months. Infarcts are seldom fatal. As many as 75 percent of all intracranial hemorrhages, however—those that occur in the subarachnoid space and those that spill into or begin in the brain itself—result within hours or days in death.

When Ferrier had seen the last of his office patients on Monday afternoon, when his dictation was finished, his calls completed, and the thick stack of charts initialed, he returned—alone—to the hospital. I waited for him in the empty office, rummaging through the journals that had recently arrived, reading the current cartoons he and Putnam and the secretaries kept posted near the coffee machine. It was the first time in nearly a year of visits that I had declined an opportunity to trail behind him, to watch while he earned his living, observing his successes and embarrassing him with my presence when he occasionally did something dumb. But this was not a quick trip across the street

to look at a CAT scan, or to test the strength and reflexes of
a patient about to be operated on, or to quiet the seizures
of someone who had been brought into the busy arena of
the emergency room. This time Ferrier would simply sit in a
dimly lit lounge filled with sofas and overstuffed chairs. He
would simply talk with Jayne Welty's family about whether
she should be allowed to die. I was somehow certain that I
should not monitor their conversation.

"Sure, you can come. They've seen you with me before,"
Ferrier had told me as he hurried out the door. Earlier, it
had seemed as if their decision was already almost made, and
there had been no indication that Jayne's husband, her parents, or her two sisters would argue she must not be taken off
her respirator, that a miracle must be awaited. Nonetheless,
their decision, if they were to make one, was a profoundly
private matter. So I decided to stay behind.

Ferrier's role in the slow and quiet conversation would
be to answer their questions; he would outline the possibilities for organ donation if they were interested; he would
presume what Jayne's future would be *on* the respirator, if
they asked him to; he would listen as each one spoke. The
conversation would be a quiet one and there would be long
periods of silence. If Jayne's family had already found the
strength to reach a decision, the meeting would be short and
Ferrier would simply accede to their wishes. If they disagreed
about what they should do, or if they could not bring themselves to speak the words that seemed like a kind of sentence,
the meeting would be long and awkward and achingly sad.
If the family members seemed divided, or if they simply

could not decide what to do, Ferrier would offer no opinion except to suggest that they wait a few more hours, then meet again. If it seemed certain that they believed Jayne should be taken off the respirator but could not bring themselves to say so, Ferrier would likely lend the weight of his position in support of that conclusion. If Jayne's husband pressed him for his own opinion at that point, Ferrier would surely say, "Well, if it were my wife . . . ," as a prelude to saying that Jayne simply had no hope.

During my months with Ferrier, I had known of similar meetings he had had with families facing the same terrible options. I had been surprised to discover that the possibility of taking a patient off a respirator or of forgoing heroic treatment was not a great ethical and legal dilemma for him or for the hospitals that housed his patients. As life-sustaining technology had become increasingly sophisticated in recent decades, both medical and legal practitioners were now aware that horribly traumatized bodies could be kept "alive" virtually indefinitely. Yet there was growing and widespread agreement that there were few ethical, emotional, or economic reasons to use that technology for weeks or months or years simply in the name of the Hippocratic oath. A physician would still be legally accountable if he chose to inject poison into a patient or, perhaps, to withhold intravenous food, but to remove a patient like Jayne from a respirator would not be construed as "mercy killing." It would instead be seen simply as what it was: a decision made by the patient's family, in consultation with a physician, that a particular type of treatment should be stopped because it could no longer improve the patient's condition. Ferrier had never so much as hinted at concern about whether he conceivably could be charged with committing euthanasia, and the people who staffed the intensive care units seemed to treat decisions to end life-support as sadly inevitable occurrences. Death was as common in their wing of the hospital as was birth in the obstetrics ward, and recognizing hopelessness seemed to them to be as critical a part of their jobs as recognizing when and how they could help.

Ferrier now could no longer help Jayne, but he could be a bit of help to her family, speaking to them not so much as a counselor but as someone who had been part of similar situations, who knew what could be expected if her nostril tubes were removed and what could be expected if they were not, someone who had witnessed many others struggle with the same decision in this matter of life and death.

An hour and a half after he had gone to talk with Jayne Welty's family, Ferrier and I sat drinking scotch in the bar of the old Victorian hotel downtown, his whiskey served neat, as had become his habit when he lived in Britain, mine served with the requisite American "rocks." There was nothing left to be done with the day. The teams playing the Monday night game on the big television above the bar didn't interest us, so we simply stuck to the scotch, eating a supper of sandwiches in the big upholstered chairs that flanked a round black cocktail table.

"Things like this are always easier when it's been several days since the accident," Ferrier said. "Not that they are ever easy, but after the family has seen several days of no response, it's easier for them to deal with the possibility that their wife or daughter isn't going to come round."

"Why don't you always, as a policy, leave the patient on life support for a set length of time before you do anything?"

"Because each situation is different. And for practical reasons. I think we all approach it very cautiously. We try to be absolutely honest about a patient's chances, but we don't even bring up the issue of life support until we feel that there is just no hope—until brain death or terrible disabilities are certain. And when we bring it up, when I bring it up, it's because it would be cruel to do otherwise. The patient is dead, his brain is, even though the heart may be pumping away like nothing ever happened. And to get heroic at that point just doesn't make any sense. It's very expensive; it puts enormous strain on the family, and it doesn't serve any purpose. Death is already a fact."

"How can you make a reliable diagnosis of brain death?"

"It's a bedside diagnosis. You do a variety of tests to check for even the subtlest kind of response—response to pain being one of the most critical. If a patient has no response to deep pain, no grimace, no attempt to pull away, if the gag reflex is absent, no caloric response—the ice water in the ears—no doll's eyes, pupils fixed and dilated, no attempt to breathe on his own, off the ventilator, that patient is in pretty grave shape. But someone with all those findings sometimes can still breathe on his own or can slightly move his eyes if a bit of his brain-stem function is still intact. Jayne is still triggering the respirator on her own, but left on her own, her intake is quite poor. They did another EEG late this afternoon. A flat-line EEG is almost eerie, the tracings just these steady horizontal lines, absent of anything. And they did a nuclear brain scan while I talked to her family. It's a procedure we don't use a lot these days, but it can still be helpful occasionally. It tracks the movement of a radioactive material that's injected into the bloodstream. None of the material got to her head; there's no blood flow to her brain from any vessel. It's so swollen that the pressure is keeping it out."

"And her family knows the results of that?"

"They know everything. They want to spend tonight with her, her husband does. I'm not sure her parents will stay all night. And they decided to donate her corneas and her liver; her kidneys, too, if they don't fail in the next twelve hours."

"What about her heart?"

"I called the transplant team at the university—they'll come up and take the organs—and I'm sure they'll see if there's a recipient for the heart."

"I wonder if her husband knows the whole story."

"Stan Singleton was waiting in the hall when I went back to the hospital. I guess he and Bill talked for an hour or so, and I'm sure Bill suspects something, but . . . I hope Singleton didn't spell out too many details. I don't know what purpose they would serve at the moment. Bill was crying a lot this evening; I'm sure her death has begun to sink in."

"Is she dead? Right now?" I asked.

"She . . . she's brain dead, yes, which, from my perspective means that *Jayne,* Jayne the person, is dead. Parts of her body are still functioning, but. . .. Death can be pretty relative.

Muscles can contract for hours after a heart stops beating. They are as functional as ever. Are you still alive because some of your muscle fibers still respond to stimuli?"

"What will the records show as her time of death?"

"Oh, the time when her heart stops beating, I'm sure."

We talked on into the autumn night, staying inside the hotel, sinking deeper into the wing-back chairs, discussing death and infidelity. I confessed to Ferrier that Jayne was the first person I had ever been attracted to who might already have been dead. "With my luck," he said, smiling, "I'm just thankful that I wasn't in Singleton's shoes."

"Would she have made it if he had brought her in right away?"

"Who knows. It was a big rupture and it did a lot of damage immediately, I'm sure. But Stan Singleton's going to have to deal with that for a long time, isn't he? Medically, though, I'm not sure that if we had seen her two or three hours earlier it would have made a lot of difference. With smaller ruptures, you need to clip the artery early to limit the trouble it's going to cause, but with a major rupture, you inevitably get so much pressure from the bleed and so much swelling from damaged tissue that the whole brain is heavily traumatized. If the swelling damages the brain stem, then that's pretty much the end of things. You've got to have a fairly intact brain stem to be conscious; it just controls too many vital functions."

When I asked him about the viable treatments for nonfatal kinds of strokes, Ferrier explained that with the exception of surgically clamping arteries and removing hematomas following rupture—procedures that are only sometimes done, in cases where a bleed is still in progress or where the hematoma is threatening a critical local area like the brain stem—or the administration of anticoagulant and antiplatelet drugs to prevent further thromboses, treatment of stroke victims is largely rehabilitative. "If you infarct most of your left hemisphere, bringing back your speech is pretty problematic. Some function often returns when the edema, the swelling, is reduced; sometimes damaged nerve cells are able to sprout new dendrites, new connections that effectively reprogram certain functions—and speech and physical and occupational therapy play a fundamental role in that process. It's the therapists and the families who really get stroke victims back on their feet."

He asked me if I remembered Eddie Ruiz, the man he had been called away from lunch to see sometime during the previous winter, a man who had suffered a sudden left-sided weakness while he was shoveling to reach a water main. I remembered Eddie Ruiz—jovial, wisecracking despite the fear that must have beset him, his left arm and leg shockingly limp and uncooperative. CAT scans performed that winter afternoon had shown swelling in Eddie's right frontal and parietal lobes—his nondominant hemisphere—and an angiogram had shown a severely occluded right common carotid artery. Sensation and movement in Eddie's left arm and leg had slowly returned over the next few days, his loss of function presumably the result of a "transient ischemic attack," a short-term loss of blood to the brain that is not sustained long enough to cause an infarct. But Ferrier and Dennis Mitchell, a vascular surgeon, had recommended a carotid endarterectomy—a surgical scraping of the artery's internal walls—fearing that, without it, a major infarction was probable. The surgery itself had posed a risk of sending an embolus into his brain, of causing the kind of infarct they were attempting to prevent, but it was a risk that they and Eddie had decided should be taken.

Eddie awoke from the surgery with severe right hemispheric deficits—his left arm and leg nearly immobile, the left half of his face numb and uncontrollable. He spent the following two months in the rehabilitation wing at St. Luke's Hospital, regaining enough use of his left leg to allow him to walk with a cane, trying to relearn the reading and calculating skills the stroke had taken from him, trying, with only limited success, to regain cognizance of the left half of his body.

"Eddie's a good example of how much better we often are at managing stroke with therapy than with surgery. Not that the surgery was a drastic mistake; I think that without it he stood a strong chance of totally occluding his carotid and maybe causing himself even more trouble, but we'll never know about that. Since the infarction from the surgery was in Eddie's nondominant hemisphere, he didn't lose his speech. But, of course, when he spoke, he could use only half his mouth and tongue, so his speech sounded flat and slurred. But what was amazing to observe—and he wasn't unique by any means; you see this with most people who have nondominant strokes; it's a phenomenon called ignoral—was that he totally lost recognition of his left side and of the left half of the world. If you asked him to follow the words he was reading with his finger, the finger would move to the end of one line, then would only go back to the middle of the next line. He had his full field of vision, but he just no longer *knew* about his left. You could touch his right hand and ask him what it was, and he'd tell you it was his right hand. If you asked him what his left hand was, he'd say, 'oh, it's, uh, it's,' and he couldn't tell you. If you moved it over to his right side, he'd say, 'oh, it's a hand.' One time, I asked him to draw a clock with the hands set at four o'clock. He drew the hands correctly, and the right half of the clock was circular, but the left half was flat. When I asked him to draw nine o'clock, he couldn't do it. He just couldn't visualize nine o'clock."

"How do the therapists work with those kinds of problems?"

"With patience. It takes a long time. You repeat things endlessly and you teach the patient little tricks, little habits that help him to notice things, to be aware of them. People will eat from only half the plate, or put on only one shoe, or only comb their hair on one side; women will put makeup on only half their face. But by the time Eddie left the hospital, he had improved a lot. He had enough use of his left side that he could walk with a cane, and he could follow a whole line of print, and he was learning how to avoid leaving food in the left half of his mouth—but that much took two months to learn. I saw him in the office a few weeks ago. He was getting around pretty good, complaining about how in the world they expected his OT to be able to teach him how to cook when she didn't even know what *menudo* was."

"You said something about how critical the brain stem is, or how it's sensitive to stroke."

"It's not particularly prone to stroke, no, except that, re-member, hemorrhages are prone to occur in deep brain ar-eas, like the brain stem. The complication is that the brain stem is so vital to basic brain function. It serves as a kind of alerting center, to keep you conscious, to keep you asleep or awake and aware. Also, it's a conduit for motor and sensory tracts, connecting the cerebrum and spinal cord. Sometimes it's called the 'reptilian brain' because all reptiles, and the birds and mammals that are descended from them, have brain stems. That's about all reptiles have—nothing com-plicated. But, I guess, if you're a lizard out cruising the rocks, you probably don't need much. With people, you need a hell of a lot more than the brain stem, but you also *have to have* the brain stem. Even a big hemorrhage or lots of edema up in the cerebrum, or in the cerebellum that sits behind it, can exert enough pressure to shut down your brain stem and pretty well close out your account. And infarcts or hemorrhages within the brain stem are usually disastrous.

"Putnam's got a patient—who I'm rounding on while Putnam's lecturing at the university this week, by the way—a guy in his fifties who had a brain stem stroke early this sum-mer, June, I think. He infarcted his lower brain stem and was brought in with steadily progressing symptoms—one-sided

facial weakness, difficulty swallowing, then difficulty moving his eyes, then no body movement at all, no speech, virtually nothing. It's really a sad situation. He seems to be
receptive; he can hear and understand what you say. His
eyes stay open, and they're fixed in central gaze, meaning he
cannot move them from side to side, but if you ask him to
look up or down, he can move his eyes with seeming ease. It's
very difficult to know just how intact his intellect, emotions,
and other higher functions are. The presumption in this
kind of situation is that you become a kind of child, or less
than a child—very dependent, living for the moment—but
we just don't know—except to know, in his case, that he can
follow eye movement commands and can communicate a bit
of information with eye movements. I mean, compare him
with Jayne. He is definitely *not* brain dead; his brain stem
still has enough function for him to survive, but God, he's
locked inside himself."

A long computer printout stretched from one end of
the wall to the other, its thousands of Xs forming
large letters that read GET WELL SOON, SAL. WE MISS
YOU. Salvador Maldonado, wearing a hospital gown and
pajama bottoms, his dark, handsome face freshly shaved, lay
curled on his side when we walked into his room at St. Luke's
Hospital on Tuesday morning. An IV line was taped to his
forearm; a fatter catheter tube snaked across his mattress,
attached to a urine bag that was pinned to the bottom sheet.
His eyes were open, unblinking, his lips slightly parted. Ex-

cept that he had no tubes in his nose, he appeared to be in the same grave condition that Jayne Welty was in—surely this man was not responsive, surely they would decide that his brain, too, was dead. But when Ferrier moved around the end of the bed and crouched a few inches away from his eyes, he said, "Good morning, Mr. Maldonado," as if Sal Maldonado might have been able to say good morning in reply. "It's Dr. Ferrier. Remember me? Remember that Dr. Putnam is down at the university this week? How are you today? Look up high for me so I know you can hear me, Mr. Maldonado."

Sal Maldonado's eyes, his irises so dark they were hard to distinguish from his pupils, rose smoothly up, then down again. "Raise them one more time, Mr. Maldonado," Ferrier urged, and he obliged. "This time," Ferrier said, his words spoken slowly, "I only want you to raise your eyes if your wife has been in to see you this morning. Raise your eyes if your wife has come to see you today." His eyes did not move; Ferrier waited but there was no response.

While Ferrier was checking his muscle reflexes with a hammer—they were brisk, indicative of the damage to the upper motor neuron tracts in his brain stem—a nurse walked into the room, and Ferrier asked her if Mr. Maldonado's wife had been to the hospital yet that day.

"No. She almost never comes till the middle of the afternoon, does she, Sal?" The nurse put her hand on his shoulder and squeezed it before she turned away. "I'll be back after a bit," she told him.

It was astonishing. If he was aware that his wife had not yet come that day, then surely he was aware of everything that transpired within that small room. Surely he could see the photographs of his wife and children that were taped to the wall, surely he could read his huge get-well card, and could hear the conversations of the nurses as they bathed him and changed his sheets. He *was* in there, wasn't he? He was locked in, as Ferrier had said, unable to initiate any kind of communication, unable to say please bring me a radio to help me get through these interminable days, or to say he was cold and needed a blanket—able only to say yes or no by lifting his haunting eyes.

But there was another possibility. Perhaps his eyes remained motionless because Ferrier's question about his wife was too complex, too difficult for him to understand. It was certain that he understood enough to raise his eyes in response to simple commands, but was he really aware of who had been to see him and who had not? Perhaps his response—the absence of one—had only meant that at that moment his wife was not within his field of vision, or even that the word *wife* no longer had any meaning. It was frightening. How could anyone know how much he knew, how much he perceived, how much of him still lived behind his eyes?

Ferrier brushed back Sai Maldonado's hair, then held his hand as he said good-bye, telling him he would see him in the morning. The dark eyes now seemed somehow desperate to me, but they did not move again before we left.

"He's really in there, isn't he?" I asked Ferrier as we walked to the nurses' station.

"Oh, he definitely has some comprehension, there's no question, but—"

"My God. Imagine if his thinking processes are totally intact. What must it be like for him day after day?"

"I'm almost afraid to ask too many questions," Ferrier said. "Do you think he'd raise his eyes if we asked him if he wanted us to kill him?"

I waited while Ferrier scribbled a note into Sal Maldonado's fat chart—page upon page, three months now of pages, each one recording his blood pressure, his temperature and pulse, recording the daily amounts of glucose that were administered intravenously and his output of urine and feces, recording the sad fact that his condition remained essentially stable.

"He's had a small pneumonia or two, a couple of other complications, and I know that Putnam tried to talk with his wife about whether they shouldn't consider those complications kind of fortunate, as a blessing, in effect, something that would allow him to die. But she and the rest of the family, from what Putnam said, wouldn't hear of it. They want absolutely everything treated as aggressively as possible. They're waiting for a fucking miracle."

"Could he come out of it?" I asked. Could his brain stem somehow recover enough to let him move and speak and swallow again? Could this man's mind ever be unlocked?

Ferrier held the heavy door open, waiting for me to reach it. "You mean, do I believe in miracles?"

Yes, Ferrier believed in the miraculous brain itself. But no, he did not believe that Sal Maldonado's brain stem would somehow recover, that he would simply "wake up" one day, say hello to his wife and good-bye to the nurses who now had cared for him for months. Yet Sal was by no means in the same condition that Jayne Welty was. Her brain had entirely ceased to function. With the assistance of an artificial breathing apparatus, her heart continued to beat, but it could not pump blood into the organ that had made it possible for her to move, to think, to speak. Her brain had ceased to be, and her family had decided not to hold her body hostage to their grief.

At least part of Sal Maldonado's brain remained alive, however. Because of the severity of his stroke, Ferrier could not know how much of his higher cortical function remained intact, but Sal certainly could respond to simple commands, and that meant his brain was at least minimally capable of receiving and decoding spoken stimuli and of initiating a muscular response. Sal, in contrast to Jayne, was very much alive. He was breathing without assistance, and neither Ferrier nor Putnam would have argued that for him there was no hope. But both men characterized that hope as only a very small one, a thin theoretical hope that he might one day move his arms or speak.

In asking his family to consider whether they should be unaggressive in treating the pneumonias he had already suffered, and the infections that would inevitably beset him in the future, the two doctors were asking a very difficult and profound question. It seemed extremely unlikely that Sal's condition would ever improve, and if it did not, was his life now enough of a life to warrant heroic measures to sustain it?

At least for now, Sal's family answered that it was. At least for now, Sal could raise his eyes in recognition of his wife; at least he could lift his eyes in greetings to his children, and for them that was miracle enough.

Before Ferrier saw Jayne Welty in the intensive care unit at County Hospital, he saw three other patients on the wards, two of them Putnam's. The third patient he checked on was Wayne Byers, the stoic, nearly silent man with melanoma, who had been admitted to the hospital ten days before. Wayne had begun to take his Dilantin regularly again since I had last seen him— racked by seizures in the emergency room. The seizures had abated for two weeks, but then they had begun again, a normally therapeutic level of Dilantin in his blood now unable to quell the chaotic firing of nerve cells irritated by his swollen tumors. In addition, Wayne had begun to become confused for short periods of time, not knowing where he was, or even who he was, ignoring the friends that now seemed to be strangers. Ferrier and the oncologist had agreed that Wayne now needed to be hospitalized, and Ferrier was currently trying, with some limited success, to raise his dosages of Dilantin, and now Tegretol as well, to levels that would again stop the seizures, high levels that inevitably made him very drowsy and even more lethargic than before. There would be no more surgery, Wayne's doctors had decided; and the chemotherapy, apparently unsuccessful, would not be tried again.

Wayne was asleep when we walked into his room. Small bandages still covered his surgical scars; his scalp was still bald, his face gaunt, his skin pale and chalky. A copy of the newspaper he no longer worked for lay on the tray beside his bed.

"I won't wake him up," Ferrier said in a whisper. "We'll come back after lunch. Chart says he hasn't had a seizure for, well, not since the night before last. Thirty hours or so. Maybe we're getting—" Ferrier's beeper suddenly sounded; he reached for it and silenced it. Wayne stirred but did not wake up, and we made our way out of the room.

It was Bonnie, a secretary at the office, who was trying to reach him, and Ferrier called her from the nurses' station. She told him Barbara Bishop had just telephoned, saying she urgently needed to talk to him. Bonnie gave him the number and he placed the call, listening briefly, saying little before I heard him say, "good, I'll see you then." He hung up the phone and turned to me, looking a little shocked, astounded, his querulous expression suggesting that the news was not good. "Barbara Bishop. She said the jury was back by eight-thirty this morning with a verdict. It took them just thirty minutes and they awarded her two . . . *million . . . dollars.*"

"You won," I said.

"They didn't award me anything."

"But you helped her get it."

"Two million bucks. That's outrageous. That's *obscene,* for God's sake. I mean, yes, she's disabled, but Jesus!"

"Maybe you did too good a job."

Ferrier shook his head, mumbling something as he stepped away to make a note in Wayne Byers's chart. We walked to the stairwell when he was finished. "That verdict, what in the hell . . . I just can't believe it," he said, sounding genuinely disturbed.

"Oh, you know, they'll appeal. She probably won't end up getting that much."

"I feel like a whore," he said.

Two million dollars did seem like a lot of money, but surely Barbara Bishop deserved compensation for her injuries. Except for her misfortune of having been in the drunken driver's path, her brain would not have been damaged—her memory would not have faltered, her intellect would not have lost its once-sharp edge, her temporal lobe, scraped by her skull when she hit the windshield, would not have become prone to sparking seizures. Her accident was not her fault, the deficits it left her with were not of her own doing, so didn't the jury's award represent a certain justice? It seemed to me that it did.

In contrast, was anyone at fault when Sal Maldonado's brain stem suffered its terrible infarct? Did Eddie Ruiz deserve compensation for the surgery that caused him to abandon the left side of his world> Who was culpable when Jayne

Welty's hemorrhage destroyed her brain? None of their three strokes, each one a cerebrovascular *accident,* was caused by another's negligence, so it was fair that none of them would receive compensation, was it not? None of the three of them were *victims* like Barbara Bishop, were they? Well, yes, it seemed to me that they were—victims of nothing more than the capricious risks of living, perhaps, but victims, nonetheless. Jayne Welty was the victim of a congenitally weak cerebral arterial wall. Eddie Ruiz, like millions of people, was the victim of atherosclerosis, and a victim, too, because he lived in a time when occluded arteries could not be surgically cleared without running a horrible risk. Sal Maldonado, surely a victim, surely proof that justice has no meaning in matters of health, suffered enormously simply because a primitive part of his brain, robbed of its blood supply, had forgotten how to function. Their three profound misfortunes did not seem so different from Barbara Bishop's, after all. Crossing the wrong intersection at the wrong time, Barbara was a victim of chance. But Sai, Eddie, and Jayne were injured by chance as well.

During my visits I had met many patients whose brains had been injured, their deficits caused by trauma instead of by infectious agents, tumors, compromised immune systems, or mysterious degenerative processes. Stroke, too, was a kind of trauma, and I tried to consider whether trauma was fundamentally different from disease, and it didn't seem that it was.

I had met, for instance, one of Ferrier's fellow physicians, a general practitioner whose spinal cord had been severed when his motorcycle roared off the edge of a mountain highway, a man who was now a paraplegic, able to practice medicine but embittered by his disability, embittered by the phantom pain in his groin and his legs that constantly beset him.

I had met an eighteen-year-old boy who, during the course of an operation to remove a subdural hematoma, had been a victim of a surgical drill that malfunctioned and bore too deeply, tearing his middle cerebral artery and infarcting much of his left hemisphere, leaving him wheelchair-bound, epileptic, and asphasic, his chances for an independent adulthood very slim.

I had met an oilfield roustabout whose facial bones had been shattered by a flying wrench and whose brain had been so severely concussed that he had not worked for a year, still suffering constant dizziness, loss of appetite and libido, sleeping sixteen hours a day, unable to do the most menial chores without first finding a way to get angry, his rage temporarily giving him the energy to mow his lawn or to do the breakfast dishes.

I had met a twenty-three-year-old woman with severe cerebral palsy—fixed and permanent brain injury caused by trauma at birth—who always wore a helmet to protect her head from the falls that accompanied her constant seizures, who could walk but could not speak, making herself understood only by grunting and pointing with her finger at objects that intrigued her, who received good care, and even affection, in a state-supported group home, and who might live in a kind of suspended infancy for many more years to come.

These four and many others whose brains and spinal cords had been traumatized in accidents, most of whom saw Ferrier only once or twice a year, their chronic but stable conditions not requiring the constant attention of a neurologist, seemed little different from his patients who suffered disease—those who were made numb and ungainly by multiple sclerosis, or tremulous by Parkinson's disease, or immobile by ALS, or whose clogged and corroded arteries resulted in sudden strokes. All illness was accidental, wasn't it?—whether injury or disease, whether caused by a car wreck, an invading virus, or by some cellular twist of fate— all illness occurring for no purpose, arriving uninvited, enduring with no justice.

In the lounge near the ICU, Jayne Welty's family waited. Her parents, holding hands, sat on a small couch across from a television set that was turned off. Her sisters, both younger than Jayne, one of them still a teenager, sat in straight-backed chairs, both wearing skirts and makeup as though they had dressed up to say good-bye to their sister. "I'll see you in just a minute," Ferrier said to them, momentarily leaning into the room.

Ferrier looked at Jayne's most recent EEG—performed at seven that morning, the fourth EEG since she had been admitted—and he studied her chart at the nurses' station before we walked into her room. Bill Welty sat in a folding chair at Jayne's bedside, holding her limp hand, his face looking worn and weary, his expression almost vacant, his tears long since exhausted. "Bill," Ferrier said, "good morning. Were you here all night?"

Bill nodded. "Morning."

Ferrier walked to the opposite side of the bed. He peered into Jayne's eyes but did not take his ophthalmoscope out of his briefcase. He, too, took her hand. "The EEG that they did early this morning doesn't show any change. It's flat-line, like the last one was. I'll do some final tests here in a minute as well, but everything we discussed last evening still seems to hold. Her urine output is slowing down a lot, which is something we would expect to happen at this point, but if her kidneys are going to be intact enough for transplant, they have to be taken soon—and, of course, that decision doesn't have to be final. You all may certainly change your minds. But assuming you don't, the transplant team is due here at about nine-thirty."

"I think everybody feels the same way they did last night," Bill said. "I'll go check with them again though. Jayne and I talked one time about transplants. I'm sure she'd want to try to help somebody else. It's the one thing that " Bill couldn't speak for a moment. "It I'll be in the lounge," he said, his voice quaking with a sadness that seemed to envelop him and Jayne and Ferrier and me as well. For the first time ever, in that instant, I had an inkling of what that kind of loss must mean, a glimpse of grief's bleak and consuming blanket. Bill delicately laid Jayne's hand and forearm on the bed, as though he might injure her if he were not careful, then he stood and walked out of the room.

I had not wanted to intrude on Jayne's family the night before, yet there I stood at her deathbed, surely intruding now, observing as her family ended their vigil, not needing to be there, but wanting to be there for reasons I could not explain. I had never seen a patient whose heart had stopped, and in the years before, the bodies I had seen after death were only bizarre embalmed mannequins, waxy facsimiles of the people they had recently belonged to. At death, a body would be different, I presumed. The transition from life to death would be sudden, definite, dramatic in its clear finality. Life—glorious, incomprehensible life—would simply stop, and the silence of death would be unmistakable. A body at death would be the one thing in the world that would be truly straightforward, cold, and utterly uncomplicated.

But Ferrier claimed that Jayne was already dead, that death had taken hold of her a day or so ago. If he were right, then even death had no simplicity. Jayne's skin was still warm and supple, her heart still pumped, her breasts still heaved with each intake of breath. Yet her open eyes suggested nothing; they were devoid of expression, offering no hint of ever having glittered with delight, of having mirrored understanding, of ever having seen.

Ferrier held Jayne's forehead and quickly turned it from side to side, watching the eyes, observing that they remained totally fixed. He did not inject cold water into her ears again, but he did press his pen against the nails of a finger and toe, again getting no response, seeing no trace of movement, no grimace, nothing but the open, empty eyes. Ferrier turned off the respirator and left it off for a couple of minutes, confirming that Jayne herself was not breathing, before he turned it back on. He pressed Jayne's hand between his palms before we walked out of the room.

In the lounge, everyone in the family was standing, each person's face looking apprehensive, uncertain about what was about to happen, unsure of what was expected. Ferrier shook Jayne's father's hand, and the hands of her sisters, then asked them if Bill had explained that the transplant team would arrive in about twenty minutes. They nodded. "We feel good about it," Jayne's mother said.

"What will happen," Ferrier explained, "is that they'll arrive— and you all might want to spend some time with Jayne before they do—then we'll ask you to come back here while they briefly take her into surgery. They won't be taking her heart; there wasn't a matched recipient, but she'll stay on the respirator while they remove her corneas, and the kidneys, and the liver. When they've finished, we'll take her off the respirator. She isn't breathing on her own anymore, so when it's gone, she probably will stop breathing rather quickly. And, of course, just as soon as all that's done, you can go back in again. I'll be here, so let me know if there's anything you need, okay?"

"Mother," Jayne's father said to his wife, "let's go see Jayney for a minute." His eyes were wet; his wife had begun to cry and he took her by the arm. Bill and Jayne's sisters stayed behind. "Thanks," Bill said to Ferrier, shaking his hand, unable to say anything else. Jayne's sisters were tearful now, too, and Ferrier hugged them both before we left them alone.

We spotted Stan Singleton, standing alone, near the door into Medical Records at the opposite end of the corridor and we walked to meet him. "Doctor," he said, "I don't want to get in their way. I won't bother them, but I . . . wanted to be here, at least. When I called in last evening, Bill said they were going to take her off the respirator this morning. Is she still—?"

"Right now we're waiting for the transplant team from the university. The family decided to donate her organs. When they're finished, then we'll take away the life support."

"And she'll die?"

"She'll be on her own. She isn't breathing on her own now. Off the respirator, she probably won't breathe at all, but—"

Stan Singleton started to cry. "She was such a wonderful. . .." His tears made it hard for him to speak. "She. . . ." We stood beside him, saying nothing, offering him nothing but our silent presence until the three men who made up the transplant team turned the corner into the corridor—the three of them wearing scrubs and carrying two red and white coolers, looking as they walked toward us like surgeons planning a picnic. Ferrier reached for Stan Singleton's arm, saying, "Listen. This wasn't your fault. Call me in a couple of days, will you?" Stan nodded, and Ferrier escorted the three men down the hall and through the doors into the ICU.

At the door of Jayne's room, Ferrier briefly outlined for them Jayne's accident, the surgery, and her deteriorating status since. Beverly, Jayne's nurse, followed them into her room to help them transfer her onto the cart that would roll her into surgery.

Jayne's family waited in the lounge again, all of them still standing, embracing one another, saying little except to assure themselves that she would have wanted it this way. Ferrier told them he would come back for them in just a few minutes before he went to the nurses' station to begin dictating a death summary. The three surgeons spoke briefly with Ferrier when they returned from the operating room, then left, their coolers containing Jayne's gifts. I followed Ferrier and Beverly into the room where Jayne had been returned. The bedcovers were pulled up over Jayne's shoulders now; her hair was mussed from her short journey; her eyes, missing their corneas, looked strangely flat and opaque. There were sucking, gurgling sounds when Ferrier and Beverly, working together, pulled the tube that had reached to her stomach, and she gasped—or seemed to gasp—as the second nostril tube came up from her lungs. Jayne's strong heart beat for four minutes after Ferrier closed her eyes.

A GIFT IN GILLELEGE

An excerpt from BEETHOVEN'S HAIR

Paul Hiller, journalist and music scholar, had been keenly interested over the years to read the infrequently published volumes of the monumental Life of Beethoven that American Alexander Wheelock Thayer had begun work on more than a half century before, a biography, unlike most of its predecessors, that had been intended to describe the composer's life as it actually had occurred. Soon after Thayer had initiated the project in 1849, he had enlisted the long-term assistance of writer and historian Hermann Deiters, whose principal task it would be to edit Thayer's writing and translate it into German, the appropriate language in which the exhaustive biography should be published, Thayer believed. The two men had succeeded in completing three volumes—addressing the composer's life through 1816—when, following years of failing health and a mounting writer's block, Thayer had died in 1897 and the task of completing the project had fallen to Deiters alone. Deiters had been able to finish the biography's fourth volume in the weeks before to his own death in 1907, then it had fallen to his colleague Hugo Riemann to complete the fifth and final volume, to reedit its predecessors, and to over-see the publication in 1917 of the definitive, five-volume set, a biography that in the end succeeded stunningly in its scope, its scale, and its "devotion to Beethoven the man," as Thayer long ago had hoped it would—a work that proved to Paul Hiller and thousands of kindred Beethoven devotees that the composer had been, in fact, all the more remarkable for his flawed humanity. His was human music, not the work of a god of any rank, and therein lay both its mystery and its enormous, enduring appeal.

Paul Hiller, age eighty-one, white-haired, still hand-some, and not at all the corpulent man his father had been, died on January 27, 1934, soon after suffering a stroke at his home at 31 Eifelstrasse in Cologne. At his bedside were his wife Sophie, her age unknown, and his two younger sons—Edgar, soon to be twenty-eight and an opera singer like his father and grandmother before him had been, and Erwin, then twenty-six and an actor, both sons still living at their parents' home. Unknown to them and residing in Berlin at the time was their half brother Felix, fifty-one, who had grown up in Chemnitz, and who had supported himself as an artist in his younger days before becoming a composer, continuing in the tradition of his paternal grandfather. Three days after Paul Hiller's death, a paid obituary appeared in a Cologne newspaper, the small no-tice bearing a thick black border and headed by a simple black cross. "After a life of rich artistic creativity," it read, righteous up to his death, our unforgettable dear husband and father, Herr Paul Hiller, music writer, passed away unexpectedly . . . at the age of eighty-one. He died firmly believing in his Savior. In accordance with his wishes, we have laid our beloved departed one quietly to his final rest in the Southern Cemetery in Cologne. In deep sorrow: Sophie Hiller; Edgar and Erwin Hiller. We ask friends to abstain from condolence visits.

Paul Hiller had worked as a staff writer for the Rheinische Zeitung for a quarter century, a position he had held until eight years before, yet it was not that newspaper in which his family chose to have the obituary published. Neither did it appear in the Kölnische Zeitung, the periodical that had published Paul's memorial article on the centenary of his father's birth. Instead, the obituary had been purchased in the Westdeutscher Beobachter, and therein lay the first of many subsequent mysteries. Why did Paul Hiller's family choose to note his passing in the Cologne newspaper that was the most zealously pro-Nazi at that moment? Had Paul Hiller borne ill will toward the newspaper where he had worked so long, and was this choice therefore evidence of some spite? Or did the family members choose to publish the obituary in the Westdeutscher Beobachter specifically in order to help mask their Jewish identity, to protect themselves from harassment and the growing threat of violence? Could that attempt at concealment account as well for the

use of the cross and the short notice's two separate references to Paul Hiller's—and by inference his family's—devout Christianity? Ferdinand Hiller and his wife, Antolka,
had become converted Lutherans almost a century before,
and their son therefore was at least a nominal Christian, yet
by all accounts his parents' conversion had been one only of
convenience. For four generations by now, the Hildesheim
family had called itself Hiller in order to help it assimi-
late into middle-class German society as well as circumvent
the very real possibility of persecution. Were the posting of
Paul's obituary in a pro-Nazi newspaper and the repeated
references to his Christian faith merely the continuation of
a lamentable but necessary family tradition carried out this
time in frighteningly dangerous times? . . .

T he cavernous Danish National Archives contain no
     evidence indicating that a German emigrant named
Sophie Hiller or either of her two sons, Edgar or Erwin,
were admitted to Denmark between 1934 and 1943. Neither
do the archives contain a record establishing that Sophie's
stepson Felix Hiller was one of the thousands of German
refugees who had passed through Danish immigration prior
to the outbreak of the war. It is possible, of course, that
one—or even all—of them were admitted under false iden-
tities. Hundreds of refugees present in Denmark in 1943 entered the country by clandestine means and without official
sanction, and therefore no record of their presence has ever
existed.

What is irrefutable, however, is that the lives of this single family steeped in music had been ruptured in a way that would have been utterly unimaginable as recently as 1934, the year in which Paul Hiller passed away. The available evidence makes it appear certain that none of the Hillers remained in Cologne in 1943, and the reappearance of the locket likewise makes it possible that at least one of them escaped to Denmark before the late-summer of that year, when the Nazis seized martial control of their occupied country and set about the scurrilous business of deporting Jews. But would Sophie, Edgar, or Erwin Hiller have been readily identifiable as Jewish in a country where that designation was deemed insignificant in comparison with the grave importance it had borne in neighboring Germany? Once in Denmark, would the Hillers have shunned their Jewish ethnicity as a further means of self-protection? Or conversely, might they have sought out that country's small community of Jews as a way to draw vital assistance and support from others who similarly were hunted? Might a member of the Hiller family have been among the large crowd that had gathered at the venerable Copenhagen Synagogue on the morning of September 30, 1943, to hear Rabbi Marcus Melchior's stunning announcement?

> Last night I received word that tomorrow the Germans plan to raid Jewish homes throughout Copenhagen to arrest all the Danish Jews for shipment to concentration camps. They know that tomorrow is Rosh Hashanah and

our families will be home. The situation is very
serious. We must take action immediately. You
must leave the synagogue now and contact all
relatives, friends, and neighbors you know are
Jewish and tell them what I have told you. You
must tell them pass the word on to everyone
they know is Jewish. You must also speak to all
your Christian friends and tell them to warn
the Jews. You must do this immediately, within the next few minutes, so that two or three
hours from now everyone will know what is
happening. By nightfall tonight, we must all be
in hiding.

This extraordinary information had come to the rabbi
from C.B. Henriques, a supreme court barrister and long-
time leader of the Jewish community, who had received it
from Social-Democratic party chief Hans Hedtoft, who, in
turn, had been personally warned by German shipping at-
taché Georg Duckwitz that a Nazi aktion was imminent.
Duckwitz first had risked arrest for treason on September
8 when he had attempted to intercept a telegram cabled to
Berlin by his close friend Werner Best, the Nazi's plenipo-
tentiary in Denmark, in which Best had recommended to
Hitler that now was the right time to deal decisively with
the nation's Jews. Duckwitz had failed in that endeavor, but
when, ten days later, Hitler had ordered the abductions and
deportations to commence on October 1, Duckwitz had
been unable to stay silent. It had been solely his decision of

conscience that had given members of the Jewish community the single day's notice, during which time they had been
able to hide or to flee, his decision alone that had mobilized
the resistance movement and thousands of hitherto passive
Danes. Before nightfall on September 30, a determined, if
impromptu, nationwide effort to rescue Denmark's Jews
was underway.

Messengers immediately were mobilized in Copenhagen
and smaller cities and towns to spread the critical word,
volunteers knocking on every door they came to because
theretofore there had been no general awareness in Denmark
of who was Jewish and who was not. Lutheran ministers
made urgent telephone pleas to their parishioners to shelter
Jews however they could; resistance leaders began to marshal
the aid of merchant fishermen whose boats could begin to
ferry Jews to safety; boy scouts and members of hunting
clubs combed woodlands in search of refugees who had
sought the limited cover of trees, attempting to direct them
to harbor towns where boats might await them; everywhere
hospitals suddenly were filled to overflowing with patients
whose names were listed as Hansen, Petersen, or Jensen, and
as word reached the hospitals about families who were precariously hidden—or not hidden at all—ambulances quickly were dispatched to fetch them.

Taxis that otherwise would have been plying Copenhagen's cobbled streets on an early autumn afternoon now
sped through the quiet countryside en route to the fishing
villages that ringed the Øresund coast; and seaside trains,
too, were packed as though the summer holiday season sud-

denly had recommenced, their hushed, grim-visaged passengers wearing as many clothes as they could fit beneath their heavy coats. Fishing ports like Rungsted, Humelbæk, Helsingør, Hornbæk, and Gilleleje began to swell with their new arrivals, townspeople opening their shops, their barns, attics, and living rooms to guests who had been utterly unexpected the day before.

Perhaps because it was farthest from Copenhagen and the perceived threat of the Gestapo, but also certainly because the train dead-ended there, the village of Gilleleje on the northern tip of Sjælland soon felt a particular surge of temporary inhabitants. On Tuesday, October 5—five days after the rescue effort had hastened to life—the evening train into Gilleleje carried 314 people instead of the three dozen it normally did, the Gilleleje stationmaster penciling the word "Jews" beside the number he scribbled in an effort to explain the flood of passengers. But these were not the first refugees to reach the town of 1,700 inhabitants; many had arrived in the preceding days and already had boarded fishing boats docked in Gilleleje's small harbor and safely crossed to the port of Höganäs in neutral Sweden, a dozen nautical miles across the wind-chopped expanse where the narrow Øresund met the open waters of the Kattegat Sea.

The first eight refugees—two families from Copenhagen who had not needed to wait for Rabbi Melchior's urgent announcement to sense that flight from the Nazis was about to become their only option—had escaped across the sound in the early morning hours of Wednesday, September 29. Hidden by shopkeeper Tage Jacobsen and his wife, then ferried to Sweden by retired fisherman Niels Clausen, who had lost a leg and had not been to sea for several years, but who had agreed to transport them nonetheless, the four adults and four children had been interrogated by police in Höganäs on their arrival, then quartered in a boardinghouse.

By Friday, October 1, dozens more refugees had arrived in the village. The Gilleleje Inn had been filled, as had the Badehotel, despite the fact that its owners, townspeople said, were open about their pro-Nazi sentiments. So many people who plainly hailed from somewhere else had begun to walk the streets that nervous residents began to invite the strangers into their homes, and grocer Gilbert Lassen opened the summer houses for which he acted as caretaker to refugees as well, certain that their owners would approve of his largesse. Before long, frightened Jews anxious to flee Denmark, their names almost never mentioned to their hosts, had been sheltered virtually everywhere in and around the village—in garages and lofts, in sheds and warehouses, at the hospital, the boatbuilder's yard, the waterworks, and the brewery.

Fishing cutters and oceangoing schooners from the large Gilleleje fleet had sailed unpredictably but often during the first days of the rescue. The passengers they took on board paid what they could for the short voyage to safety, the fisherman accepting payment simply because it had been irresistible not to demand it, but also because they had risked their boats, their livelihoods, even prison if they had been apprehended by the feared Gestapo. Knots of huddled refugees had waited at the docks for hours in open daylight in the beginning, then simply had walked on board a readied boat. But before long their swelling numbers, as well as the sheer numbers of embarkations, had necessitated that runs largely had been attempted late at night. The ships made the crossing without the benefit of lights, and soon thereafter departures from the harbor gave way to safer and more surreptitious launches from the beaches that lay east and west of town, a half-dozen refugees at a time loaded into dinghies in the seconds between the crash of each successive wave, then ferried out to the Maagen, the Tyborøn, the Haabet, the Fri, or the Wasa waiting in deep water.

Instead of setting a course due east to Höganäs, captains of the erstwhile fishing vessels had tended to sail north into the Kattegat as they departed the Danish coast, and only had steered eastward across the sound once they reached open water, where the likelihood of encountering German patrol boats had been even slimmer than it otherwise was. And once the trickle of refugees had reached a steady flow, the neutral Swedes—openly favoring the Allied powers now that Nazi military fortunes had begun to ebb dramatically—had done what they could to make the fishermen's round-trip journeys simpler. Swedish naval vessels made rendezvous with the Danish ships a mile or two out from the welcoming coast, their human cargo transferred on narrow gangplanks from one wave-pitched ship to another before being delivered to the Swedish harbor.

But then on the morning of Wednesday, October 6, Gestapo chief Hans Juhl, based in the nearby port of Helsingør and sniffing trouble, declared all the harbors of north

Sjælland off limits to anyone who did not possess a valid fisherman's card; he instructed members of the Danish civilian coast-guard to monitor carefully all activity along the shore—although the guard's allegiance to him was tenuous at best—and Juhl and his men began to make periodic raids on harbors and suspected hiding places in hopes of catching the Danes in what they perceived as blatant acts of sabotage—the secreting of hunted Jews out of Germany's grasp.

Wednesday morning dawned dreary and overcast, a light rain continuing from the storm that had raged in the night, and a hard southeast wind still swept across the village's thatched and tiled roofs, then out into a troubled sea. The more than three hundred refugees who had arrived by train the night before—together with those already in town but who had not yet found their way to Sweden—were dry and momentarily safe, at least, if not entirely comfortable in makeshift lodgings throughout Gilleleje and its surroundings. By the estimate of a group of townspeople meeting at first light at Oluf Olsen's butcher shop, as many as five hundred Jews whose lives were in real peril were hidden at the moment. So many refugees had descended on Gilleleje that new locations in which they could hide were becoming distressingly scarce, and the local leaders spoke urgently about how best to deal with an increasingly grave situation. Should the refugees be moved far inland somehow? Should someone try to get word to resistance organizers in Copenhagen that Gilleleje already was packed to overflowing with people who could not sail to Sweden because the Gestapo had grown determined at last to stop them? Should the townspeople attempt to organize a single, large, but inherently very risky transport, boarding most—or even all—of the refugees onto one of the large ships that had sought shelter in the harbor during the long storm? Would the captain of one of those ships agree to the dramatic plan?

Grocer Gilbert Lassen attended the meeting at Olsen's shop; so did fishmonger Juhl Jensen, high school teachers Assenchenfeldt Frederiksen and Mogens Schmidt, Pastor Kjeldgaard Jensen, and Christian Petersen, chairman of the parish council. At least six out-of-towners also were present: a man named Nielsen who sold insurance in nearby Hillerød; Niels Thorsen and Jean Fischer, resistance activists and students at Copenhagen's Technical University; Arne Kleven, a star football player a few years before, now a union administrator, and writer for the underground newspaper Nordisk Front; as well as Henry Skjær, the renowned, 44-year old baritone from the Royal Danish Opera. Neither the well-known Kleven nor Skjær were Jewish and therefore their lives were not in danger, but they, like the students, had become very active in organizing the escape during the preceding week, and both had arrived in Gilleleje on the packed Tuesday evening train, together with hundreds of people in flight for whom they now had assumed more than tacit responsibility.

At the close of the early-morning meeting, the ad hoc rescue committee agreed that although the effort would entail serious risk, the option that made most sense was to arrange a large-scale transport and to do so as soon as possible. The students were charged with collecting money from the refugees to pay for their passage, and the teacher Schmidt volunteered to go to the harbor to convince the captain of at least one of the storm-sheltered ships that the bounty he would receive for a two-hour detour to Sweden would be well worth the short-term risk to his ship and crew. Although twenty vessels had anchored in the small harbor during the night storm, the only skipper whom Schmidt could find in the harbor area was Gunnar Flyvbjerg, captain of a large, family-owned schooner named the Flyvbjerg. But for the seductive fee of 50,000 Danish kroners, the captain and his mates readily agreed that they would make a single run to Höganäs, departing at one o'clock that afternoon. The hold of the Flyvbjerg was empty, and although its passengers could not be comfortably accommodated en route, many hundreds of refugees—perhaps even everyone in town who was desperate to go—could come aboard.

News of the impending transport spread immediately throughout the village, and in only an hour a worrisome number of refugees had begun to gather openly along the docks at the harbor, anxious about how many people the schooner could carry, and eager to assure themselves of passage. The organizers had planned to escort people to the waiting ship only in small groups, but the rush of refugees to the harbor by late morning meant that scheme had to be abandoned before it even began. Instead, hundreds of people simply swarmed the harbor area by midday—men, women, and children of all ages bundled in heavy clothing, their faces etched with fear and uncertainty, many attempting to manage suitcases, trunks, and baby carriages. Townspeople gathered too, if for no other reason than that nothing like this ever had occurred in Gilleleje, and everyone—whether bound for Sweden or simply there to see the refugees on their way—knew that Gestapo Juhl and his men might arrive from Helsingør at any moment, trapping the Jews at the water's edge before they could board and be gone.

At last people were allowed to begin making their way along a narrow breakwater to the place where the Flyvbjerg was moored, then to begin boarding. The crowd surged toward the stone jetty that would lead them out to the ship; people struggled to maintain their places in line; and although some were safely onboard after a time, the process was terribly slow. To the dismay of many, a fisherman began to try to direct the crowd, and when someone shouted, "Throw him in the harbor! He's an agent!," others misunderstood and began to scream, "The Gestapo! The Gestapo are coming." In the seconds of panic that ensued the rumor soon seemed true, and even the Flyvbjerg's captain quickly was convinced that the Nazis were bearing down on his ship. He started his schooner's motors, pushed away the desperate people who still struggled to board, then cast off, passing beyond the encircling breakwaters in only a moment and heading out to sea, stranding hundreds on the jetty, hundreds more still on shore.

Although 182 refugees ultimately reached Sweden aboard the Flyvbjerg that day, perhaps 300 more did not. Despite the fact that the Gestapo had captured no one, the transport plan had failed. For the moment, at least, the hundreds of terrified, perplexed, and angry people—a few separated from family members who now were en route to Höganäs—were ushered inside the big repair shed that stood at the foot of the jetty, and a frenzied meeting soon was underway to try to determine what to do next. No one had been captured, but it now seemed clear that future embarkations as large as the one just attempted, whether disrupted by Nazis or not, surely would pose similar logistical problems. A carefully crafted strategy for getting small groups efficiently onto ships had to be devised, but in the meantime, the Jews simply had to be shrouded from sight.

A small group of refugees briefly had been held at the village church during the morning while they had waited to board the Flyvbjerg, and it seemed to make sense to hide a larger group there once again. In an empty loft above the nave, perhaps a hundred people could be concealed—for a long time, if necessity demanded—and before the meeting broke up, Arne Kleven, the union administrator and writer, agreed to escort a group of refugees to the church and lock himself inside with them in order to assure them that they would not be forgotten. It was a promise that was to become all too easy for him to keep.

During the Sunday morning service three days before, Reverend Kjeldgaard Jensen had read to his parishioners the pastoral letter that had been issued by the bishops of the Danish Lutheran church in response to the crisis. It was the duty of church members, the letter instructed, to protest against the persecution of Denmark's Jews because

Jesus had been a Jew, because persecution was contrary to his command to love one's neighbors, and also simply because persecution "is contrary to the conception of justice that prevails in the Danish people." Pastor Jensen himself had taken the letter very much to heart: he had joined the efforts of the ad hoc organizing committee; he had made the church and the parish hall readily available for the hiding of refugees; and then, late in the afternoon on Wednesday, October 6, he went to the church door, loudly spoke the word håbet, "hope," the password that proved he was a friend, then was let inside by Arne Kleven. He climbed the steep and narrow stairs to the loft, then announced to the many people gathered there that as vicar of the sacred place where they now waited, he would protect each one of them with his life if called upon to do so.

The spirits of the people now sheltered in the loft had been crushed when the chaotic scene in the harbor stranded them on shore, the Flyvbjerg, some of their friends, even family members, embarking for Sweden without them. Many of them had spent all the money they possessed to secure passage on the Flyvbjerg, and despite assurances from townspeople that they would not be asked to pay again, they could not be entirely certain that that would be the case. They had been told as well that they would remain in the cold, dark, and airless loft only until townspeople could plan a way for them safely to board the Jan, another of the several schooners that had sought safety in the Gilleleje harbor the previous night, and whose captain also had agreed to transport refugees. This time, the plan was for the Jan to leave the harbor, then weigh anchor well offshore; small groups of refugees would be ferried out to the ship in dinghies in the dead of night from Smidstrup Strand, a secluded beach east of town. Kleven told the refugees that they would be transported that night, if possible. The organizers apologized for their discomfort, but they assured the huddled and desperate Jews—as Pastor Jensen had done—that they diligently would protect them until they were safely on Swedish soil.

In addition to the sixty or so anonymous people who had made their way to the loft from the harbor under Arne Kleven's escort, another group of nameless refugees who had just arrived in the village now sought the shelter of the church as the dreary day gave way to night. Before leaving Copenhagen earlier in the afternoon and traveling in taxis and private cars to Gilleleje, Henry Skjær, the opera singer, somehow had gotten word to a group of fleeing Jews about the planned transport aboard the Jan and had told them that they should seek shelter at the church until the secret operation was underway. Earlier, Marta Fremming, a nurse and wife of Dr. Kay Fremming, one of the town's two physicians, had come to the parish hall—a block away from the church—to inform Grete Frederiksen, who lived in an apartment on the premises, that this new group—numbering as many as sixty people themselves—would arrive about dark, and so they did, in single carloads, beginning at six p.m.

Although no record survives directly linking Marta Fremming to Henry Skjær, it seems virtually certain that they must have worked jointly to bring the new group of refugees to the town and to the church. What is sure is that the unmarried Miss Frederiksen welcomed the new arrivals to the parish hall when they knocked on her kitchen door and spoke the password "hope." She made the first two dozen people as comfortable as they could be in the parish hall itself, where they spent the evening in its dark and unheated central room; the others she escorted to the church loft, where they brought the total number of people now hidden there to perhaps ten dozen.

Virtually everyone in town, of course, knew that the church was filled with Jewish refugees. Throughout the afternoon and evening, people brought blankets and coats, tureens of soup, even a roast. But as soon as night descended, it became impossible for those who were hidden to eat because it was simply too dangerous to turn on even a single light. Buckets were placed in a corner to serve as makeshift toilet facilities, but neither could they be located once night fell and the interior of the loft grew dark as a cave. The temperature hovered barely above freezing; people's hands and feet went numb; and the place was eerily silent—more than a hundred people packed into the small attic space, saying nothing for hours on end, not even daring to whisper, the only sound the incessant ticking of the clock in the tower, its maddening repetitions seeming to mock the refugees' precarious fate.

It is not clear when it happened, but at some point prior to midnight, Dr. Fremming was called to the church to attend to someone who was ill. He may have arrived with Red Cross workers, and perhaps he was called instead to the parish hall. Neither is it known how long he stayed or whether he still remained when a series of knocks were made on the heavy door. "Get out! The Germans are coming," those who were knocking whispered loudly, but whoever these people were, they did not utter the password, and Arne Kleven therefore did not open the door, and neither could he take credence in their warning.

At about midnight, however, the Gestapo did descend. They beat on the parish-hall door with pistols drawn; they spoke the password, and when Grete Frderiksen cracked the door to see who it was, a Gestapo officer shoved his boot in the opening to prevent her from slamming it shut, then a host of troopers burst into the place, readily capturing all the Jews who were hidden inside, only a few officers needed to detain the refugees there while the rest left for the church. Positioned beside the barred church door, Kleven could hear for a second time loud knocks and a shouted warning that the Germans were on their way—the admonition coming this time from Grete Frederiksen's brother and fiancé, whom she had been able to alert by escaping out the parish hall's kitchen door. But for the second time too, these men, speaking Danish, had not known the password, and so Kleven determined that he should do nothing more than search for alternative hiding places in the church, or for another exit, neither of which he could find.

Yet there was a tiny door concealed behind the altar, and Pastor Jensen was attempting to open it from the outside in order to alert Kleven and those in the loft of the immediate danger when a Gestapo agent positioned nearby spotted him. In hopes of gaining a bit of time, Jensen told the Gestapo that church sexton Aage Jørgensen possessed the only key to the building, and, accepting his story, he and Gestapo Chief Juhl made their way to Jørgensen's house, where Jørgensen too helped stall for precious minutes by insisting that the key was a tricky one, and that perhaps he should come open the door himself, but the officers would have to wait while he dressed, he told them, and his dressing would be slow because his back was very bad.

Previously, the Gestapo had carried out its raids without the assistance of the thousands of German soldiers stationed in north Sjælland, but the barricaded church appeared to be a big enough prize that the Gestapo chief now ordered troops from a nearby garrison to provide assistance, and by about four a.m., the exterior of the church was flooded by light from automobiles and troop-trucks, and was surrounded as well by battle-ready soldiers. The long night of despair suffered by the people in the loft now appeared to be ending in utter horror, but from downstairs Kleven did his best to assure the refugees that their fortress would hold. Because Kleven's key was pressed into the lock from the inside, the sexton—with the small and impatient Gestapo chief at his side—was unable to open the door, and still more terrifying moments passed before Juhl announced at the door that he now had no choice but to fire-bomb the building: the refugees either would be forced out by the ensuing smoke, or they would burn to death, or they could spare themselves and open the door. It was their decision, he shouted.

At five a.m., Arne Kleven took a deep breath, steeled himself for whatever was about to follow, then opened the heavy door. People in the loft above him had begun to plead for him to do so, and he too knew that hope now was lost. "Where are they?" Juhl cried as he burst into the small church. "You can damn well find them yourselves," Kleven replied, and it was only seconds later when men armed with machine guns bounded into the loft, aimed blinding lights on the huddled, frozen figures they encountered there, then forced them out of the loft, into the night, and down the sloping street to the parish hall where, together with the refugees who had been captured earlier, they waited eight more hours before they were loaded into canvas-topped troop-trucks bound for the Horserød prison camp near Helsingør. A hundred and twenty Jews had failed in their desperate effort to reach exile in Sweden, and virtually all the townspeople of Gilleleje now ached with the belief that they horribly had let them down.

We will likely never know precisely when, or where, someone fleeing for his life or for hers gave Kay Fremming a coiled knot of Ludwig van Beethoven's hair, held safe in a wood-frame locket. The identity—and the unexplained motive—of that person long may remain a mystery as well.

Although rumors swirled around the small harbor town for months, even years afterward that Dr. Fremming had been given something precious by one of the hunted refugees, he was a quiet and always insular man who appears never to have spoken openly about a most unusual gift he received on or about October 6, 1943. Nor did he ever affirm, on the other hand, that he had agreed to hold and guard the locket until its owner returned for it sometime hence. Yet whether the lock of hair was a profound offering of gratitude or simply someone else's keepsake, which he agreed to hold in trust until the day when it could be reclaimed, it is sure beyond any doubt that this fragile bit of the corporeal Beethoven fell into Kay Fremming's possession sometime during those few days of determined heroism on Denmark's sea-buffeted shore.

Despite the absence of certainty, there are clues, at least, with which it is possible to piece together a scenario—or several of them—that bring the giving of the lock of hair into plausible focus. Marta Fremming did confirm long ago that the lock of hair was given to her husband in the midst of those most momentous days in Gilleleje's history. It is certain as well that she and her husband were active in the collective effort to protect the Jews who rushed to their town in hopes that they could find a way to freedom in Sweden. And the fact seems inescapable, more specifically, that Kay and Marta Fremming were in contact, if not careful collaboration, with opera baritone Henry Skjær, who had urged refugees to travel from Copenhagen to Gilleleje on the afternoon of October 6, instructing them to go to the church to await passage to Höganäs on the Jan.

What is not known positively is whether Dr. Fremming and his wife also hid refugees in their home or at their clinic sometime during the days of the rescue, although that probability seems quite high as well—the lock of hair conceivably given to the doctor by someone he had begun to get to know and whose debt to him seemed great. Other questions, too, remain:

Why was Copenhagen resident Henry Skjær, already a luminary in the small and rarefied community of Danish music, so intimately involved in the rescue cause in Gilleleje, a provincial town that in those days was about three hours away from the city by train? Unlike Arne Kleven, whose union and journalism background made him a ready sort of activist, Skjær's profession and his notoriety, on their face, do not make it appear obvious that he would have been eager to be involved. Did he, like Kleven, travel to Gilleleje and attempt to help people he did not know simply out of a heightened personal sense of moral and patriotic duty? Or was Skjær endeavoring to assist one or a few persons in particular—colleagues, friends, family members? Although people clearly remember that Skjær was present at a hastily called meeting in the early afternoon of October 6, soon after the Flyvbjerg's abrupt departure from the harbor, his whereabouts during the remainder of the day and the ensuing awful night are unknown. What is certain is that Henry Skjær informed people in Copenhagen—either in person or, more likely, by telephone—that the Jan would sail from Smidstrup Beach, and that its passengers would wait at the Gilleleje Church to be taken to the ship. But did he, in fact, give that information to the person who then chose to flee to Gilleleje carrying with him or her the lock of hair?

Indeed, might that person have been 35-year old Edgar Hiller, also a professional singer, who had been employed by the Cologne opera when the record of his whereabouts was interrupted back in 1935? Were Henry Skjær and Edgar Hiller—resident in Denmark under a false name for some years perhaps—musical colleagues, even close friends? With Skjær's help, was Edgar Hiller hidden at the Fremming's house? Or did the doctor attend to him, or a family member, when he was called to the church? Did the donor somehow become aware that the doctor himself was much enamored of music and that he was an accomplished flutist as well?

These questions beg still others like them, yet they can be distilled into three elemental and enduring queries: Why did the locket's owner choose to give it up in Gilleleje? Why did Kay Fremming forever remain so silent about the circumstances of the giving? And was it Edgar Hiller, in fact, who gave away the lock of hair his grandfather had cut from a great man's corpse?

COWBOYS & IMAGES

An excerpt from COWBOY

There is a dry and bedeviled corner of the American West that has seen a lot of cowboys in its time. It is a high and rocky triangle of terrain bounded roughly by the brown waters of the Colorado, Dolores, and San Juan rivers, and it straddles the states of Colorado, New Mexico, and Utah. It is a haughty kind of country-ugly and enticing, beautiful and forbidding. It nurtures a little grass, and it engenders a perplexing loyalty.

When the Spanish explorer-priests Dominguez and Escalante passed through the region in 1776, they thought the land appeared capable of providing pasture for many cattle. The first Hispanic ranchers settled in as the nineteenth century opened. A group of Mormon stockmen followed in the 1850s. And a long and steady migration of Anglo-American cattle and sheep raisers began in the 1880s. But the region never became a cattle empire, as vast reaches of Texas, Nebraska, and Montana had become. It seemed destined instead to spawn as many kinds of cowboys as numbers of cows. After Zane Grey visited the coarse canyon and mesa country early in the twentieth century, he made the area the setting for *Riders of the Purple*

Sage, a seminal Western novel and one of the most popular ever written. The sandstone spires of Monument Valley were the dramatic backdrop for John Ford's epic Westerns of the 1940s and 1950s. Novelist Louis L'Amour imagined a frontier locale called Shalako in the region's ponderosa uplands that was the setting for many of his hot-iron horse operas. And recent Westerns like *True Grit* and *Butch Cassidy and the Sundance Kid* took shape among the region's meadows and mountains, arroyos, and desert ridges.

Today, cattlemen with more misery than money, and their cowhands whose lives are carefully crafted anachronisms, still do push belligerent beeves across Cowboy Wash and Red Horse Gulch, Expectation Mountain and Disappointment Valley. The region remains a place where men in sweat-stained straw hats lean long over the blades of their irrigating shovels, where Anglo, Hispanic, and Indian cattlemen and cattlewomen cut hay in the torrid summer, then feed it to cattle in the cold calamity of winter. It is a place where raucous rodeos are still the year's grandest celebrations, where men who have to ride earth-movers and oil well-supply trucks instead of horses to earn their keep dance to country swing tunes into the early morning with beer-drinking, coy cowgirls whose names are tooled onto leather belts. It is a brash and callous country where cowboy is a very versatile word—not just a noun but an adjective and a ubiquitous verb as well. It is a place of enduring dreams and a few pompous delusions, and it is the place where this book unfolds.

But this book is not about historical cowboys alone, or the troubles of contemporary ranchers, or the six-shooter cowboys of books and movies, or the weekend wranglers on ranchettes who struggle to sustain a personal connection to the wild spirit of the West. It is, instead, a book about all of these and especially about how these four kinds of cowboys are entwined by the rope of myth, about how the images of each one are related to, and are dependent on, the others. It is a book about how America gave birth to the cowboy, then observed him with astonishment, about how we have continually remade the cowboy, molding him to suit our needs, and about why the complex figure of that horseback boy somehow endures on the frontier of interstellar space.

The mythic cowboy, the cowboy whose image has been shaped by history, fiction, and folklore, is unquestionably America's predominant symbolic native son. His myriad images have come to represent the American ideals of individualism, strength, and courage; and his imagined role in the settlement of the West is a national metaphor for the American commitment to action, work, and achievement. Yet the mythic cowboy is not anchored in the history of statesmanship or military service. The first cowboys were not presidents or generals, explorers or philosophers. They were laborers-lower-class boys who, beginning in the 1850s, hired on to work in a saddle on the back of a horse—rounding up thousands of wild Texas cattle, branding and castrating them, then pushing them east into Louisiana and the Deep South, west toward California, and finally north to the railheads that connected the open plains to the population centers east of the Mississippi. Most of the historical cowboys—who were called *vaqueros* and drovers until the flow of cattle out of Texas had almost stopped—were hard-working hands who endured the caprice of weather and the crush of isolation. But they were not heroes. They were of no greater collective historical significance than the men who baled cotton or built the railroads, the loggers or longshoremen or farmers. The cowboys became legendary figures almost by accident—and only because something in their personal images, their nomadic lifestyles, and their elemental connection to animals and the wide reach of the western land was intrinsically appealing to millions of Americans. The flesh-and-blood trail boys were transformed into the proud and strapping characters of the cowboy myth not because they were historically important, but because they were made symbolically important. The courageous and capable mythic cowboy, the footloose and unfettered man of the saddle, came to symbolize the kind of person Americans liked to believe they were, or dreamed they might become, and cowboy fantasies grew far more vivid in the public's mind than did the realities of cowboy life. Early balladeers sang,

The winds may blow
And the thunder growl
Or the breezes may safely moan; A cowboy's life
Is a royal life,
His saddle his kjngly throne,

But they weren't celebrating the truth of that claim. No, they were delighting in the fanciful notion that it might indeed have been so.

T he man who first began to give the cowboy symbolic stature, who first presented a heroic cowboy image to an easily persuaded public, had never been a cowboy himself. If he had, he might have felt that trail hands were simply too ordinary, their jobs too mundane, and their impact too local to ever become the stuff of legend. But William F. Cody, the actor and showman who had grown up in the frontier West and had been a buffalo hunter, scout, and Pony Express rider, understood that Easterners had been fascinated by the frontier expansion into the western half of the continent and that their interest flourished even after the railroads and telegraph lines had united the regions and fences had formed an enormous gridwork across the prairies. When Cody formed the traveling Wild West show, he was aiming to make himself rich by offering reenactments of frontier adventures, struggles, and triumphs to people who had already begun to view the settlement of the West as an allegory of the whole nation's achievements and aspirations. According to The Wild West's printed program, each show would "present an exacting and realistic entertainment for the public amusement. [Cody and company's] object is to picture to the eye, by the aid of historical characters and living animals . . . the wonderful pioneer and frontier life in the Wild West of America."

Cody presented Indians and homesteaders, stage drivers and scouts, mounted cavalry and skilled sharpshooters, performing entertaining "spectacles" that were billed as portrayals of real events from the bold frontier. In his efforts to keep his audiences captivated by the notion that something grand and transcendent had taken place when the new nation pushed westward, the showman tried to imbue every one of his frontier figures with an aura of profound significance. To complete the myth, Cody even claimed that the motley wranglers who looked after the show's livestock were stirring examples of the skill and fortitude that life in the West demanded. Cody's cowboys rode bucking broncs, bulls, and buffalos to demonstrate their talents in the saddle and to prove their daring. They "rescued" stagecoaches to show their gallantry and courage and fine moral character.

The audiences responded so enthusiastically to the cowboys that Cody decided to gamble on making one of his wranglers a star attraction. He chose William Levi "Buck" Taylor, a Texas-born trail hand who had worked on Cody's Nebraska ranch. Cody assured spectators that Taylor was not a ruffian, as most cowmen were presumed to be. In fact, Cody said, his handsome cowpoke was "amiable as a child," and he called Taylor, who could indeed perform impressive riding and roping maneuvers because he was "the King of the Cowboys." Taylor was an immediate hit, and Cody quickly began to highlight his wrangling skills; posters and newspaper ads featured Taylor and other strapping cowboys; dozens more western horsemen were added to the troupe, and the cowboys rode near the head of parades and processions, just behind the heroic figure of the long-haired showman himself.

With the publication of *Buck Taylor, King of the Cowboys* in the Beadle Half Dime Library in 1887, the cowboy's image was well on its way to being permanently transformed. Buffalo Bill's Wild West show, and its more than a hundred imitations, played a principal role in crafting an image of the cowboy as a good and decent fellow, but it was Erastus Beadle, the successful New York publisher of mass-circulation "dime novels," who made the cowboy's life exciting enough to sustain the public's attention. Since the early 1860s Beadle had been producing cheap thrillers—stories of the exploits of pirates, rogues, detectives, and a sort of composite western character who was often called a "border man." Cody himself had been the subject of hundreds of pulp stories—more than five hundred Buffalo Bill stories were eventually published—but it was the short, sensational novel about Buck Taylor that focused immediate attention on a new kind of frontier figure—a mounted fighter and adventurer who rode nowhere without his six-shooters strapped to his hips. The fictional gunfighters in the thousands of thrillers that followed occasionally used ropes to scale cliffs or to tie up the desperadoes they captured, but their principal tools were their long-barreled revolvers. Their cows, the beasts that had given rise to their profession, had strangely disappeared.

When Philadelphia lawyer Owen Wister published *The Virginian* in 1902, the first full-length, "serious" cowboy saga, cattle were similarly missing from the scene. The Virginian was handsome, strong, and stoic. Whenever the need arose, he too could quickly fill his hands with iron; he brought outlaws to justice and won the heart of the heroine. But unlike Buck Taylor, he was often silent and essentially mysterious. Yet something about the Virginian was immensely appealing. The quiet force of his actions became a model for the thousands of fictional cowboys who followed him.

The action-filled life of the cowboy received enormous attention in the early twentieth century. Frederic Remington and many other painters discovered romantic and adventurous images in the cowboy, his horse, and the wild land he rode across. Zane Grey, Max Brand, Ernest Haycox, Clarence E. Mulford, and other novelists wrote formulaic Westerns that emphasized gunplay and hard-riding excitement. "Action, action, action is the thing," said Brand. "So long as you keep your hero jumping through fiery hoops on every page you're all right . . . There has to be a woman, but not much of a one. A good horse is much more important."

Action was obviously a staple in the early films as well, and cowboy stories seemed naturally suited to the cinema. Galloping horses, fiery gun battles, and the majestic sweep of a far horizon could be vividly depicted on screen. Stories about the winning of the West had an epic quality to them, and the Hollywood movie industry made the western horseman its focal heroic subject. At the same time, a new entertainment that combined the pageantry of the old wild west shows with the athletic contests that had become a common form of recreation for western ranch hands—extravaganzas variously called roundups or stampedes or rodeos—became popular across the nation. Boys and girls in stylized western dress who performed tricks and competed for prize money by riding, roping, and wrestling cattle and unbroken horses became emblematic of the early *vaqueros* and drovers. Like the cowboys in books and the cowboys who rode the ranges on the silver screen, the rodeo riders were also connected to the trail boys, but the tether was only a tenuous one. In just two decades after the last longhorns were trailed out of Texas, the popular image of the brave and capable cowboy bore only scant resemblance to the scrappy seed stock of his breed.

Buffalo Bill and the Beadle stable of writers succeeded in transforming the cowboy from outcast to idol late in the nineteenth century. But the evolution of the cowboy into a symbolic figure of national significance was a twentieth-century phenomenon. Although he has his roots in a poignant and specific period in the history of the nation, the mythic cowboy has been a continually evolving character, adaptable to any era and to many needs. Owen Wister's reserved Virginian gave way to William S. Hart's emotional and ambiguous film cowboy who often turned from a life of crime to one of virtue.

Then, Hart's popularity was usurped by a succession of huge-hatted, handsome cowboys like Buck Jones, Lash LaRue, Ken Maynard, and Torn Mix, who were almost unimaginably good and bashful fellows, cowboys who made a booming business out of delivering women from their peril. Then cowboys who could sing as well as they could swing a rope came on the scene—Tex Ritter, Gene Autry, Roy Rogers and the Sons of the Pioneers—gaudy, silk-shirt-ed cowboys who turned the guitar into a ubiquitous Western prop, and who forged an enduring connection between country music and the image of the cowboy. John Wayne transformed the chaste and incorruptible cowboy into a man who was happy to fight with fists and guns and anything else that was handy, who swore, spat, and swilled whiskey on occasion, the kind of cowboy who would even sleep with a lonely schoolmarm or an alluring *señorita* if he found the time between his fights. But Wayne's cowboy was a moralist nonetheless, a hero in common men's clothes, very different from the violent, anarchic cowboys who followed him, epitomized by Clint Eastwood's amoral drifters and anguished outlaws.

The American culture has responded with interest and affection to many other kinds of cowboys during this time, cowboys who have been angry and comic, daring and inept, handsome and homely, corral-bred boys who have never left the country, and city slickers in Lucchese boots and belts with diamond buckles. We have popularized many different kinds of cowboys because we are many different kinds of people and because the cowboy, as a mythic figure, reflects our own images of ourselves more than he reflects any verifiable truths about himself. The cowboy is, in effect, the American Everyman, and as such he is as anonymous as he is identifiable, as obscure as he is ever present. When Americans—even people who live in the cowboy-covered West—are asked to name cowboys, they name figures like Buffalo Bill, the cowboy's first public relations man, or Tom Mix, one of the first Western matinee idols. They mention

Charles M. Russell, a prolific painter of cowboys; Shane, a cowboy gunfighter in a book and a later movie; John Wayne, the classic film cowboy; Hoss Cartwright, a mammoth and memorable television cowpoke; Larry Mahan, a rodeo star; and even Ronald Reagan, an actor, president, and gentleman rancher of wide renown. Each is a recognizable "western" figure, a man who has presented an image that we identify in one way or another as cowboy, yet each is very different from the others, and none has ever earned his wages working cattle.

There are still a few of those cow-connected boys around. There aren't many of them, but they can still be found in places like Twin Bridges, Montana, and Tuscarora, Nevada, in Alpine, Texas, and Anadarko, Oklahoma. They are skilled practitioners of their craft, suffering isolation like the first cowboys, but they too have been whittled and honed by the images of our imagined cowboys. They wear wide, unwieldy hats like Tom Mix did instead of the flopping-brimmed felts that the range cowboys wore; they strum guitars like Gene Autry did (the early trail hands played fiddles) and listen to Porter Wagoner or Toby Keith in the cabs of their pickup trucks. They read Louis L'Amour novels at lunch breaks, watch Western movies late at night on their girlfriends' TVs, and are as affected and afflicted by the romantic image of the Marlboro Man as are other Americans, perhaps even more so, because the idyllic appearance of his western way of life is something that some of them can begin to approximate in their own.

There are cowboy purists of note who swear that these modern-day horsemen are the only real cowboys among us, spurning the drugstore and disco varieties as phony facsimiles of the lads who work on the land. But real is a dangerous word to use in connection with cowboys. It implies authenticity and a specific standard of comparison. If the historical trail ranger or drover is that standard, then there is little similarity with any contemporary figure to whom we can attach the label cowboy. Today's working cowboys tend beeves, as did the first cowboys, of course. But rodeo cowboys much more readily share the early trail hands' nomadic life style; the cowboys who roam the country bars and honky-tonks share the drovers' inclination to celebrate in nearly suicidal fashion; and the West's roughnecks, truck drivers, drillers, and welders are the modern-day descendants of the trail boys who worked because they had to, and who took up that dirty, grim, and grueling job because it was the only work they could get.

During the roughly 120 years that the word cowboy has been in widespread use, it has as readily described fictional figures, entertainers, and laborers as bona fide boys in the saddle, and it has referred as much to a style of perceiving and presenting oneself as to a cow-centered way of life. Instead of trying to discern who is the real cowboy among the many imposters, this book assumes that each of the century's cowboys is a genuine article. It contends that whether he rides the short-grass prairies, the interstate highways, the Hollywood backlots, the decrepit small-town arenas, or the fanciful terrain of writers' imaginations, each cowboy belongs to a fine fraternal breed, to a culture of cowboys characterized by dreams of freedom and images of a western land where every man has a purposeful part to play.

In John Ford's 1962 film, *The Man Who Shot Liberty Valance*, James Stewart is Ransom Stoddard, a Westerner who becomes a United States senator after he is hailed for killing a hated outlaw in a street duel. Years later, when the aging Stoddard reveals to a group of newspaper reporters that he did not actually kill Liberty Valance, one reporter stands and tells him, 'This is the West, Senator. When the legend becomes fact, print the legend."

The West has provided fertile ground for the nurturing of legends since the first explorers trekked across it in the sixteenth century in search of the fabled cities of gold. Fantastic stories about the land's horror and its beauty, about the savagery of its native people, and about incredible opportunities for finding wealth began early to envelop the frontier with an aura of mystery and excitement. The people who ventured west, who endured the perils of the wilderness and who experienced its joys, appeared bolder, braver, and more full of life than those who had not tested themselves on the frontier. In the middle of the eighteenth century there were no movie stars or sports heroes to read about, to emulate, and to adore. It was the adventurers who captured the public's imagination and who held its attention.

Considering the cowboy's status as the final frontier figure, as one who experienced the demise of the wilderness and the subsequent birth of a cattle-based culture and economy, it is easy to understand why the nation was reluctant to forget him. The cowboy, once transformed by Cody and dozens of pulp writers, became vivid and vibrantly attractive to millions of people. He was envisioned as the symbolic bearer of civilization into a region that was just beginning the slow but inevitable civilizing process. Something important was under way in the West, and Americans latched on to a symbolic figure that could help make the transition comprehensible to them, that could justify the force and furor of settlement and imbue it with a sense of glory.

The cowboy, the mounted adventurer in exotic western garb, a common man with uncommon skills, was the ideal representation of the bold man of the West. But because cowboy history was sketchy, because the facts surrounding the trail drovers were few in number and were drab and passionless, the created cowboy, imbued with excitement and honor, assumed the symbolic role. The cowboy that was crafted by Cody's showmanship and the sensational dime novels began to occupy a niche in the nation's folkloric imagination even while the final trail drives were under way in the late 1880s. The cowboy as historical fact had been replaced by a cowboy as mythical force.

What people believe is real is ultimately far more important than what actually is real, if indeed what is real can ever be accurately ascertained. It is the conviction that the folkloric cowboy whom we have been told was noble and brave has become of greater significance than the historical cowboy. "Human kind cannot bear very much reality," wrote T. S. Eliot, and in the case of the cowboy it is clear that as a people we have been unable to bear the truth that the earliest cowboy was nothing special. We needed a folkloric image of him to help enliven and legitimize the history of the western expansion; we needed to revere and remember him in order to stay proud of the past. And so we transformed the cowboy and his history into myth.

But myth, in the present context, is not make-believe. It is not a fable but a cultural force, a collectively agreed-upon way of explaining why things are the way they are and how they came to be that way. Myths are, in effect, the ways in which we agree to order the world; they are the simple and familiar stories that we use to explain the complex events of human existence, stories that bridge the gap between the actual way in which things occur and the way in which we understand them.

It is, for example, literally true that early cowboys used guns sparingly and not very accurately, but it is mythically true that cowboys were adept and agile gunfighters. It is literally true that range cowboys and Indian peoples had only occasional contact with each other, but it is mythically true that cowboys and Indians were bitter enemies. Iowa-born actor Marion Morrison appeared in over 140 films under the name John Wayne—a literal truth. John Wayne was and is America's cowboy hero—an example of the power of myth. The images of all our cowboys are diverse and sometimes divergent, and cowboys are sometimes as superficial as they are widespread, yet the American cowboy is transcendent. The mythic cowboys ride out beyond the fence-lines of time and place, and all of them are true, even if they never lived among us.

THE LADY AND THE TOWER

No true American patriot can countenance any such expenditure for bronze females in the present state of finances, and hence, unless the Frenchmen change their mind and pay for this "gift" themselves, we shall have to do without it. — Editorial in the *New York Times* in opposition to plans for the Statue of Liberty, September 1876

Is the city of Paris to permit itself to be deformed by monstrosities, by the mercantile dreams of a maker of machinery; to be disfigured forever and to be dishonored? For the Eiffel Tower, which even the United States would not countenance, is surely going to dishonor France. — "Protest Against the Tower of Monsieur Eiffel," published in *Le Temps*, February 1886

Her copper-clad skirts had begun to rise above the slate roofs of the city two years before, and by now all of the colossal woman and the 30-foot torch she held in her hand towered above the beguiling Paris of the Belle Époque. You could readily see her—proud, inscrutable, lifting the torch high as if to help illumine the City of Light—from the Arc de Triomphe just four blocks away, from the heights of Montmartre in the northeast and even from the broad green lawn of the Champs de Mars across the Seine in the south, at a site on which the creators of the huge statue lately had begun to imagine that a latticework tower seven times her size would rise one day.

But for the moment, the lady—whose copper façade, exposed to Paris's moist riverine air, already had begun to take on a distinct green patina—joined the domes of the Sacré-Cœur and Invalides and the spire of Notre-Dame as the city's tallest structures. For the moment, she remained a proud if perhaps unlikely Parisian, yet both her nationality and her place of residence were about to change. On the evening of May 21, 1884, the Franco-American Union—the confederation of politicians, businessmen, and philanthropists who had struggled for years to reach this culminating and very grand day—hosted a formal dinner in celebration both of the statue's completion and the pending transfer of its ownership to the people of the United States. The opulent feast's guest of honor, of course, was Alsatian sculptor Frédéric-Auguste Bartholdi, who—two decades before—first had imagined creating a gigantic, lamp-bearing woman who would keep watch in

Egypt rather than America. In attendance as well were two of the most world-renowned Frenchmen of the era, Count Ferdinand de Lesseps, a much-journeyed diplomat and the storied builder of the Suez Canal, as well as the esteemed bridge and building designer Gustave Eiffel, who recently also had engineered the wrought-iron framework that allowed the 100-ton sculpture of the lady to rise high above the rue de Chazelles.

It seems unlikely that Eiffel—utterly self-possessed but an essentially private man, one whose modest bearing belied a quick and supple mind—offered anything by way of a formal comment following a final course of sorbet au Kirsch and cigarettes, but it is certain that both Bartholdi and Lesseps did, the former finding it irresistible not to remind the sixty gentlemen in white tie in attendance that although, admittedly, it had taken them some time, together they had rather deliciously proved wrong legions of skeptics in both France and America. "For a long time," intoned the man whose piercing eyes and full dark beard helped draw attention away from the weak chin about which he was deeply self-conscious, "malicious and critical spirits considered our work an 'elephant,' as they say in the United States—one of those burdens you don't know how to get rid of."

For a long time, people in France had found it difficult to understand precisely why France should give the gift of a metal lady to the new country across the ocean and harder still to comprehend why its citizens should pay for its ample cost. And Americans in turn had found it almost impossible to muster continuing interest in the curious, if substantial gift that had been in a seemingly endless state of being given for so many years by now. But at last, the lanky Bartholdi wanted to remind his colleagues, the extraordinary statue that honored America's commitment to liberty and newly symbolized the vital friendship between the two nations would rise in New York's harbor as proof that great and complex projects could be accomplished. And he wanted the men who by now had begun to enjoy their Madeira and cigars—since neither wives or paramours had been invited to the august event—to remember as well how essential to the project's success the passionate involvement of Count de Lesseps had been, a man whom Bartholdi praised as both "an exceptionally well-endowed and beneficent fairy" and "the great heart and mind of France."

In the moments following that fulsome introduction, Lesseps, a still-athletic if white-maned 78-year old, rose to accept the accolades and congratulate the statue's sculptor in turn and briefly echo his sentiments about the role the copper lady would play far into the future, one of reminding people everywhere—not solely in France and the United States—of how precious freedom was and how precarious its cause often could be. Then Lessep's subject quickly shifted to his true obsession of the moment—to his fierce determination to complete construction of a second great canal before his days were done, this time one that would cut across the narrow neck of Panama and once more make the world a dramatically smaller place, just as the opening of the Suez Canal had done fifteen years before.

His audience soon was utterly absorbed by the count's description of the arduous task of cutting a broad canal through Panama's rough and densely tropical terrain, and no one in attendance—many of whom had loosened a waistcoat button or two by now—seemed concerned that Monsieur Bartholdi's statue, officially titled Liberty Enlightening the World, was being feted with talk of dredging machines and malaria, torrential rainstorms and the Americans' obviously wrongheaded determination to build an Atlantic- and Pacific-linking canal across Nicaragua instead. Lesseps, large and leonine, was a man of both courage and complex vision—and his persuasive skills were second to none, it was said—and few among the dinner guests required assistance in understanding that the statue was a piece of careful diplomacy as readily as it was a vast collection of pig iron and copper sheathing, and that its gift to the United States curiously might serve the cause of the Panama Canal as readily as it would the glory of France and the bonds of international amity.

If people in the United States believed they were deeply indebted to France for the statue, perhaps they might be inclined to accept as a given as well the truth that great entrepreneurial and engineering projects—whether canals or astonishing statues or the very high tower that the brilliant Monsieur Eiffel and his assistants had begun to imagine as the centerpiece for the coming centenary celebration of France's revolution—really ought to be left to the French themselves, clearly the best builders in the world. Perhaps Bartholdi's lady and Eiffel's tower, monuments in metal, might play important adjunct roles in ensuring that France would command a vital strategic link between North and South America—and between the two vast oceans—for centuries to come.

Frédéric-Auguste Bartholdi, Gustave Eiffel, and Ferdinand de Lesseps first had collectively encountered each other in Egypt in 1869 and it was the industrial marvel of the recently opened Suez Canal that began their decades of association. The count was eager to show this newest wonder of the world—and his personal triumph—to people from home, of course, and Eiffel, then a 37-year old engineer who was hungry to make a mark for himself, and who had come to Egypt to deliver a consignment of locomotives on behalf of France's General Railway Equipment Company, was fascinated to observe how steam shovels and dredgers had gouged a hundred-mile river across the Isthmus of Suez in only a decade. Bartholdi, two years Eiffel's junior, had come to Egypt as Lesseps's personal guest. Two years before, the count had become captivated by the young sculptor's bold proposal to build a monumental lighthouse at the Port Said entrance to the canal in the form of a robed woman holding aloft a torch. Egypt Carrying the Light to Asia the statue would have been called, but despite Lessep's enthusiastic support for the project, it had collapsed when the Egyptian government failed to allocate the necessary funds to construct it. Yet although that enterprise had been thwarted—or perhaps, said cynics, simply had been transformed into another lady lighting another place—you can imagine the rich pleasure the three builders of things large and lofty must have taken as they stood on the deck of Empress Eugénie's royal yacht as members of the official French contingent celebrating the linking of the Red Sea with the Mediterranean, each of the three the sort of men who could not help but dream great dreams and work tirelessly toward their realization, each man the kind for whom it seemed perfectly reasonable that a way could be found for huge ships to sail through the desert sand.

In the spring of 1884, however, a mountain of work remained to be done on many fronts before any of the three briefly could rest on their laurels. Bartholdi's statue still was not guaranteed a suitable pedestal at the site on Bedloe's island in New York harbor that he long ago had selected, then finally had secured, and it wasn't unthinkable that the statue simply would be dismantled and packed away if the Paris burghers grew tired of it blocking a street. The tower that in five years' time would bear Eiffel's name and climb high into heaven and astonish the world still was nothing more than a pencil sketch on brown paper executed by Maurice Koechlin, a young draftsman in Eiffel's firm. And at the moment, Lesseps's Universal Interoceanic Panama Canal Company was in desperate need of a quick infusion of cash.

In two years of work under the harshest kinds of conditions, cutting through the rocky Panamanian divide called the Culebra had proven to be a gargantuan and very expensive task, and Lesseps now hoped French citizens would rush to purchase the new issue of stock his company recently had offered and thereby keep his steam shovels digging. He had offered the Paris press a copy of his dinner remarks in the hours before the feast, in fact, in the hope that its publication would further spur the public's interest in the venture and the proffering of its investment francs. But the months ahead would prove to be dramatically difficult ones.

Two more confounding years would pass before Bartholdi's statue at last stood high on a granite pedestal and began to keep watch over New York's harbor, welcoming a steady stream of immigrants to America's shores. In three more years, Lesseps would turn to Eiffel to salvage the increasingly disaster-plagued Panama Canal project, and Eiffel—to his deep regret—would agree to come to its rescue at precisely the same time his namesake tower was rising, and being met by public ridicule, beside the Seine.

In time, the statue that no one really wanted would become a powerful and enduring symbol to generations of immigrants of what made the United States unique among all nations, symbol of a country that believed in individual freedom and opportunity more than it believed in anything else. In relatively little time, the tower that had been dubbed "a truly tragic lamppost, a high and skinny pyramid of iron ladders," would become not only a monument to the glories of industry but also the foremost visual representation of the city of Paris and all of France as well, an elegant spire wrought out of iron that seemed, quite wonderfully, to link earth to sky and material to imagination. In time, both Lesseps and Eiffel would be charged with crimes in connection with their dealings in Panama, and although both would be exonerated to some degree, the stains on their reputations would remain. America ultimately would be forced to abandon its plans for a canal in Nicaragua in favor of completing the failed French project in Panama, and international relations would be altered forevermore with France's retreat from a position of prominence in the New World.

The Statue of Liberty and the Eiffel Tower, two odd and utterly non-utilitarian structures, have, nonetheless, come to matter enormously in the collective consciousness of the people of the two countries in which they stand, and their senses of themselves and their perceived missions in the world. The two structures were exceedingly complicated to build and are now impossible to imagine the world without, both created at a time when the advent of wondrous machines and the remarkable things that could be made with them seemed to make gods of great builders and to portend that the future would be a very bright place.

At the time the story begins, Americans and the French had pledged themselves to an inviolate friendship, one that had emerged out of bloodshed of their separate eighteenth-century revolutions. Largely because of those shared revolutionary roots, the citizens of both countries viewed themselves as being essentially modern and unrestrained by the past, and they shared as well an enduring—if often denied—belief in their pre-eminence over other nations. Yet the people of France and the United States were dissimilar in striking ways as well. While the French placed great stock in collective action, national glory, and the importance of culture, the new Americans more highly valued self-reliance, entrepreneurship, and individual comfort.

The French prized philosophical inquiry while Americans vaunted their practicality, and if the French appreciated leisure, cuisine, artistic endeavor and intellectualism, Americans in turn cherished hard work, simple food, relaxed manners and the equalizing role played by commonplace standards—something the French saw as cultural mediocrity.

Both countries shared complex yet vital relationships with Great Britain—the French linked to the great colonial power by geographical proximity, the Americans by the kinship of language. They shared too an enduring uncertainty about whether, like Britain, they ought to play broad and expansive roles in the world at large, and they also shared the memory of recent and terrible war. The United States had remained united, but only at huge cost, in 1865 at the close of a bitter and deeply scarring civil war, one that twenty years later still left little taste in Americans' mouths for military adventuring in other parts of the world. In 1871, France had suffered a humiliating defeat in its ill-advised war against Prussia and had been forced to surrender to the Prussians its eastern provinces of Alsace and Lorraine, a loss that continued to gall the French fifteen years after the fact, but also cautiously remind them that in the future they ought to press forward to war only when war was utterly unavoidable.

In the long aftermath of those separate conflicts, both the United States and France finally had rebounded economically and with renewed commitment to the ideals of their revolutions, and it was industry much more than politics that instilled in the people of both countries a compelling vision of the coming twentieth century. By the middle 1880s, the industrial might of both nations rivaled—and in many ways surpassed—that of the British, and there appeared no limit to the glories that coal and steam and iron could contrive. Cities like Paris, Pittsburgh, and Cleveland, Marseilles, Buffalo, and Lyon were alive with the stink and rattle and clang of immense optimism, and the pall of smoke that draped each city seemed to blithely and quite happily obscure the past. To observers in other nations of the world, the peoples of France and the United States appeared to be making great leaps forward at often-astonishing speed, and within the two nations themselves a sense of destiny began to build, then to become contagious.

It was out of the belief that God observably blessed the bold and the industrious that these two great shrines to the age, its meaning, and its values were conceived and created—the Statue of Liberty a memorial to the idea that kings and despots never again could shackle the dreams and passions of free peoples, the Eiffel Tower a latticework temple to what creative minds had discovered and achieved by now and everything that remained possible to them far into the future. In the months following the May 1884 banquet that marked the completion of the enormous statue—her high-held arm 45-feet long, her aquiline nose nearly as tall as a man—many of the august group who had celebrated that evening began to plan in earnest a grand international exposition in Paris in the summer of 1889 that would, according to the fair's general manager Georges Berger, show our sons what their fathers have accomplished in the space of a century through progress in knowledge, love of work, and respect for liberty. We will give them a view from the summit of the steep slope that has been climbed since the Dark Ages. And if one day they should again descend to some valley of error and misery, they will remember what we did and they will remind their children of it, and future generations will thereby be more determined than ever to climb still higher than we have.

What men like Berger, Bartholdi, Eiffel, and Lesseps could not know, of course, was that the hundred years that followed the fair, the anchoring of the lady in the new land, the stunning erection of the tower, and the completion of the canal that linked the oceans would be a century filled with unimaginable error and misery. What they could not know was that France and America would remain vigorously linked, yet also separated by jealousies, suspicions, and competing creeds. Yet their common belief in the vital consequence and enduring importance of building shrines to the best human accomplishments and the loftiest human ideals would prove throughout that same century to have been both bold and wise. This is the story of two monuments that the people of the United States and France did not need but have come to deeply depend on, of two symbols whose multiple meanings and symbolic significance have grown over time as if they too were hammered out of cast iron and copper, the story of a time—not utterly unlike our own—when the bold and audacious construction of a lady and a tower changed two nations, the nature of their friendship, and the rest of the world forever.

In the summer of 1865, French law professor and politician Édouard-René Lefebvre de Laboulaye hosted a private dinner for a small group of friends who, like him, were ardent supporters of the return to republican rule in France as well as the nearly century-old republican government in the United States that recently had survived a terrible civil war. Among those in attendance at Laboulaye's home on a hot August evening and who heard him suggest that France surely should give the United States a gift of some sort commemorating the common republican bond between the two countries—as well as celebrating the end of the war and the survival of the American union—was Frédéric-Auguste Bartholdi, a young sculptor from the eastern province of Alsace who passionately wanted to make a career for himself as the creator of public monuments on a scale far greater than ever had been attempted before. But nothing immediately came of Laboulaye's suggestion, and the idea simply might have died had not Bartholdi determined six years later, following his service in the disastrous Franco-Prussian War, that he should visit America, gauge interest there in the erecting of a monument to liberty, and perhaps even secure a site.

When the steamship Pereire on which Bartholdi was traveling entered New York harbor on June 21, 1871, he was immediately convinced that the harbor itself was the ideal location for a monument, and he wrote enthusiastically to Laboulaye with the news: "At the view of the harbor of New York, a definite plan was first clear to my eyes . . . In this very place shall be raised the Statue of Liberty, grand as the idea which it embodies, radiant upon the two worlds." Bartholdi enclosed a sketch with his letter, one envisioning a gigantic robed woman holding a torch high in her hand, her head crowned by a ring of individual rays that emanated liberty itself perhaps. The sketch was remarkably reminiscent of the design Bartholdi had created four years before for a lighthouse at the entrance to the Suez Canal, yet he believed that this at last was the project that actually would lead to such a lady's construction.

The Romans often had depicted liberty as a woman, he knew; a female figure symbolizing truth was common among French freemasons, and, of course, in 1830 French painter Eugène Delacroix had depicted liberty as the mythic "Marianne," a bare-breasted and brave young woman carrying the tricolor flag in one hand and a musket in the other. For his part, Laboulaye had hoped for a monument that somehow more concretely expressed the bond between France and the United States, yet he remained supportive in his communications with the sculptor, in largest part because as long as French citizens remained burdened with the heavy taxes owed Prussia in the aftermath of the war, he felt certain the time was not right to begin a campaign seeking their contributions for a gift to the United States.

It was 1875 before Laboulaye, whose liberal republicans by now had won control of the French parliament, formed what he named the Franco-American Union, comprised of the current French and American ambassadors to their respective countries, elected officials, and a number of prominent and wealthy individuals who could give the union a kind of immediate cachet, as well as, Laboulaye hoped, a substantial share of the 240,000 francs Bartholdi estimated the statue would cost. In its initial appeal to the public at large, the union requested contributions of any size from every corner of France in order to complete the statue and present it to the United States the following year, in time for the centennial celebration of American independence, a goal which was immediately unrealistic, and which appeared utterly unreachable soon thereafter when repeated fund-raising events fell flat on their faces.

In America, where Laboulaye hoped a similar group would form to raise funds for the massive pedestal the statue would require, progress was slower still, and several prominent American newspapers expressed suspicions of French motives as well as outright opposition to any U.S. government involvement. When Bartholdi ultimately exhibited Lady Liberty's full-scale hand and her torch at the 1876 Centennial Exposition in Philadelphia—as part of a several-pronged effort to muster enthusiasm that certainly wasn't building in New York—the New York Times, which earlier had railed against Bartholdi and the project, now decried Philadelphia's act of "piracy," and urged New Yorkers to do everything they could to see the statue realized. When the hand and torch were moved to Manhattan at the close of the centennial exposition and placed in Madison Square Park—where they remained for six long years—the newspaper once more turned critical, suspecting that other pieces of the lady might eventually appear in other parks but that Bartholdi's ultimate plan surely was to swindle honest Americans.

In February 1877, both U.S. houses of Congress unanimously approved a resolution granting the right for the statue to be placed on Bedloe's Island, near the New Jersey shore, formerly the site of an army installation. But the American Committee for the Statue of Liberty, the group of private U.S. citizens attempting to raise money for its huge pedestal, was having no better luck than were their French counterparts, and it began to appear that the statue likely never would be funded. Then, in an act of desperation in France, the Franco-American Union persuaded the government to sanction a special lottery, and in July 1880, the union announced that it successfully had raised more than 600,000 francs, then formally notified the American committee and the U.S. government that Bartholdi and his assistants would begin constructing the statue immediately, as well as pleading between the lines for stepped-up efforts on the other side of the Atlantic to get the pedestal paid for and built so the lady would have a place to stand when she arrived.

Over the course of the next four years, the challenge for Bartholdi became the actual construction of the copper lady, something he always had believed was possible, but to which he had devoted only minimal attention until now. Soft and malleable copper, it was clear, was the right material for the statue's skin, but its weight would be enormous. Feeling sudden and dramatic pressure to make good on his promises, the sculptor rather belatedly sought expertise in the complexities of load-bearing, wind resistance, tensile strength, and the best design of its interior framework from his acquaintance Gustave Eiffel, whose wrought-iron bridges throughout Europe, the Middle East, and Asia as well as the recently completed Bon Marché department store near Paris's Luxembourg Gardens had brought him huge renown. Eiffel, then forty-eight, was a master at innovation, and he was immediately intrigued by Bartholdi's most-unusual project.

Of greatest concern to Eiffel was the fact that Lady Liberty would be dramatically buffeted by winds; she would need to be very flexible as well as able to withstand summer expansion from heat, and the contraction caused by the winter's bitter cold. Iron was the logical material for the inner framework, but if iron and copper came into direct contact, the galvanic action of the two metals would result in the statue's collapse in only a few years. Working closely together with Bartholdi to ensure that the interior framework would precisely fit the statue's outer copper skin, Eiffel and his team designed and then built a central pylon comprised of four giant girders, each nearly a hundred feet high, interconnected by a latticework of bracing and struts. For the statue's upraised arm, a second forty-foot structure had to build, this one at a complex angle that required extensive counterbalancing on the vertical pylon. Reaching out from the two pylons were a total of 1,830 light iron ribs that linked the copper sheeting to the frame by means of a series of simple copper "saddles," which wrapped around the iron ribs before being riveted to each exterior copper plate, the iron insulated from the copper with both asbestos and shellac. It was a design that allowed the iron ribs to act like springs, ensuring that the copper lady could flex with the dictates of weather—that she could both stretch and breathe—and that the girders themselves carried virtually all of the statue's weight.

In order to precisely shape each of the statue's 350 copper sheets, Bartholdi initially worked from a four-foot high clay model, which he then refined in a series of larger plaster models, culminating with a final form that was fully one-quarter the finished statue's size. From the largest plaster model, workers built wooden lattice molds against which the soft copper could be hammered into shape, but before any hammering was done, incredibly precise measuring was required to ensure that—at four times the model's size—every sheet perfectly fit its neighbors. Each section of the statue had fifteen hundred reference points, and each reference point required six separate measurements, meaning that each section received nine thousand measurements before workers were sure that the lattice molds were properly shaped and ready to receive the sheets.

In October 1881—on the hundredth anniversary of the Battle of Yorktown, in which French and American revolutionary forces defeated the British in the decisive battle of the Revolutionary War—U.S. ambassador to France Levi P. Morton drove the ceremonial first rivet for the final assembly of the statue, which took place in the wide cobblestone street outside Bartholdi's warehouse and workshop near the Arc de Triomphe, and the statue at last began to rise, sixteen years after it first had been imagined by Édouard-René Lefebvre de Laboulaye, who would not live to see its completion. Nearly three years would pass before the lady would stand tall—and entirely complete—in Paris's rue de Chazelles, the surrounding rooftops reaching only to her knees. On July 4, 1884, French and American officials climbed the spiral staircase that wrapped around Eiffel's framework and in the sunlight at the lady's crown signed documents officially transferring her ownership to the United States—which was a serious problem, because still the United States had no place to put her.

By the summer of 1884, the pedestal on Bedloe's Island had been designed—by French-trained architect Richard Morris Hunt—and excavation of its foundation was underway, but the American committee charged with funding the pedestal remained woefully short of its $250,000 goal. Americans just weren't interested in the statue, it seemed, and even many wealthy New Yorkers who were potential benefactors declined to come to the project's rescue and make the completion of the project a cause célèbre; industrialist and philanthropist Andrew Carnegie—an immigrant who might have been stirred by the lofty rhetoric of the statue's advocates—agreed to contribute, rather reluctantly, only five hundred dollars. But another immigrant at last came to the rescue.

Joseph Pulitzer, a Hungarian-born newspaperman whose St. Louis Post-Dispatch had become one of the country's most respected papers, recently had purchased the New York World from financier Jay Gould, and had transformed it into a defender of the common man. Pulitzer loved a good editorial fight and to champion controversial causes as well, and when work on Bedloe's Island ceased for lack of funds in March 1885, Pulitzer could not control his anger.

It would be an irrevocable disgrace to New York City and the American republic to have France send us this splendid gift without our having provided even so much as a landing place for it. There is but one thing that can be done. We must raise the money. The World is the people's paper and it now appeals to the people to come forward and raise the money. Let us not wait for the millionaires to give this money.

Pulitzer vowed to print in the World the name of every individual who gave so much as a nickel to the cause, and in only five months, the newspaper raised the remaining $100,000 needed for the pedestal from 120,000 individual contributors. If the members of the committee who had needed seven years to raise a like amount were more than a little embarrassed, they also were grateful, because for the first time in twenty years, there appeared to be no impediment now to the statue's placement on the island that Bartholdi long ago had hoped would be its home. And rather magically, there was something in Pulitzer's appeal that at last ignited true American interest in the statue as well; he had shunned high-minded rhetoric about the meaning of the statue in favor of pleading for the little guy to show up the wealthy elite, and, in the process, somehow the statue began to seem to belong to the people—the common people of France and the United States—although it certainly hadn't until now.

Its home ready for it at last, the statue was carefully dismantled on the rue de Chazelles and placed, piece by piece, into 214 wooden crates, which were loaded aboard the French frigate Isère. On June 19, 1886, two hundred thousand people watched the odd cargo arrive in New York harbor, and a massive parade up Broadway marked the occasion. Fifty-six thousand additional dollars ultimately had to be wrested from the U.S. treasury in order to pay for the reconstruction of the statue and the grand dedication ceremony that was scheduled for October 28. Bartholdi himself pulled an enormous French flag away from the face of the statue on that dreary, rain-soaked autumn day, and the gathered dignitaries—all men—cheered the unveiling of the gigantic lady whose name was Liberty.

Women had been barred from the island for the occasion because, ostensibly, it was too dangerous for them, but a ship containing disgusted members of the New York State Woman Suffrage Association cruised the harbor nearby, both as a way of attempting to participate in the proceedings and in protest. It would be fully 34 years before women were granted the right to vote in the United States, and 59 years would pass before women—symbols of liberty—finally could vote in France.

As the Statue of Liberty rose to an astonishing height of 152 feet in Paris's rue de Chazelles in the spring of 1884, people of every sort—but builders in particular—had begun to look skyward with longing. Surely in the miraculous modern era people could climb even farther into the sky than did Bartholdi's copper lady. Marvelous inventions seemed to be dramatically changing the world every day: seven years before, an American had invented the telephone; then a Frenchman had invented the phonograph before an American somehow invented it as well, the same fellow who next came up with the incandescent electric lamp. Three years earlier, a Frenchman developed an automobile powered by steam; then an American invented a camera that made it easy for ordinary citizens to take photographs; first New York and now Paris were lit by electric street lamps, and a French physician recently had announced development of a successful vaccination against rabies. There seemed to be no end to what scientific achievement could make possible, and it wasn't surprising therefore that people in Europe and the United States had begun to believe a structure could climb 300 meters into the heavens.

A decade before, engineers in America had hoped to build a 1,000-foot (304.8 meters) tower for the 1876 Centennial Exposition in Philadelphia, but both financial and structural concerns had kept their plan grounded; then in 1881, a French engineer returned from a trip to the United States with plans to build a masonry "sun tower" 300 meters high on whose summit would be mounted a floodlight capable, he claimed, of turning nighttime Paris into day.

But it wasn't until 1884 that Émile Nouguier and Maurice Koechlin, young engineers in Gustave Eiffel's world-renowned firm, first sketched a high tower that seemed to have some likelihood of actually being constructed. Their plan envisioned a single massive pylon comprised of four truss girders splayed out at their base and joined at the summit, linked by crossbeams at regular intervals, a structure of incredible stability—but one that was a little lackluster, believed Stephen Sauvestre, an architect in the company. To their design he added masonry feet for the tower, massive ornamental arches that linked the girders at the first level above the base and seemed to invite passage underneath, and a glass bulb at the summit that lent it a lighthouse's kind of completion. It was Sauvestre's amended design that first caught Eiffel's true attention and sparked his interest in the tower's possibilities. In September 1884, he took out a patent on the design in association with his employees, then promptly bought exclusive rights to the design from them.

It was a measure of Eiffel's influence in Paris that when a competition to build a centerpiece tower for the planned 1889 Exposition Universelle that would celebrate the centenary of the French revolution was announced on May 1, 1886—just as Eiffel's framework for the Statue of Liberty was being permanently erected on Bedloe's Island in New York—that the competition guidelines just happened to specify a wrought-iron tower dramatically like the one Eiffel already had patented. Nor was it surprising when Eiffel's design was selected the winner from among the competition's 107 entries. Ever a shrewd businessman as well as an engineer, in January of the following year Eiffel signed a contract between himself, the national government, and the city of Paris, granting him a 20-year concession on income the tower would generate and 1.5 million francs in construction costs—only about a quarter of what the tower would require, but making it possible to begin construction immediately in order to meet the deadline of the exhibition's opening in little more than two years.

A team of forty engineers and designers in Eiffel's suburban Paris factory immediately set to work on the 3,600 workshop drawings that would be required in order to manufacture the tower's 18,000 individual elements, then 150 "terra firma" men set to work machining, cutting, and drilling each cast-iron piece to an accuracy of a tenth of a millimeter before they were preassembled to a size that the horse-carts hauling them across the city to the Champs de Mars would allow. At the construction site, a team of 250 men were on constant show to the legion of city dwellers who were fascinated by the tower's progress—slow at first as massive foundation holes for each tower's four piers had to be dug down below the bed of the nearby Seine before the tower itself could begin to rise—then far quicker as teams began to assemble the myriad pieces of iron that comprised each pier.

Although the forthcoming exposition and its focal tower already had been heavily publicized, of course, it wasn't until the four latticework piers began their ascent that cries of opposition to the project began to be widely heard, and it was the city's artistic and intellectual elite who were most exercised about the horror—and the shame—the tower would bring to belle Paris. In a joint statement published in Les Temps, a group of forty writers, artists, musicians, and architects voiced their collective outrage that the nation of France was allowing to be built a ghastly contrivance that even commercial and crass America would not sanction—that was how horrible the prospect of the tower was—and further railing against "the construction of the useless and monstrous Eiffel Tower in the middle of our capital, which public malice, often a sign of commonsense and a spirit of justice, has already baptized the Tower of Babel." Other pamphleteers dubbed it a "truly tragic lamppost;" an "iron mast with solid rigging, unfinished, confused, deformed;" "this high, thin pyramid of iron ladders, a disgraceful and giant skeleton;" even "this hideous, gridded pylon, this infundibular grating."

Eiffel was significantly wounded by the criticisms, in part because they pricked at his belief that everything he built was inherently good, but also because he genuinely found the tower graceful, even beautiful, and he responded to his critics by pointing out that "there is in the colossal an attraction, a special charm, to which the ordinary theories of art can hardly be applied." In other words, the tower's size alone lent it a certain majesty, and whatever the attitudes toward it were, the tower continued to rise at an astonishing pace.

A 30-meter high wooden scaffolding supported the rising piers until they were joined by the first platform, where four restaurants, a post office, and a promenade were planned, then new scaffolding supported the climb to the second platform, where the newspaper Le Figaro planned to publish a special daily edition during the months of the exposition. Steam cranes that climbed the same rails that later would be used for the tower's elevators hoisted each iron element into place, where a team of four men waited to secure it: a "mate" would heat each rivet in a small forge, then toss it to a "stake holder" who drove it into two aligned and predrilled holes; the "riveter" struck the head of the rivet to temporarily secure it once it was seated before a "hammer man" permanently flattened it with a maul. Two-and-a-half million rivets in total bound the tower together by the time it was topped out in early January 1889, only twenty-one months after its erection began.

But now Eiffel and his associates encountered their first real crisis—the apparent likelihood that elevators would not be ready in time to lift the exposition's visitors high into the air, which was the tower's purpose, after all. Vertical, hydraulic-driven elevators had been in use for some time, but never to climb a structure as high and to carry as many passengers as Eiffel's tower would necessitate. Further complicating matters was the fact that the four piers of the tower arced upward at a long curve to the tower's second level, and current technology necessitated that elevators climb vertically. The simple solution would have been to construct elevator shafts in the center of the open arcade between the feet of the four piers, but although Eiffel was being accused of being a lowly engineer who cared nothing about aesthetics, he would not even discuss that option because, he believed, it would ruin the tower's artistry. Instead, he issued a call to the four most-renowned French elevator firms to rapidly solve the problem of lifting passengers up the arcing piers, then waited in vain for a response.

Waiting as well was Elisha Otis, an innovative American elevator designer who was certain that he alone among the world's engineers could solve Eiffel's problem. Otis was so sure, in fact, that he designed a system—a very big and very complicated half elevator, half cog railway powered by hydraulics—specifically for the tower, then waited for Eiffel to come calling. Because the terms of Eiffel's contract specified that every element of the tower be French material built by French manufacturers, Eiffel struggled with a number of lesser solutions until at last he had no choice but to ask exposition officials to make an exception and allow him to ask—rather late—for American help. Otis was delighted to be called on, and although his elevators were not ready to ferry passengers on the exposition's opening day, May 1, 1889, they were in operation six weeks later, and ultimately worked so well—so swiftly and quietly—that the elevators themselves subsequently were highlighted as one of the most marvelous U.S. technological exhibits at the exposition.

More than eighty national pavilions and exhibit halls greeted the first of what ultimately were more than thirty-two million visitors to the Exposition Universelle de 1889, including the vast Galerie des Machines designed by Ferdinand Dutert, inside of which literally thousands of pumps, engines, and motors devoted to what seemed to be every conceivable human endeavor cranked and whirred and bedazzled the excited crowds who flocked to see them. Yet unquestionably, the thing that every fair visitor most wanted to see—and to climb—was La Tour Eiffel, and Eiffel himself felt hugely vindicated by the immediate popularity of the structure that had been so scorned only a year before and that successfully had broken the 300-meter barrier that many engineers had vowed could not be achieved. Writers now labeled the tower "a shepherdess keeping watch over her flock of bridges," a "beguiling sky guitar," as well as the most astounding structure ever built in France, America, or anywhere else in the world. And it was a measure of how difficult it would be top it—literally as well as figuratively—that when Chicago's Columbian Exposition opened three years later, its centerpiece was merely engineer George Ferris's rotating passenger wheel, a clever invention, yes, but for the moment, the French reigned supreme among the world's builders, and Gustave Eiffel was king.

Two years following the anchoring of the Statue of Liberty on Bedloe's Island and fully a year before he personally crowned his completed tower with the French tricolor flag, a supremely confident Gustave Eiffel agreed to come to the technological rescue of his colleague Count Ferdinand de Lesseps, whose sea-level canal project across Panama had fallen into deep trouble.

At the 1879 International Interoceanic Canal Study Conference in Paris, Eiffel had been one of only eight outspoken participants out of 135 gathered engineers, businessmen, geographers, and entrepreneurs who lobbied against Lesseps's plan to connect the Atlantic and Pacific at sea level, favoring instead a canal comprised of a series of steel locks that, in effect, would allow ships to rise over the 400-foot Culebra range. Buoyed by the massive support for his plan—and angry with Eiffel for his opposition to it—Lesseps began construction of the sea-level canal in 1882 with only $6 million of the $24 million his company's accountants initially estimated the project would cost. By 1885, the Culebra had hardly been dented and the French government refused to authorize the issuance of public bonds to supply Lesseps with the enormous amount of new capital he required. Increasingly desperate, Lesseps toured the United States in support of the long-delayed completion of the Statue of Liberty as a means of mustering American support for the canal as well.

Yet the private citizens of both countries remained wary of investing in the venture, despite Lesseps's stellar reputation as a Grand Français and a man who could work miracles of every kind. By 1887, Lesseps had succeeded in his efforts to see the Statue of Liberty completed, but his canal project was far behind schedule and entirely out of money, and at last the count admitted that the only practical way for ships to cross Panama was via a series of locks—locks which Eiffel curiously had designed and patented at the same time he had begun to build his tower.

Eiffel tarried three weeks in deciding whether to accept Lesseps's plea for help, then, in November 1887—with his attention presumably monopolized by the requirements of erecting the tower—he signed a $27.4 million contract with Lesseps's Universal Interoceanic Panama Canal Company to construct a ten-lock canal system on a scale never remotely attempted before and to complete the project in only thirty months—only slightly longer than the time needed to erect the much simpler tower in Paris. It was an astonishingly ambitious plan, one that most observers believed would be impossible—if the legendarily prudent Monsieur Eiffel had agreed to it, that is—and in August 1888, only six months after beginning work, Eiffel's 6,000 canal workers had excavated 630,000 cubic yards of Panamanian earth, putting them fully ten months ahead of schedule. The French government at last agreed to allow Lesseps to float the bond issue it had denied him three years earlier, infusing the project with $51 million in new capital and making it appear that once more—with the same flamboyant and very public success he was experiencing on the Champs de Mars at the moment—Eiffel was accomplishing the impossible.

But on December 14, Lesseps's company filed for bankruptcy, having already sunk a billion and a half francs—nearly $300 million—into the project. A civil tribunal officially dissolved the company for which Eiffel had gone to work, but Eiffel found it so difficult to believe that France would allow a project obviously in its long-term national interest to go under that he ordered his company to continue working until the spring of 1889, when French officials advised him that there was no hope that the company would ever be paid for the $1.4 million in work it had done since the bankruptcy had been declared. As the splendid Eiffel Tower reached its summit in March, and final work was completed for the opening of the exposition in May, Eiffel reluctantly and still disbelievingly abandoned the most ambitious undertaking of his career.

Following a long investigation, Count Ferdinand de Lesseps and Gustave Eiffel were indicted on charges of swindling and breach of the public trust on November 21, 1892, and a scandal of unparalleled portions burst open in Paris, one that ultimately demonstrated that Lesseps's company had paid an astounding $4.4 million in bribes to help keep its financial troubles secret. In March 1893, Eiffel was found guilty of misusing funds entrusted to him and was sentenced to two years in prison and a fine of $4,000. Eighty-seven-year old Lesseps, senile by now, was sentenced to a five-year prison term. Both sentences ultimately were overturned and Lesseps died eighteen months later entirely unaware of the scandal. But for Eiffel, its indignity ensured that he never would build another great project. He focused the remainder of his long life on his operation of the tower, which was an enormous financial success, as well as important weather and aerodynamic experimentation, much of which the tower itself made possible.

In 1904, the United States government purchased the remaining assets of Lesseps's Panama Canal company for $40 million. Now an entirely American project, construction of a lock-system canal based entirely on Eiffel's plans began that year and was completed a decade later. Its control of the crucially important new shipping route ensured the United States's greatly enhanced international prominence, not only in the Americas but around the world. And, conversely, France's retreat from a vital geographic and strategic presence in the New World initiated both its real and symbolic retreats from the decades of international power and prestige that had seemed so assured in the recent past. Only a few years before, at the time when the Statue of Liberty sailed to America and Eiffel's tower rose to the delight and astonishment of the whole world, a wonderful new age of machines had commenced, it seemed certain, and so, too, had a competitive and difficult kind of friendship between France and the United States, an era in which the glories of which humankind now was capable seemed perfectly captured in those two iconic structures—a copper lady and a very tall iron tower whose importance would only continue to grow.

BEAUTIFUL ISLANDS

An excerpt from the novel

We had the sky, up there, all speckled with stars,
and we used to lay on our backs and look up at
them, and discuss about whether they was made,
or only just happened.   — Mark Twain, *Huck-*
leberry Finn

Seeing Colorado from space was like looking back with new uncertainty on a place you've known forever but have never understood. Late spring snow still draped the high spines of the San Juans and the Sangre de Cristos, and the valleys spread like disheveled rugs between the ranges. Yet I couldn't see the towns that I knew were tucked into the folds of the mountains and that sprawled across the sage-strewn plains. I couldn't see Durango, my hometown, couldn't gauge by a gridwork of streets where the house must be. My father had joked with me over the phone before the launch, promising he would go outside and wave into the sunlit sky; and I bet he actually did wave a time or two. But I never waved back because it was hard to imagine that he was actually somewhere in my field of vision—an indiscernible speck in faded jeans and house slippers standing on the cement slab by the back door. And it was hard to imagine that the entire rumpled and wind-scoured region wasn't just some glorious gas station map that had been wrapped around the sensuous curve of the earth. That canyoned and summited corner of Colorado was profoundly familiar to me, but from the silent vantage of space it looked like someplace that was worlds away, forever inaccessible.

Colorado had seemed plenty far enough away from Houston as well, and I had considered flying up for a visit, but I finally decided to drive. We had spent about ten days in debriefings following the flight, and then NASA sent Bill Grimes, Cathy Cohn, and me out on the promotional circuit for a couple of weeks, so the idea of throwing some quarts of beer into a cooler and heading across the hard, anvil-hot prairies of Texas sounded strangely appealing. I stopped at Pe-Te's for lunch on the day I left, mentioned I was heading north for a few days, then chewed on pork ribs while Pe-Te told me about the time he almost froze to death hunting elk above Pagosa Springs. I laughed, told him I figured Cajuns ought to stay the hell out of the high mountains for the general safety of us all, then had him make me a couple of barbecue sandwiches for the road.

I hadn't seen the kids since the day before the launch and I wanted to stop in Austin to take them out for a hamburger or something, but Peggy had made it clear that I was never to stop by unannounced, and I was afraid that that *Texas Monthly* jerk would be there, so I simply blew the kids a kiss as I drove up 290 into the Hill Country, promising myself that we'd have a real reunion on my way back. I had been a father in absentia for only a couple of months, and it was a role I wasn't very good at. When I was away from Matt and Sarah, as I was most of the time now, it was hard not to convince myself that I was a bastard for not being with them. Yet when we were together, I always seemed to be glancing into mirrors, wondering if I appeared to be a good father to the rest of the world, rather than simply paying attention to those two remarkable little people. Peggy and I had at least succeeded with them, hadn't we? At least our children were evidence that our twelve years together had had some meaning, a more precious legacy than simply a couple of fat photo albums too painful now to open. As I drove through Dripping Springs and on through the secure and sultry darkness, eating Pe-Te's sandwiches and listening to a country disc jockey dedicate songs to "all you boys high-ballin' out on 1-20," it seemed to me that driving those whining eighteen-wheelers on all-night hauls wouldn't be a bad occupation. But by the time I got to San Angelo I was so road weary that I was already looking for a new line of work, and I stopped at the Holiday and got a room.

The bar, called the Branding Iron as I recall, was still open, but empty except for a guy who looked as if he had rough-necked for ninety years and his girlfriend in vinyl pants. The bartender probably would have been just as lovely even if it weren't after midnight and if I weren't alone and awkwardly lonely. We talked while I drank better scotch than I usually drink and while she began to clean up the bar. I told her I was from Houston, and she told me about the time she and her best friend, who lived there now, had gone to a club on Richmond called Cooter's, how they had quickly discovered that every male in the place was rabidly on the make.

"Did you take anyone up on it?" I asked.

She grinned, shook her head, and dipped two glasses into the rinse sink. "It's quite a world out there, isn't it?"

When she asked me what I did for a living I told her I was an engineer, my standard reply, but I was immediately sorry I hadn't tried the truth. It was late; she just wanted to get home, no doubt, and I was just another engineer. I finished my drink, went to my room and fell asleep with what seemed to be the undeniable knowledge that had she known I was an astronaut she would suddenly have found me irresistible and certainly would not have gone home.

In the morning I was glad to be waking up alone, glad to avoid saying a cold and sober goodbye in the unforgiving fluorescent light of a motel room, anxious to drive as fast as I could across the sere sweep of west Texas. I ate breakfast in Big Spring, made Lubbock by eleven, then rolled northwest toward New Mexico among the polled Herefords and Brangus cattle, the stubbled cotton fields, and the scattered, persistent pump jacks sucking oil out of the smooth skin of the plains.

My father would be full of questions, I knew, and I wanted to get to Durango before it got late. He and Mom had gone to Canaveral to watch the launch that Tuesday in May, and I was able to have lunch with them and the kids in the crew quarters the day before, but it was an awkward way to see them. They both seemed surprisingly nervous, and I was paying most of my attention to the kids. When I got back to Houston, Dad told me over the phone that Mom had decided she just couldn't watch the liftoff, shutting her eyes and squeezing his hand until that crackling roar of the solid boosters reached them. She opened her eyes, he said, expecting to see the orbiter augering into the alligator marshes. But all she saw was those beautiful sun-bright streams of exhaust as we arced out over the Atlantic.

When I got to Durango, I wanted to tell my parents how glad I was that they got to see that sight—knowing their son was sitting atop those shrieking rockets. I wanted them to know that I owed them a lot and that I really was trying to be a decent adult, but I didn't know how to say it without my words sounding like the maudlin verse in a greeting card. Still, I hoped I would find something I would be brave enough to say.

By the time I got to Albuquerque, the stupefying Texas humidity was gone, the sooty air in the city was hot and powder dry. Just outside Bernalillo I picked up a young Navajo who was standing by the side of the road with one arm outstretched, the other clutching a paper sack. He wore a T-shirt that said kiss me in red paint that was meant to look like lipstick, blue running shoes, and his long hair, black as space, was folded and wrapped with a cotton ribbon. He said he was going to Nageezi, and I told him I could take him that far. When I asked if he was a student, he said no and then was silent.

"Where are you going?" he asked as we passed the turnoff into the Jemez Mountains.

"Home," I said. "Durango."

"What do you do for a job?" he asked, now seeming ready for conversation.

"I'm . . . an astronaut. I work for the government." This time I told the truth.

"Oh," he said, then was silent again. I could see a flannel shirt and the brown spine of a book in his sack but I couldn't read its title. The red hills were spotted with squat piñon trees, and the dark layers of the distant mesas were distinct in the evening light.

"Do you go to the moon?" the young man asked after a while.

"No. No, we only go into earth orbit these days."

"Why do the other astronauts go to the moon?"

"Well. I think the main reason they went was to see if they could get there. It was exploring."

"Oh," he said. "Do they like the moon very much?"

"I think they were glad to get back."

"I bet," he said.

When I stopped on the shoulder of the road across from the trading post at Nageezi, I asked him if he lived nearby.

"Over behind that round hill," he said. The spare ground, covered with small sage and saltbush and dry chamisa, stretched away in a series of shallow depressions and stunted hills. I held out my hand and told him my name was Jack. We shook hands and he said, "Good luck if you go to the moon," before he shut the door.

As I drove on in the advancing darkness, I couldn't help but wonder what the moon means to a Navajo teenager who lives in the barren, lunar landscape of the San Juan basin. I wondered whether he was the sort who would figure all we got out of Apollo was the boxes of rocks, or whether flying out to another world would seem as reasonable to him as hitchhiking to Albuquerque and back. I looked out the window for the moon and found a pale crescent in the western sky—not a cratered sphere caught in the empty sea of the solar system, just a new moon, small and intangible, suspended above the Carrizos.

I was tempted by the Lotaburger in Bloomfield but realized I could get to Durango in less than an hour, so I stayed on the road, anxious and wide awake, glad to be arriving in the enveloping and quiet night. I stopped on the bridge at the base of Cedar Hill and peed between the rusted tangle of trusses into the river, the same river I'd grown up beside, then crossed the state line and headed for town. Yard lights like the pinpoints of stars spread across the flat farm country, and the bright streetlights at the southern edge of town lit the new shopping mall and the five acres of asphalt that surrounded it, its empty parking lot making the whole enterprise appear out of place and unneeded. The sight of it also made me realize that this wasn't a town I knew well anymore. It would always be home; it would always belong to me in a strange, emotive sense. It was probably a possession I would never really know again, yet I could never sell it or give it away.

It looked as if every light in the house was on when I turned off Seventh Avenue into the steep driveway. The sagging basketball hoop and the backboard with a rectangle outlined in electrician's tape had been gone for fifteen years, but it still surprised me to find them missing. And there was a new Subaru they hadn't told me about. But just as I was about to get in to investigate the new car, Dad opened the back door.

"Don't leave," he hollered. "You just got here."

I closed the door of the car and walked over to give him a hug. He had taken his collar off and his white T-shirt was visible through the open front of his black shirt. His eyes were bright in the dim light, but it was obvious that he had tempered the wait with a tall highball or two.

"Hi, Dad," I said while he held me. "Nice car."

"Wonderful to have you," he said, and when we pulled apart his eyes were wet. "Come on. Your mother's anxious to see you. Yes, we're really going to enjoy it. I'll take you for a ride tomorrow."

My mother met us in the laundry room. I gave her a kiss, assured her that I had done nothing but eat all day, then wandered through the house, sizing it up like some sort of prospective buyer. Dad handed me a drink in the living room, and there was one for himself in his other hand.

"Sit. Sit," he said. "How was the drive?"

"Good. Just what I needed. But it's a big trip."

"You've had your share of those lately," Mom said, her voice and her smile betraying a pride in me I didn't think I deserved. "Did you stop in Austin?"

"No. They weren't expecting me. Peggy's pretty firm about me scheduling my visits."

"But they're your children as well," she said. "Sometimes I don't think she's as aware of that as she should be." She seemed startled by what she had said, a little embarrassed, then quickly added, "—but the kids were thrilled with the launch. Matthew tried to be the picture of nonchalance about it all, but by the time they got us up on the roof of that building to watch he could hardly stand still. I think he was really kind of afraid."

"Sure, he was," Dad said. "We all were. But then you were off, and it looked like everything was going to be all right. It was hard to believe you were really inside it."

"How did Sarah react?" I asked.

"She was a real trouper," Mom said. "I don't think she expected all the noise and so much steam and smoke. She asked me if it hurt you, and I told her it didn't hurt a bit, which was probably something of a white he, wasn't it?"

"Not really. You are pretty well crunched into your seat for a bit, but it's all so quick. I hope neither of them got too upset. I probably should have been more careful to explain to them what to expect."

"They were fine," Dad said. "Just fine." He paused to sip his drink. "You and their mother have put them through all kinds of new experiences in the last six months, and that launch was undoubtedly one of the better ones."

"It didn't take you long to bring that up," I said. "You're welcome to give me your usual pastoral line about how these things are so hard on the children, Dad, but you ought to give us a little more credit."

"Don't you two start in," Mom said. "Let's leave that alone, Richard. Jack's barely in the door."

Dad stared at the print of the Georgia O'Keeffe painting of the church at Ranchos de Taos, a Christmas gift from his parishioners a few years before, then took a long drink of his scotch. He had always played silence to great effect, its tension his reliable ally. I had learned long ago to give him as much of it as he wanted, so I said nothing, but I winked at Mom as she went out to the kitchen.

When he was ready to speak again, he cupped his glass in his hands, leaned forward in his chair, and spoke quietly, his words coming as if they had been rehearsed: "Your mother and I went through some very difficult times during the years I was in seminary. You and Mary were barely out of diapers; she was still nursing Michael. We had to live on next to nothing. But the worst of it probably was that I felt that if I was going to be a priest I had to somehow prove my sainthood. I was going to be wearing a collar and that was going to change everything. When we fought, I tried to make her feel guilty for fighting with a holy man." He smiled. "I'm sure I was a real joy to live with. I've kind of assumed that something similar happened last year with you two. You being too busy getting ready for the flight. Peggy feeling that you had abandoned her for a spaceship."

"She was the one that did the abandoning, Dad. I didn't run off with some asshole from Austin."

"No, I don't think you abandoned her, Jack, and I doubt she really meant to abandon you. But now that your flight's over, things might seem rather different to both of you."

"You are a nosy bastard, aren't you?" I said, grinning when I said it. I knew I wasn't prepared to have him solve my marital problems so early in my visit.

"I'm in the nosy business. We clerics begin with the presumption that absolutely everything is our vital concern. That's probably why we seem so damn overbearing."

"What about that?" I asked, obviously changing the subject. "Are you really going to retire?"

"I've decided not to decide. If the Holy Spirit wants me to stay at St. Mark's after I'm sixty-five, he'll just have to let me know by keeping me alive. I guess Mom told you we buried Hal yesterday?"

"No. . ." I didn't know what to say. "The cancer?" He nodded, his eyes got wet again, and he pulled on his nose. "They thought they had it licked. Then about a month ago they did a biopsy of a little spot in his stomach—positive —and they sent him to Denver for more tests. It had spread all through his lungs and liver. He was in the hospital here for about three weeks." Dad ran his fingers through the thick hair at his temples. The skin on the top of his head was taut and pink. "When I went to see him on Saturday, he asked me whether I would rather see him die in a hospital bed or die catching trout. So, Sunday afternoon I got him dressed and snuck him out a service entrance. We drove up to Rockwood and I put him in a lawn chair next to the bank. He fished for almost an hour before he got too weak. The river seemed like such a tonic."

"Did he catch anything?"

"No," Dad said, "but he didn't mind. He died back at the hospital that night. Asked all about your flight, Jack. He was looking forward to seeing you. He said he sure would put that on his list of things to do before he died."

"It ought to be on everyone's list," I told him, wishing I could say something about Hal and how I was so sorry.

"I told Hal they ought to send burned-out priests on space missions. I bet one weightless orbit would be better than all the retreats you could ever stand. Say, I was kind of hoping that at coffee on Sunday maybe you'd talk about it a little. Everyone is very interested."

"And that way you'd cleverly get me to church."

"You can't blame a fellow for scheming a little."

"I guess it wouldn't hurt me," I said. "You sure you don't mind having a heathen address your flock?"

"Oh, I'll be keeping my eye on you," he said, then smiled as Mom came back into the room. "He said yes to my proposition, Dorothy. I only had to agree to a five-figure sum."

"Perfectly reasonable," she said, "if you'll really let him talk. No annoying interruptions."

"Dorothy!" Dad said. "You've got me confused with one of your other men of the cloth. I—"

"You be still," she said. "That kind of talk doesn't become you. And I think I'll call it a night."

"We haven't even heard about the flight yet. Come sit down. Your son has grand things to tell us."

"I'll hear everything in the morning. Good night, Jack," she said, bending over to kiss the top of my head. "And good night to you, Father Healy."

Dad blew her a kiss, then watched her disappear down the hall. I refused his offer of another drink, then changed my mind when he got up to help himself to another. He had always preferred to let my mother go to bed without him, it seemed, staying awake, drinking and reading until his head collapsed into the corner of the recliner and he slept. I remember that when I was still home I would often get up in the middle of the night and find him slumped in his chair and snoring, a book by Teilhard de Chardin lying in his lap. I always wanted to close his book, to take his watery drink to the kitchen, to nudge him and send him off to bed, but I never did. Time after time, I just turned off the lamp that stood beside the chair, then slowly made my way across the carpet, leaving him alone in the darkness.

But that night there was my mission to discuss, and his book stayed shut, and I drank with him into the early morning. He wanted to hear about the reason for the countdown delay, wondered whether we were aware of how much media attention we were getting, asked me all about the EVA, how the backpack worked, and what it felt like as I flew away from the orbiter. I remember that when I was in high school kids used to tell me what a good listener he was, but that ability to listen always seemed limited to the hours he wore the collar. I don't think Mike or Mary or I ever thought he paid any sort of rapt attention to us. But that night, he was undeniably entranced by my descriptions of the flight. Space seemed to be a subject that tapped the inveterate tinkerer in him as well as the starry-eyed theologian. He was enthralled with the thought that humans could go to inhuman realms, and the idea of seeing the earth spin in the blackness seemed almost sacramental to him.

"When we saw those first pictures on TV of you and Bill Grimes out there, completely away from the shuttle, I couldn't believe it. Your mother and I both had big tears streaming down our faces. I mean, good heavens, there you were in absolute space. I thought, what a very lucky man he is."

"I know I am," I said. "Whenever I had a second just to drink it all in, that was what crossed my mind. Why do I get to do this? I felt so damn . . . fortunate. Why not Mary or Matt . . . or Hal McGinnis?"

"Matthew's time will come. He'll have a hell of a life. And Hal . . . I'm going out to see Jane tomorrow, by the way. Losing her dad on top of everything else has been quite a blow. Hal's brother and his wife were going to leave today. Come with me. I told her I'd try to drag you along."

"Sure. I'd like to," I said. I told him about how we had finally snared the satellite, and then I demanded a bed.

"Off you go," he said. "I'll be along in a bit."

The next morning, I asked my father if he had heard from Mike recently as we drove west out of town, crossing the runoff-swollen river, then twisting through the bare canyon that was still and shadowed in the morning light. Mike had called from Denver on Tuesday, he said, and he seemed to be doing better. He was working at a bakery in the mornings and spending his afternoons at St. Andrew's, helping in the kitchen and cleaning the room where the street people slept, their canvas pads strewn across the checkered linoleum floor.

"As long as he stays on the Thorazine, he seems to do just fine," Dad said. "But then for no reason he'll stop taking it, and I'll get a call that he's threatening Father Long with a Buck knife because John takes his mind away while he sleeps. John Long has been tremendous with Michael. You remember John, don't you? We wanted to bring Michael to the Cape with us, but since he finally seems to be getting settled, we decided we'd better not. And I'm sure Mary was sick about not being able to come."

"She called a couple of days after I got back to Houston," I said. "Vintage Mary. She was certainly not going to be overly impressed by some expensive federal enterprise that smacks of militarism, but she did say she wished she could have seen the launch. I told her I hoped there'd be another one sometime. The next time, she said, she could guarantee she wouldn't be strapped with a ten-month-old."

It was still hard to imagine Mary as a mother. She had not married Robert until she was thirty-three, and the daughter, named Adrian, had not arrived until a few days following Mary's thirty-ninth birthday. She would be devoted to her child, I was sure of that—she would be patient and endlessly understanding, and her fascination with Adrian's progress would smother other, less captivating concerns. Yet Mary was utterly independent, and it was hard to imagine her surrendering to the mundane commitments of motherhood.

The eldest of the three of us, Mary had very decidedly emancipated herself at seventeen when she went to college in California. She seldom wrote or telephoned our parents, and her Christmas visits were always short, plagued by a kind of unspoken argument about her responsibility to her family. When Mary had her first one-person show in Berkeley a couple of years after she graduated, she didn't tell any of us about it until the show had already come down. Mom and Dad were crushed that she had not wanted them to see it, or to come to the opening, but she professed shock at why they would have even considered it, telling them her work was tentative and unfocused, missing the point entirely.

I had always struggled with the question of what I wanted to do with myself, with what would ever be worth doing for dozens of years; Michael had struggled with the neurochemical chaos inside his brain; but Mary had always been resolute. Painting was, for her, not so much a decision as an obligation. She was very critical of her talent, never satisfied with a specific piece, yet she painted, year after year, as if she were meeting the terms of a demanding personal contract.

I had never understood what she and Robert shared, nor did I know how this zoology professor and the abstract painter had ever managed to meet. When she spoke of him—on the few occasions when we talked on the telephone—she would only refer to him in the most cursory way, always saying how busy he was, how his job at Cal was all-consuming. About young Adrian, however, I was happy to discover that Mary was willing to talk at length. Adrian, it seemed, was her first creation in which she was willing to take some pride.

My father said he was sure Mary was still painting, but that since she had stopped teaching when Adrian was born, he was worried that their financial situation was getting rather pinched. Yet he was gratified and a little relieved to hear from Mary that a gallery in San Francisco had recently sold two of her large paintings.

The highway met Cherry Creek and followed its twisting course beneath the snow-shrouded peaks of the La Platas. The aspen were in leaf; the trees swayed in the warm breeze of early summer, their white trunks straight and thick and knotted. Dad turned onto the dirt road in Thompson Park, the tires of his new blue car churning a column of dust behind us. He waved at a rancher in a straw hat and tall rubber boots who was irrigating a green hay field, then drove another mile before turning into the lane that led past the barn and the hay shed to the house. Jane, dressed in jeans and a snap-button shirt, her dark, gray-streaked hair held up with a silver clip, was tossing scratch to red chickens when she saw us. She emptied the grain from her bucket and came over to the car, hugging Dad first, then holding her arms out to me.

"Hello, spaceman," she said, "You don't look like it's harmed you." Her broad face was tan and smooth, her smile as disarming as ever. "Welcome back to solid ground."

I told her it felt good to be back. Her shirt was rolled up to her elbows and she saw me glance at the smooth stump at her right wrist. I had heard about the accident, of course, and I knew that her hand was gone, but the visual evidence was nonetheless an unsettling surprise.

"Oh yes, you haven't seen this," she said, lifting the stump up to my eyes. "What do you think? Some people pierce their ears. I chop off my hand." Always brash and uninhibited, Jane had no doubt thrust the evidence of her misfortune into dozens of people's faces in the months since she had lost her hand and her husband.

"Very becoming," I said. "I like it. How are you getting along?"

"Well, if it wasn't my goddamned right one it wouldn't have been so bad, but I swear it's like trying to work with five toes and an ax handle this way. But . . . all things considered, I—"

"She's doing beautifully," Dad said. "I saw her saddle a horse when I was out the other day and she didn't seem to have any trouble."

"But you didn't see it roll off his back when I stepped in the stirrup, did you?" She grinned, told us to follow her into the house, and I watched her as she turned and marched toward the back door. I had always been attracted to Jane; we had even dated—both of us feeling a weird incestuousness about it— during one summer when I was home from college, but I was surprised to find that as a one-handed widow now pushing forty Jane seemed so strong and so alluring.

Kenny had been dead for almost a year; she had been hospitalized for two months and had worn a back brace for two more. Her hand was severed by the hitch of the horse trailer when it landed beside the overturned truck. Kenny was also thrown out of the pickup and was crushed by the side of the trailer. Both horses lived for over an hour before a state patrolman finally took out his revolver and shot them. The neighbors got the last cutting of hay in, and Jane hired an immigrant from Chihuahua to feed for her that winter. Dad said she wanted to sell the cows and half the place. As we sat down at the kitchen table, she told me she planned to keep the horses and to stay out in the park indefinitely.

"I had thought about finding a house in town for Dad and me, but I didn't really want to live in town. Now that he's gone, I'm sure I'll stay put. I saw you on TV, Jack. Couldn't really tell it was you out on your spacewalk, but you looked great floating around inside the shuttle. You guys must have had a terrific time."

"I doubt they got a lick of work done," Dad said.

"Strictly recreational," I told them; then I said something to Jane about her dad. Hal and my father had been friends since Dad first arrived at St. Mark's. But unlike Dad, Hal was always as captivated by the skies as I was. He and I used to spot constellations and watch lunar eclipses in my parents' backyard, and I was fascinated by his stories about the Northern Lights from his years spent in Alberta. I got a telegram from him in Houston years ago on the day the first Viking lander touched down on Mars. It just read, we made it! best, hal.

"He watched your launch at the hospital," Jane said. "He told all the nurses and technicians that he had a friend flying on the shuttle and that they, by God, couldn't sedate him."

"When we got back," Dad said, "he had to hear every last detail about the launch. I brought him one of those souvenir hats that says NASA, and he wore it in bed while we watched the landing." He paused. "I'm going to miss that man."

"Me too," Jane said; then she got up from the table. "Shoot, it's after eleven. It's not too early for a beer, is it?" She went to the refrigerator. "Come on. We'll take these out to the porch."

"I'll meet you there," I said. "I want to go look at your horses." I took a beer and walked through the corrals by the barn and out into the pasture. Four horses grazed on the bromegrass near the south fence. They picked their heads up and studiously watched me approach. A bay mare finally took a few steps in my direction, then stopped when she noticed I wasn't carrying a grain bucket. When I reached her, I rubbed her neck and let her smell the bottle to prove it was nothing of interest. The other three, still wary of a hatless man in khaki pants, kept their distance. A second mare, surely ready to foal, had a big, bell-shaped belly, and her steps seemed labored as she moved along the fence. I ought to be a horseman, I thought. I ought to trim hooves, attend the births of pinto colts, spend weekday afternoons in smoky sale barns, and tell inquiring strangers that I was a stockman when I hung my hat on the racks in the local cafes. The bay mare, still not convinced, grabbed at the neck of the bottle with her mouth and hit it against her teeth. She stepped away, and I turned back toward the barn. I could see Jane and Dad sitting in a swing on the porch, and I waved but they didn't notice. The sun was high in the cloudless sky, and the sweet aroma of the cottonwoods wafted up from the creek. A magpie scolded me from a fence post, and the horses went back to the grass.

I couldn't hear what Dad was saying as I came around the corner of the house. Jane nodded and said, "Yes, I suppose so," then waved to me to join them.

"That mare looks like she's about ready," I said.

"I hope so, poor thing. She's so uncomfortable, especially now that it's getting hot. She's a sweetheart. This is her first foal. I'm a little nervous about it. Knowing me, I'll probably end up with a huge vet bill for having him come watch a perfectly normal birth. I told your dad I'm going to ride the roan up to the cabin tomorrow to get some of Dad's things. You can have Brenda, that bay that likes you, if you want to come."

"The cabin?"

"That hunting shack of Dad's up in Echo Basin. Want to?"

"Yes. I do. But you have to promise not to laugh at me when she makes me look ridiculous. I haven't been on a horse in ages."

"I thought all you Texans could cowboy," Dad said.

"Maybe all those Texans can," I said. "I just use their license plates. What time?" On the way to the car, Jane suggested I come out about noon; she said she'd have the horses trailered and the whiskey packed in the saddlebags.

"Don't get him too relaxed," Dad told her. "I've got him reserved for Sunday morning."

"I'll take care of him," she said. "And thanks, Dick. You've been awfully sweet to us, to me," She pushed the door of the car shut, and the way she looked at my father in that instant made me aware of how close the two of them had become. Something in her face, too—perhaps it was the sorrow it still reflected, perhaps it was a nascent hint of happiness—made my feelings for her seem like a sudden infatuation.

At dinner that night, my mother was worried about Mike, about whether he would end up in the hospital again, and I told her I had thought about going up to Denver before heading back to Houston. I hadn't seen Michael in almost two years, and I wasn't particularly anxious to see him again and to hear his incoherent stories. But Mike was doing very well, they said, and I admitted that it would be good for the two of us to be back in touch.

Mike was only two years behind me in school and we had been close until I was a junior or senior in high school. I was student body president and was, no doubt, rather impressed with myself, and I began to be horribly embarrassed by a brother who would lean for hours against the tiled walls of the science-wing restroom because, he said, the kids in the hallways wanted to steal his clothes. Mom remained Michael's great ally during the two years he tried to go to college, and although Dad had read a seemingly endless series of articles and books about schizophrenia, he, like me, responded to Mike with a certain exasperation.

"It would mean a lot to Michael if you could stop for a day or so," Mom said. "He really needs to know he has a family who cares about him." My mother's voice always assumed a terrible sadness when she talked about Michael, the child to whom, for reasons I doubt even she knew, she had always been closest, the son whose private anguish had deepened her love and protection. When she spoke with concern about Michael, I always wanted to give her a kind of comic hug and to tell her with unfounded optimism that he was going to be just fine. But I never did, perhaps because I somehow sensed that she knew a contradictory truth.

"I'll call and find out when I have to be back. I'd enjoy the drive through the mountains. Mike and I could catch up on a lot of things. And doesn't Jane's offer to ride up to Hal's cabin sound great?" I asked, getting away from the subject I knew they were desperate to talk about, but the one that I somehow couldn't address.

I borrowed a pair of boots from Dad on Saturday, and he insisted that I take his straw hat as well. I told him I'd feel a little stupid in a cowboy hat, but he convinced me that without it the sun would burn me up. When I got to Jane's, the horses, as promised, were in the trailer, and she had sandwiches for us to eat in the truck. She asked me to drive, and I'm sure she noticed how timidly I negotiated Mancos Hill. I was more at ease on the Forest Service road that led into the basin, but pulling the heavy trailer was unsettling and the conversation was often cut by my silent attention to the road.

"I could see the La Platas from orbit," I said to break the silence. "They were just a minuscule white group of ridges, but they were easy to spot. It's funny. I felt so proprietary about this place, seeing it from two hundred miles up."

"Do you want to go again?"

"I'd love to. But working for the government gets pretty gruesome. You never know what in the hell they've got planned for you. And ass kissing is the only real talent you're required to have. If Peggy and the kids moved farther away, I'd have some real second thoughts. There was a time when all I ever imagined doing was teaching astronomy at some little college somewhere. Now that possibility seems so remote I can hardly imagine it. Maybe I'm destined to become a beer distributor, like all the other ex-astronauts."

"I was sorry to hear about you two splitting up, Jack. I always assumed that you two really had made that pact that everybody aims for. But . . . did it have something to do with her finally deciding she had to see if she could walk without a net? Not that it's any of my business."

"What do you mean?"

"I know what it's like to live in somebody's shadow. Kenny was Mr. Wonderful around here, on every committee and invited to every social event, the heartthrob of all the horny young wives whose husbands were getting fat. They all thought I was just this weird complication in his life, an aloof bitch who wouldn't even join the bridge clubs. I was in the hospital, but they told me that at his funeral they had to set up loudspeakers in the parish hall and out in the courtyard so everyone who came could hear the service. Poor Kenny. He would have loved to know he could draw that kind of crowd. He wanted to run for county commissioner. Now that he's gone, people just can't associate me with him anymore. It's the first time I've ever really felt like an individual, I guess."

I pulled the truck to the edge of the road when Jane motioned toward the sign that marked the trail. "You and Peggy probably do have something in common," I said. We backed the horses out of the trailer. Their saddles were already on, so all I had to do was to fumble at getting the curb bit into Brenda's mouth and tie the nylon bags to the saddle skirts. I watched Jane tie a rolled canvas pannier behind the cantle of her saddle, anxious to help but afraid to offer. She mounted the roan gelding, then held the reins in her teeth while she struggled to adjust the stirrups with her left hand.

"Son of a bitch," she said. "I forgot that my irrigator used this saddle last week." She turned to me, her voice softened as if she was telling me something she wouldn't have shared with everyone. "Doctor keeps telling me it's time for a prosthesis, but, God, I don't want to wear some stupid hook or a plastic hand. I don't care how much easier it would be." I didn't know how to respond, so I was silent again.

The trail was wide as it led into the timber, and the horses walked abreast. Brenda was a good walker and seemed relaxed in the trees, but the roan, named Sport, snorted and seemed to hunt for an excuse to spook. Jane held him on a tight rein and slapped his ears with her handless arm a time or two before he abandoned his hopes for chaos. "So," she said, "you want to become a beer distributor."

"Maybe a cowboy," I said. "This seems to suit me."

"I like your hat. Makes you look like Smiley Burnette."

"It's my father's fault. The image would be more like the Lone Ranger if it was my own hat."

"That's the astronaut coming out. You want people to think you're perfect."

"But you don't buy it in my case, right?"

"This whole space business . . . I don't know," she said. "I just have never got it. I'm glad for you, Jack, I don't mean that, but isn't it just a big show? All for the patriotic glory of it?"

"My Rotary Club speech about the space program would put you to sleep," I said. "But no. I think it's pretty important. Even going to the moon made sense if you accept the idea that you ought to go wherever you can get to."

"So now we know the moon is rocky and gray and wouldn't be much of a vacation."

"There's an old book by Oriana Fallaci about the space program in the years before the first moon landing. She began her research as this outrageous skeptic, but by the end she seemed to think space travel was some sort of valiant symbolic quest. She interviewed Wally Schirra, who is your classic right-stuff kind of guy, Spartan and tight-lipped as they come. But old Wally ended up gushing to her that the moon and Mars are ugly islands. Nobody would want to live there, he said. But the reason for going to the ugly islands was to prove you could do it, so you could keep searching for the beautiful islands."

"Assuming there are some."

"Oh, they're there."

"An act of faith?"

"An act of a telescope. I mean, I don't know if we'll ever find one that has oxygen and aspen trees, but that doesn't bother me. We have to look because that's what we're programmed for—I mean, maybe even genetically. Basically, what we do as a species is poke around, snoop, isn't it?"

We rode out of the trees into a small meadow, its grass still matted by the weight of the winter's snow. A doe that was drinking in a quiet meander of the creek looked warily at us, then bounded into the stand of spruce that swept up toward the barren rock. The trail narrowed at the far side of the meadow, then made two switchbacks as it climbed through the damp floor of the forest. Sport was winded enough to be steady now, and Brenda followed so obediently that I had nothing to do but sit. The cabin, built out of pine planks that must have been hauled up thirty years before, stood on a small bank of bald rock. Loose tar paper on the roof flapped in the mountain wind, and the one window was covered with cardboard. We tied the horses to a fallen log, then looked inside.

The small room smelled musty but strangely sweet. It was dusty and dark, and the mice had made themselves at home; their dry turds were scattered across the table, the long counter, and the plastic sheet that covered the bed. Hal had left four boxes of split wood next to the rusted Ashley, and the dishes were carefully stacked beside the washbasin. Jane looked inside a three-legged chest of drawers for the things she had come for—a deerskin jacket, an old revolver, a thick roll of topographical maps, and a stack of books. She took them outside, sat down on the west side of the shack in the late-afternoon sun, and put them inside the canvas pannier. "I didn't like the idea of these things that were important to him sitting up here where they could be stolen now that he's gone," she said. I sat down beside her and could see Ute Mountain in the west, and off to the southwest, the high plateau of Mesa Verde, cut by its finger canyons. "He only liked to come here alone," she said. "I used to suggest that the two of us ride up here occasionally, but he always had some lame excuse. Then out of the blue one day he'd call and say he was on his way out the door, headed for the cabin. Always a great urgency about it. He kept that little telescope here too. But he brought it down last fall when he discovered some hunters had stayed here." She finished the packing, then took a pint of scotch out of her jacket pocket.

"You'll join me, I trust," she said before she put the bottle to her lips. "This has become quite a habit since the accident. I used to wonder why people drank alone, but I don't wonder anymore. I suppose I count Johnnie Walker among my best friends these days." She grinned and considered before she spoke again. "What's it been like for you alone, Jack?"

"I've been lucky," I said. "With the mission, I've been busy enough, gone enough that I haven't really had to face it. I'm sure that's part of the reason why I decided to drive up. I still wasn't ready to face the office routine and that god-awful empty house of mine."

Jane stared into the distance. "I haven't washed my windows for nearly a year," she said. "I leave the newspapers in rolls and stack them like kindling in the kitchen closet. Maybe this is what they mean by mourning, but I think it's inertia. It's a sort of weird inertia caused by being left alive. Like I'm numb. Like I just don't give a damn about anything. Even when we knew it was just a matter of days for Dad, I couldn't cry. I couldn't tell him the things I always assumed I would say."

I put my hand on her leg, smoothing the faded fabric of her jeans, and Jane turned to me and kissed me. She smelled wonderful, like my memories of Peggy, and she pressed herself against me. She lifted my hat off when we looked at each other again. "I'm not so inert that I couldn't make love to you," she said, her voice quiet now, its cynical edge evaporating. "I don't think I could have till.. . well. . ."

We stood and went inside the cabin. I sat on the edge of the table while she pulled the plastic from the bed. She sat on the edge of the bed, kicked off her boots, and unbuttoned her shirt with her single hand. Her breasts were tan and round and lovely, her nipples hard. "You stop wearing bras when you lose a hand," she said with a shy smile. "Come here, for heaven's sake."

I was glad to follow instructions. She must have known how much I wanted her, but for some reason I preferred to pretend I was merely compliant. I went to the bed and undressed before I touched her again. We stared at each other, saying nothing while I stood, then I curled beside her on the cold cotton bedspread. I reached for her head and found her mouth again. It had been nearly two months since I had made love to anyone, too much aching time since that strange weekend in April when Barbara Collingwood, another astronaut, and I had gone to Padre Island for the expressed purpose of coming to each other's carnal rescue. There was something similar happening with Jane and me, but bound up in it too, for both of us, were the accident and her dad and our strange connection to each other shaped by that backwater corner of Colorado. We held each other desperately, shouting and sweating, almost fighting, before we were finished and were again aware of the cold.

I pulled the bedspread over us; Jane dozed with her head on my shoulder. Her handless arm was stretched across my chest, and I could see the pale, precise scar that curled around the stump. I kissed her forehead. "Let's stay," I said. "The night. There's lots of wood."

"We'll bother the mice," she said. "Won't be much of a dinner. That . . . was the first time since Kenny. God, it seems like ages ago."

"You think your dad would mind us staying here in his private retreat?"

"If he knew you were here I think he'd arrange some sort of dispensation."

Before we got up, Jane mentioned the accident again, telling me it had been a long time before she realized she was mourning the loss of her hand as well as her husband. "At first, it seemed like such a little thing. Kenny, the horses were dead— gone forever—and my hand, well, it was nothing in comparison. Then, after a few months, I started to get angry, really mad, about being left with this stump. I was alone, and I was damn lonely, I suppose, and to top it all off, now I was some sort of freak."

"No," I said, "you don't—"

"You don't realize what it does to you, Jack. Everything you do is a big procedure, and you're reminded a million times a day of how incompetent you are. Then, finally, the resignation sets in, and that's the paralyzing part."

"But you haven't really had to give anything up, have you?" I asked, as if I had to counter with a feeble optimism.

"I've given up taking my abilities for granted," she said. "That's something more than you'd guess it would be. Before, I basically assumed I could do anything I chose. There weren't any limits. Now, the limits are the first things that cross my mind."

I built a fire in the Ashley when I got up from the bed, and at dusk I built a second fire in a ring of stones that lay off to the side of the cabin. We unsaddled the horses and Jane tied their lead ropes to a snag that looked as if long ago it had been hit by lightning. We sat by the campfire in the thickening darkness, ate two apples and a candy bar, and finished the scotch. I took Hal's deerskin jacket out of the pannier and put it on; Jane wrapped herself in a wool blanket. The crescent moon, looking as if it had leaped above Ute Mountain, had grown to nearly a quarter, and the serpentine stars of Hydra hung above it. I pointed out Betelgeuse and the bears and tried to spot the dim outline of Pegasus but could not.

Before we went inside, I told Jane that from orbit, the only way we could find the earth at night was to find the arc where the stars stopped. It seemed so strange that that sweep of total darkness, of emptiness, was the familiar earth itself, just a rocket's throw away.

Brenda and Sport began to whinny in the dead of night. When I opened the door nothing seemed to be wrong, but I waited until they were quiet before I went back inside. I don't think I slept again. I remember lying in Hal's bed until it grew light, imagining how improbable it was that I was there in his mountaintop retreat, his daughter asleep beside me.

I didn't realize what I had done—or what I'd forgotten to do —until Jane was awake, kidding me about spending my Sunday morning with an old widow-woman instead of attending my father's church. By then it was too late to make it back to town to give the talk I had promised him I would, but we hurried anyway, closing up the cabin and riding the horses back down to the truck in a flurry of preoccupied and guilty activity. At Jane's ranch, I tried to slow down long enough to thank her for the outing and the night, but she hurried me on my way, knowing better than I did, I suppose, how disappointed my dad would be.

My mother was in the kitchen when I got back to the house; she didn't say anything when she looked up from the letter she was writing at the table. I sat down in a chair across from her and asked her where he was. "He's in the backyard.

Trimming roses. But don't go out. I'm not sure he'd speak to you."

"I completely forgot," I said. "I'm so sorry. We decided to stay up at the cabin. I didn't remember until this morning, and by then it was too late to get down in time."

"He told them you suddenly had been called back to Texas. He was so embarrassed, Jack. That was the worst of it."

"Jesus. That was probably the crudest thing I could have done to him."

"Well.. .just leave him alone."

"I guess I ought to go ahead and go now that he's told people I have."

"Did you have a good time?"

"Yes . . . very, but I ought to apologize at least."

"Wait till this evening. You two can talk after dinner. Just let him garden for now."

"I better just say something and go," I said, and I got up and went out the back door. Dad was kneeling in the brown soil of the rose bed, his shirt off, his hands in cotton gloves. I sat on the grass beside him and watched him work before I spoke. His back was moist; his belly looked bigger than I had imagined it was.

"I just wanted to say that I'm terribly sorry," I said. "It wasn't intentional. We decided to stay and I forgot. I just forgot." He turned the soil with a hand spade.

"The worst thing about being a parent," he said, "is that it's irreversible." The dark soil was damp; it stuck to his ragged gloves. "I don't want an apology; don't want to accept one. It didn't matter."

"Yes it did. You asked me to do something for you and I let you down."

"You're thirty-six years old, Jack. You're free to let down anyone you want to." He still did not look at me. "That cabin meant a lot to Hal. Now I guess the wind and snow will have it ruined before long. Come back and see us, Jack."

"I guess I ought to go, shouldn't I?"

"We've had a good visit. Find your mother before you go. Give the kids a big hug for us."

"I'll give you a hug."

"Let's wait till next time," he said, patting the soil with his broad hands as I turned back to the house.

My mother was still at the table, and I told her I was on my way to Denver. "I'd like to see Mike in good shape," I said.

She got up, embraced me and held me for a moment. "I'm sorry, Jack," she said. "This family is funny, isn't it?" It was something I had heard her say dozens of times before. Whenever one of us fought with my father, whenever Mary's correspondence dwindled to months of silence, whenever the voices began to shout inside Michael's head, my mother would smile sadly and tell us what a funny clan we were. She knew, of course, that our troubles were much like any other family's. In saying we were funny, she meant to tell us how readily we could break her heart.

I got my things, drove through the quiet Sunday streets and out of town to Jane's. No one answered the door. I checked the barn and the outbuildings and walked through the near pasture. God, I wanted to see her again. I left a note taped to the door, and went back through town, drove east into the tall ponderosas and over Wolf Creek Pass. I found a phone at a gas station in Del Norte.

"Come to Texas," I said to Jane when she answered.

"How was he?" she asked.

"Hurt. Furious. Sad that he had to have kids. Will you come?"

"I'll keep you posted," she said. "And thank you."

I was in Pueblo by dusk. The interstate was almost empty, and the bare brown plains rolled away in the darkness. The moon at last lifted above the high hump of Pikes Peak, but it couldn't keep me company, couldn't keep my mind off what I had done to my father, or the way he had hurried me out of his garden. Even the recurrent image of Jane—her shirt unbuttoned, her arms opening out to me—couldn't convince me that I had ever done a damn bit of good for anyone.

SHUTTING THE RIVER OFF

An excerpt from *A STORY THAT STANDS LIKE A DAM*

The canyonlands did have a heart, a living heart, and that heart was Glen Canyon and the wild Colorado. — Edward Abbey

The unregulated Colorado was a son of a bitch. It was either in flood or in trickle. It wasn't any good. — Floyd Dominy

The river ran free in Glen Canyon for the first six years the dam was under construction, bypassing the cacophonous, swarming job site by diving into a diversion tunnel dug into the canyon wall. But by January 1963, with the vertical upstream wall of the dam already soaring 600 feet high and with the outlet pipes and the eight steeply sloping penstocks in place, it was time to shut the river off.

In consultation with his superior, Secretary of the Interior Stewart Udall, and his chief construction engineer on the site, an Arkansas-born bulldog named L. F. "Lem" Wylie, Bureau of Reclamation Commissioner Floyd Dominy had sanctioned January 21 as the day the diversion tunnel in the west wall of the canyon would be sealed. A team of ironworkers would carefully begin to close the three steel slide-gates that blocked the entrance to the 41-foot-diameter tunnel; then concrete masons, working in the wet and now almost waterless hole, would install a temporary concrete plug. Finally, 400 feet of the tunnel would be plugged with solid concrete.

The entrance to a second diversion tunnel in the east canyon wall had been dug 33 feet higher than the one on the opposite side, and since the gates in that tunnel weren't scheduled to be screwed down for a couple of months, the river didn't have far to rise before it could escape again, its downstream journey only briefly interrupted. Yet there was something symbolic about those first 33 feet of reservoir, something that assured Wylie that he and his men actually would be able to harness the son of a bitch, something that proved to Dominy and Udall that the people's money and their own political energies had been well spent.

Those first 33 feet of the lake, high enough to back water upstream about 16 miles—sending it into the side canyons of Wahweap, Antelope, Navajo, and Warm creeks—were proof of a different kind to David Brower, evidence of the heart-wrenching certainty that the canyon soon would be submerged. Brower, executive director of a small, San Francisco-based conservation organization called the Sierra Club, had traveled to Washington, D.C., on the day Glen Canyon's west diversion tunnel was scheduled to be closed, hoping that he could convince Udall to forestall what he knew someday would be inevitable. In agreeing not to put up a pitched battle against the Glen Canyon construction back when it was authorized in 1956 as part of the Colorado River Storage Project, America's conservationists had won a single concession: no dam, reservoir, or related structure would be allowed to intrude on any national park or monument.

In the case of Glen Canyon, that meant something very specific. When the Glen Canyon reservoir—now commonly being called Lake Powell—finally was full, it would send water far up Forbidding Canyon, then up a small tributary called Bridge Canyon and into the 160-acre Rainbow Bridge National Monument, a federal preserve since 1910 and the site of the world's largest and surely most spectacular natural stone arch. At the lake's maximum high-water elevation of 3,711 feet above sea level, water would sit 57 feet deep in the narrow inner channel of the canyon directly beneath the bridge. As far as Brower and his confederates were concerned, the situation was very simple: since Congress had mandated that the Glen Canyon project could not be built without adequate additional measures to protect Rainbow Bridge from encroachment, the lake legally could not begin to rise until those measures had been taken. If all of Glen Canyon could be spared in the interim, well, that would be a substantial, if temporary, additional victory.

What the conservationists wanted the Bureau of Reclamation to do was to build a dam downstream from the monument that would prevent the lake from encroaching upon it. A pumping facility would be required as well, one that would suck out the intermittent water that ran down Bridge Canyon from the slopes of Navajo Mountain—the water that had created the canyon and the bridge in the first place—and avoid the inevitable creation of a small but equally invasive reservoir on the upstream side of the barrier dam.

Dominy and the Bureau of Reclamation had been more than willing to cooperate. Bureau engineers were in the business of designing and building dams, after all, and Dominy—a charismatic kind of autocrat who liked to explain, with a grin, that he was a simple public servant—personally relished the irony that this time it was the conservationists who demanded a dam, a structure that otherwise they were invariably quick to despise. If Congress appropriated the money, Dominy would be glad to build the conservationists an impoundment they could call their own. For two years running, however, Congress had refused to approve legislation that would have made the construction funds available, and President Kennedy carefully had steered clear of the controversy, saying repeatedly that Congress should decide the issue.

As for Kennedy's cabinet member in charge of these enormously expensive federal water projects (as well as of all the nation's public lands), Udall was in favor of doing nothing, letting the lake slip under the enormous arch of Rainbow

Bridge and lap beneath its massive sandstone abutments. Since Glen Canyon Dam had been authorized, Udall had made several trips to Rainbow Bridge, first as a congressman and then as secretary of the Interior. Despite his support for every western water project that had ever floated down the congressional stream, Udall was greatly enamored of the canyon country that formed the borderlands of his native state and neighboring Utah. In 1871, his great-grandfather, John D. Lee, a legendary Mormon pioneer, had settled briefly with his seventeenth wife, Emma, on the shore of the Colorado 15 miles downstream from the place where Glen Canyon Dam now stood, and his people had been proud and influential Arizonans ever since. As far as the young Interior secretary with the piercing eyes and the burr haircut was concerned, the rocky, rough, and very remote country surrounding Lee's Ferry and including Rainbow Bridge was his country, and it was the most captivating of all the desert canyonlands. And Udall was equally convinced that if a protective dam or dams were built near Rainbow Bridge, the cure would be far worse than the disease. Roads somehow would have to be blasted into an area that currently was traversed by only a single tough and primitive trail; mesas would have to be scraped to provide material for the structures; and electric lines to provide power for the pumps would have to invade the monument as well. Udall was convinced that Rainbow Bridge would have to be destroyed if it were to be saved.

Although in those first years of the 1960s, America's conservation organizations were not at all comfortable with

Udall's record on water projects, in other respects his early stewardship of Interior had seemed enlightened compared with that of his Eisenhower-administration predecessors, Fred Seaton and Douglas "Give-Away" McKay. One thing that was very much in his favor, as the conservationists saw it, was that Udall wanted to add vast new acreage to the national park system. He wanted, in fact, to turn the postage stamp-sized Rainbow Bridge National Monument into a new 500,000-acre national park. But Udall's new park would have to include a foul little fjord of Lake Powell, and on that point, the conservationists so far had refused to compromise. It had been compromise, they reminded Udall, that had doomed Glen Canyon in the first place.

Early in the 1950s, the Bureau of Reclamation had proposed building a series of storage reservoirs on the Green and Colorado rivers in the upper Colorado basin, including a huge dam in Dinosaur National Monument up north on the Utah-Colorado border as well as the dam in Glen Canyon. Few conservationists were in favor of any of the proposed dams, but all were adamant in their opposition to the Echo Park project inside Dinosaur. As they saw it then, if any part of the national park system could be invaded, could be developed for whatever purpose, then the system itself had no integrity, and no part of the system was safe. The Echo Park proposal had to be defeated at all costs, and the logical, if lamentable, cost seemed to be withholding opposition to those proposed dams and reservoirs that did not affect or invade parklands.

After years of struggle, the West's water solons and the Bureau of Reclamation—where brash, often intimidating Floyd Dominy had not yet gained total power—agreed to scrap Echo Park in return for the conservationists' agreement that they would let the government get on with some dam building. The deal was set: Glen Canyon and five other dams would be built in areas throughout the upper basin of the Colorado River where they would not encroach on parklands; Dinosaur National Monument would be spared, and—there it was, written down in an act of Congress—"as part of the Glen Canyon Unit, the Secretary of the Interior shall take adequate protective measures to preclude impairment of the Rainbow Bridge National Monument."

On the morning of January 21, 1963, Dave Brower, who by default as well as his own force of will had become the unofficial chieftain of the nation's several conservation organizations, sat outside the office of the secretary of the Interior, hoping he would be granted a few minutes' audience. Brower planned to remind Secretary Udall of that very specific language within the Colorado River Storage Project enabling legislation, and to implore him not to let the diversion tunnel at Glen Canyon be sealed—not today and not until someday down the line when Rainbow Bridge had been blocked adequately from the rising water. But Secretary Udall did not meet with Brower that morning, not because he was entirely unsympathetic to his cause, but because that day—that day in particular—he had other fish to fry.

It was on the morning of January 21, by coincidence, that Stewart Udall had scheduled a press conference to announce his department's plans for an entirely new series of western dams, diversions, and delivery canals, a project that would dwarf what currently was being accomplished at Glen Canyon and elsewhere in the upper Colorado basin. With Reclamation Commissioner Dominy at his side, and with Brower now listening at the back of the room, Udall introduced with obvious enthusiasm and a certain public-relations flourish what Reclamation's imagineers had dubbed the Pacific Southwest Water Plan—a monumental dam, pump, and pipe system that would water vast new acreage in Arizona and California as well as deliver new supplies to the region's burgeoning cities. One of the beauties of the plan, according to the secretary, was that it would pay for itself in the end, not by the sale of water, but rather by the sale of electrical power, made possible by the deep canyons and steep gradient of the workhorse Colorado River. Hoover Dam had been generating hydropower for nearly thirty years now; Glen Canyon would begin its service in a year and a half or so; and sandwiched between them, the Bureau now planned to build two more hydropower dams, one at the head and another near the foot of the Grand Canyon. Together, the two dams would be able to produce enough electricity to pump the requisite water to Phoenix, plus surplus enough to sell to private utilities to generate the cash that slowly but surely would reimburse the government for its multibillion dollar outlay. Dominy, in fact, liked to refer to the Grand Canyon dams as "cash registers," and with them in place, the Colorado finally would come close to being entirely harnessed, a dream he had held fast to since he had joined Reclamation back in 1946.

Brower, the Sierra Club administrator, fifty years old and already silver-haired, was outwardly passive at the back of the room. He had known that something like this was in the works, and he knew certainly that Reclamation had had its eye on the two Grand Canyon dam sites for decades, but the timing of the announcement was particularly deflating. Exquisite Glen Canyon would begin to go under that day; Rainbow Bridge, a small but significant part of the national park system, seemed very unlikely—despite the Congress's stated wishes—to receive some sort of stay against encroachment; and now it was officially on the table: Dominy wanted to build two dams in the Grand Canyon, and Udall, the conservation-minded secretary of the Interior, wanted to let him do it.

It took two days to shut off the river, to get the slide-gates closed in the west diversion tunnel and to pour the concrete that would form the first of a series of plugs. Lem Wylie had never really worried that Udall would acquiesce to the dingbat conservationists and demand that he keep the Colorado running, but nonetheless, it felt good to him at long last to have the makings of a lake rising against the cofferdam that had kept the job site dry since February 1959. It wasn't that Wylie disliked the conservationists as individuals—at least not the few he had met. The Sierra Clubbers with whom he and the dam's chief designer, Louis Puls, had shared a boat ride up from Lee's Ferry back in 1956 had seemed like decent sorts. But they couldn't see the big picture somehow. They didn't understand that a project like this one ultimately benefited millions of people, and surely people were more important than a hundred miles or so of canyon that didn't amount to more than a kind of crack in the ground. And another thing about those people, Wylie would aver over a highball or two during evenings down at the modest little Glen Canyon Country Club, they simply had no idea what it felt like to be a part of a project like this, to have a real hand in building something that would stand in that hole over there forever. "I feel sorry for people who have to make their livings other ways," he liked to say, "instead of going out there each day and putting another five feet of mud on the block."

By the time they closed the west-tunnel gates that January, Wylie had overseen the pouring of 617 vertical feet of mud. More than four million cubic yards of concrete—four-fifths of what would be the dam's total volume—were already in place, and Wylie had good reason to believe he'd get the thing finished on time. He had been on board for five and a half years now, since the very beginning. He had gotten roads pushed through the desert to access the site by playing politics with the governors of Arizona and Utah; he had secured a location for thousands of workers to live by playing politics with the Navajos. He had overseen the building of the world's highest steel-arch bridge across the river, reducing a 196-mile highway trip from canyon rim to canyon rim to a quarter-mile of suspended macadam, and he had watched that government camp on the treeless, sand-bedeviled mesa east of the canyon turn into a kind of town, metal prefabs and tin-sided shacks now giving way to supermarkets, motels, taverns, and pastel-painted bungalows—this city of Page, Arizona, with its thirteen churches and nine holes of golf and 6,106 people, presently the biggest community alongside the Colorado River for 330 miles upstream and for 390 down.

Wylie, who had been bestowed the Bureau's thirty-year pin the year before and who planned to retire within another, wasn't particularly worried about what would happen to the town that had been his personal fiefdom. Reclamation was estimating that Page would shrink to as few as a thousand people once the dam and power plant were finished, but he wasn't so sure. Likely as not, the Bureau would end up building the conservationists their barrier dam near Rainbow Bridge, and that work force would keep the population inflated a while longer. Then, once Marble Canyon Dam was under way a few dozen miles downriver, the new project and its companion payroll would surely keep Page open for business. And over the long term, Wylie was convinced, huge numbers of people would come to this remote stretch of Utah-Arizona border country not just to work but to play. Lake Powell would be the biggest recreational draw in the southwestern United States. Situated halfway between Phoenix and Salt Lake City, just a day's drive from Albuquerque and Denver, a long day's drive from Los Angeles, this reservoir couldn't miss. Although technically it wouldn't be as big as Lake Mead down on the Nevada border, it would seem bigger and it would be far more beautiful. Hell, they were already making movies here. Just a month ago, moviemaker George Stevens had brought in John Wayne and Charlton Heston and hundreds more Hollywood people to shoot a picture he was calling The Greatest Story Ever Told. Page had bulged at its seams, and the wife of every lowboy driver and jackhammer man on the job had put a sheet over her head to play the part of an extra. This country looked more like the Holy Land than the Holy Land did, Stevens had told a meeting of the Chamber of Commerce, and if he was right, well, this place had a very bright future indeed.

That visitors could become enraptured by the Glen Canyon country was something Art Greene had known since the early 1940s, back when he began operating commercial boat trips to Rainbow Bridge from his Marble Canyon Lodge near Lee's Ferry at the foot of Glen Canyon. Originally, Greene had hauled his boats, gear, and paying guests in trucks 400 miles overland to the settlement of Hite at the head of the canyon, then had floated them down a hundred miles of placid river to the mouth of Forbidding Canyon, at which point they had no option but to walk six miles up the winding creek bed if they were to see the spectacular bridge. By the late 1940s, the indefatigable desert rat was using jerry-rigged airboats to carry as many as 150 people a year upriver from Lee's Ferry to Rainbow Bridge, a route that cut the length of the average trip from ten days to three. It was on one of Art Greene's upriver excursions to Rainbow Bridge, in fact, that Wylie and the Denver-based dam designer, Puls, had hitched a ride as far as Wahweap Creek and made acquaintance with their first conservationists.

It didn't take Art Greene long to realize that if these Bureau boys really were going to build a dam somewhere between Lee's Ferry and Rainbow Bridge, they would play hell with his livelihood. In 1953, with word that Reclamation's engineers had their eyes on a dam site 15 miles upstream from Lee's Ferry, but with no assurance that the dam actually would ever be built, Greene and his family—his wife and four children and their spouses—decided to take a little gamble. The senior Greene journeyed down to Phoenix to visit the state land commission, and while there he nonchalantly leased six sections of state-owned land, 3,840 acres, near the junction of Wahweap Creek with the Colorado River, just a yard or two south of the Utah border—godforsaken ground from which the state of Arizona was glad to derive a bit of income. By 1956, when the dam had become a congressional certainty and Bureau engineers and prospective bidders from heavy-construction outfits were combing the mesa tops near the site, the Greenes were serving steaks in a small cafe nearby, renting out eight stone cabins by the night, and selling a little fuel every time a pilot set his plane down on the airstrip they had bladed out of the blowsand.

In January 1963, ten years after they had arrived on the scene, Art Greene and his clan were hardly worth Lem

Wylie's worry anymore. Early on, although pleased that the Greenes had brought a vestige of civilization to that roadless and wind-scoured country, Wylie had dutifully informed them that the National Park Service would be managing the region as a national recreation area—in much the same way that it currently administered Lake Mead—and that they would have to pack up and move on because the park service had plans for a big marina there at Wahweap. Art Greene had responded that he appreciated the suggestion, but that he thought he'd stay, explaining that the state of Arizona had tendered him valid leases, and he had assured Wylie that it would all work out fine in the end because a marina was precisely what he had in mind for the place.

In the intervening years, no amount of subtle coercion or even veiled or outright threats had shaken the Greenes' resolve. The latest Wylie had heard was that Barry Goldwater, the Arizona senator who was making noises about running for president, had taken the time to go to bat for his old canyon country pal, Art Greene. Goldwater was pushing for the park service to resolve the whole hassle by making the Greenes its official Wahweap concessionaire, upgrading the de facto status the Greenes had enjoyed since 1959. And maybe that would be the simplest solution. On the day that they shut the river off, Wylie was well aware, a 200-foot-wide boat ramp already lay out on Wahweap Point waiting for water, and nearby was the Greenes' cafe and a general store, a campground, and a fancy new trailer park complete with hookups. By summertime, with all but a thousand cubic feet per second of the Colorado River languishing behind the dam, Art Greene planned to ferry tourists to Rainbow Bridge and back in less than a single day.

T he use of the Colorado for regular commercial recreation had begun almost a decade before Art Greene's Canyon Tours boats first floated the ruddy waters of Glen Canyon. It was back in 1938 that Norman Nevills, an exuberant thirty-year-old from a remote hamlet called Mexican Hat, Utah, had collected $250 from each of four far-flung passengers to conduct them in wooden boats of his own unusual design down the Green River to the confluence with the Colorado, then on through Cataract, Glen, Marble, and Grand canyons to the headwaters of Lake Mead, a trip punctuated by rough water, meager rations, and more than a few rifts between the several strong-willed personalities in tow, but one that nonetheless convinced Nevills that a career awaited him on the Southwest's rivers. In 1940, Nevills organized a Green and Colorado expedition that included Barry Goldwater—at that time the thirty-one-year-old head of his family's Phoenix-based dry-goods business—and although World War II briefly interrupted Nevill's burgeoning enterprise, by 1944 he was back on the water, beginning to make a legendary name for himself and his wife, Doris, and training numerous boatmen, infecting them with similar, insatiable passions for riding the chocolate desert rivers.

Nevills was followed in the early 1950s by several friends and former employees—that second generation of river outfitters initially carrying as many Reclamation engineers and uranium prospectors through the desert canyons as tourists. River travel was still considered a kind of crazed adventure in those days, and the few people who spent their vacations riding rapids and sleeping on sandbars were assumed to possess a decided daredevil streak. But by the second half of the decade, by the time Glen Canyon seemed likely, then certain to go under, more and more people wanted to know what was hidden in that sinuous place, wanted to see it before it disappeared, and a launch or two a week from Hite at the head of the canyon was common during the summer months.

Beginning in the summer of 1957 and continuing through 1963, the canyon also had become a kind of laboratory, a field station for archaeologists, biologists, geologists, and historians. Garbed in khaki shirts and trousers, their heads protected by pith helmets, they worked under the auspices of the park service to perform what was called an emergency survey of the region's scientific resources—the most extensive such salvage project ever attempted. Professors and students from the University of Utah and the Museum of Northern Arizona had spent successive summers in small teams scattered throughout the 160-mile reach of the canyon's main stem, as well as in the canyon of the San Juan River, the Colorado's principal tributary in Glen Canyon, and in dozens of both rivers' side canyons—combing and cataloging, making site-specific evaluations, and attempting canyon-wide interpretations, endeavoring as best they could with adequate resources but with very little time to document for posterity what had been there before the flood.

And there were others in the canyon during those summers who were determined to make a similar but more emotional kind of record. Back in 1948, writing in The Atlantic Monthly, Wallace Stegner, a Stanford English professor, novelist, and the biographer of pioneer canyon explorer John Wesley Powell, had described his own 1947 trip with Norm Nevills through San Juan and Glen canyons. A decade later, contemporary accounts of Glen Canyon had yet to appear, but a burgeoning number of writers, photographers, and artists were visiting the canyon to try to glean some lasting memory, to describe its delights and lament its numbered days. California photographer Philip Hyde, a student of Ansel Adams, had discovered the canyon country on a Sierra Club-sponsored trip through Glen Canyon in the summer of 1955, and had returned to photograph it extensively in 1962. Eliot Porter, a physician and an innovator in the bold new medium of color photography, had photographed repeatedly in Glen Canyon since 1960, twice accompanied by artist Georgia O'Keeffe, who went on to make a half dozen trips of her own into the Glen. And a young novelist named Edward Abbey, a Pennsylvanian living in New Mexico at the time—a man who in later years would become the voice most readily identified with efforts to preserve the slickrock country of the Colorado Plateau—had floated Glen Canyon on a drugstore rubber raft in the sweltering summer of 1959, a languorous and reverential sojourn he had known he would want to write about someday.

David Brower, a writer, photographer, and editor in addition to his administrative duties for the Sierra Club, had never seen Glen Canyon until long after his role in the decision to dam it had ended, but his series of trips through the canyon during the years the dam was under construction—and his mounting horror at what was about to be lost—had led to plans for a lavish book of Porter's photographs, to be edited by Brower and titled The Place No One Knew. The book was being readied for publication on the day Lem Wylie shut the river off.

Fifty-two days passed before the lake ebbed high enough for its water to slip into the east diversion tunnel, where it met three temporary outlet gates that would control downstream flows until the power plant's penstocks—their intakes still high and dry on the face of the dam—were reached by the rising reservoir. On March 13, two of the gates were screwed shut; the third gate was lowered to precisely 50 inches, just enough to allow 1,000 cubic feet of water per second to escape downstream to keep distant Lake Mead from going dry.

The snowfall in the central Rockies was the slimmest in many years during the winter of 1963, and the spring runoff was commensurately light—almost as if the capricious river wanted to remind everyone just who held the ultimate hand. By June 15, the dam stood 650 feet high; a huge 345-kilovolt transmission line was being strung from the canyon rim south toward Phoenix, and the reservoir, despite the dry winter, had risen 226 feet and was continuing to gain about half a foot per day. The scientists and salvage crews, frantic to finish their work and traveling down the canyon by motorboat, encountered slackwater more than 110 miles above the dam. Throughout two-thirds of the canyon, the riverside sandbars were submerged; the saltbush and greasewood on the terrace slopes were going under as well, and the trunks of the enormous old cottonwood trees seemed to grow right out of the rising water. At the mouth of Lake Canyon, 90 miles upstream from the dam, the water was 30 feet deep, and—a mile and a half away from its old channel—it lapped at the cliff wall below Wasp House, an Anasazi habitation built eight hundred years before.

By the middle of July, the conveyor and cableway operators, signalmen, and cement finishers had added a few more feet of mud to the block, and the end was almost in sight. Fifty miles upstream from the dam, the reservoir had backed up Forbidding Canyon far enough to spill into Bridge Canyon, and the tourists whom Art Greene guided to Rainbow Bridge had to walk little more than a mile to enter the national monument. The reservoir had risen 14 additional feet during the month, but, with the runoff receding, and with the water climbing the high, widening canyon walls and reaching ever farther up the side streams, this implausible new lake in the desert now was gaining only an inch a day.

IMAGES SPILLING FROM FINGERS

An excerpt from PICASSO'S WAR

The sole son of a tall, fair-skinned, and bearded art professor, ten-year-old Pablo Ruiz began to show a particular aptitude for drawing in 1891, by which time his parents, José Ruiz Blasco and Maria Picasso y López, had moved their son and daughters away from the dry days and clear light of their home on the Costa del Sol to La Coruña in faraway and rainy Galicia. At age fourteen, following the family's subsequent move to Barcelona in 1895, Pablo was admitted to La Llotja, a Catalan art academy that allowed him to skip its introductory courses because his talent was so clearly prodigious—remarkable enough, in fact, that his father simply stopped painting and drawing around the same time as he recognized that his son's skill already surpassed his own. Two years later, the promising artist enrolled in Madrid's prestigious Royal Academy of San Fernando, but the adolescent was bored by the quality of instruction he received, and instead spent most of his time copying the great paintings he visited daily in El Prado, as well as recording in drawings what he observed in the city's streets, cafés, and brothels.

Seventeen-year-old Pablo Ruiz contracted scarlet fever in the spring of 1898 and spent much of the following year convalescing and emotionally emancipating himself from his family in the Catalan village of Horta de Sant Joan in the company of Manuel Pallarés, a friend from La Llotja. By the time he returned to Barcelona early in 1899, he had learned to speak Catalan with impressive fluency, had decided that he would not study to become an art instructor, as his father had hoped, and he had begun to sign his work "P. R. Picasso," assuming his mother's maiden name because it had the air of Italy and the exotic about it, but perhaps also because he was like her in so many ways. People were drawn to him like they were to her: both were quite mercurial and could charm anyone they chose; he was short and dark-complected like his mother, and she had given him her round peasant's face and her dark, piercing, and altogether stunning eyes.

Back in Barcelona, Pablo Ruiz transformed himself into the companionable Catalan artist "Pau Picasso" over the course of the next five years, a time he spent reveling in the city's progressive modernista culture and establishing himself as a painter worth watching. It was also a period in which he began to travel regularly to Paris, then to spend significant time there, and in 1904 he made a decision to move to the French capital, which from all then-current perspectives was the world's epicenter of contemporary art. In Paris, the stocky and intense young man who now liked to be called simply "Picasso" came unshackled from the constraining influences of the Spanish masters. His art grew increasingly less realistic and he began to experiment with new forms of construction, composition, and perspective. Occasionally, his work was dramatically influenced by other artists—as it was early on by the Postimpressionist paintings of the Provençal painter Paul Cézanne—and at other times, his influences seemed to be solely his own boundless desire to express himself visually and his determination to do so in ever-evolving ways.

Working closely with his friend and fellow Paris painter Georges Braque beginning in 1909, Picasso developed a new form that critics later labeled Cubism. Previously forbidden inconsistencies such as differing points of view, axes, and light sources, as well as the inclusion of both abstract and representational elements in the same picture radically recast the notion of what was possible in a single painting, and both painters abandoned a centuries-old commitment to illusion as the sole means with which objects in a painting could be seen as accurate representations of their literal selves. It was with Braque as well that Picasso subsequently began to experiment with attaching paper, cardboard, wallpaper, wood, and sand to painted surfaces as a means of focusing attention on the "reality" of the work itself and not the objects to which it referred. The technique that became known as collage was perfectly suited to still life, a rather new form for Picasso, and it was curious that in addition to everyday objects, the guitar—the particularly Spanish guitar—became a favorite subject.

As the painter's reputation grew in Paris, and as his circle of influential friends greatly broadened by the onset of World War I, Picasso's legacy as an innovator already had become secured, and his work—represented by dealer Daniel-Henry Kahnweiler—now was highly sought after by collectors who wanted to buy art that they believed lay on the cutting edge. During the war, Picasso collaborated with poet Jean Cocteau, dance choreographer Léonide Massine, and composer Erik Satie to create Parade, an avant-garde opera-cum-ballet to which he contributed both sets and costumes. And after the war, it was a separate circle of friends—principal among them poets André Breton and Paul Eluard, and painters Max Ernst, André Masson, and fellow Spaniards Salvador Dalí and Joan Miró—who collectively captured Picasso's interest in their artistic attempts to blend both the conscious and unconscious realms of experience into, as Breton put it, "an absolute reality, a surreality." Drawing on the exciting new theories of Sigmund Freud, Breton—the novel movement's most passionate proponent—believed the unconscious was the wellspring of all imagination and that artists in every medium were compelled to tap it if they were to create their best possible work.

Although he never became identified as a true surrealist painter, something about the surrealists' interest in myth, dream, and the unlikely juxtaposition of the real with the imagined began to captivate Picasso in the mid-1920s, a fascination that continued throughout the rest of his life. It was in the probing of his own unconscious that a frank eroticism emerged in both his painting and the new sculptural work with which he now experimented in collaboration with his fellow Spanish expatriate, the sculptor Julio González. And also, it was the influence of the surrealists that was directly responsible for the emergence and continuing allure of the minotaur, for his deepening symbolic attraction to the bull and horse of the corrida, and even for the unfettered imaginative fancy of works like Dream and Lie of Franco.

A series of twelve pencil-and-ink sketches, each executed during two days in mid-April 1937, make it clear that Pablo Picasso—by this time not only the most renowned artist in Paris but also the world—had, in fact, finally committed himself to creating the requested mural for the Spanish pavilion at the world's fair. Yet instead of once more probing the unconscious of the little general who was bent on killing so many of his fellow Spaniards, or perhaps finding a way to depict graphically the great cause of the republic, Picasso planned, as late as April 19, to contribute to the Spanish government's overtly propagandistic anti-Franco and antifascist presence at the fair with a huge mural populated not with images supportive of the Spanish government's message, but rather with surrealistic images that would resonate solely with him. In each of the little-known drawings—discovered by researchers in the archives of Paris's Musée Picasso only in 1985—he experimented with the figures of an artist and his model, as well as the idea of a painting within a painting, a painting about a painting. In the first of the twelve sketches, blank canvases were mounted on an easel and a wall, and a sofa—over which Picasso scribbled "le canapé"—was shaped unmistakably like a penis. Two voluptuous models, arms circled around their heads, reclined in the fifth pencil drawing and floated disassociatedly from a standing artist who was turned away from them, and whose maleness was suggested by an arm and torso that could readily be interpreted as an erect penis as well. The heads of all three figures, however, were the strong-nosed female heads in profile that had fascinated Picasso since Marie-Thérèse Walter had become his model and lover six years before. The sixth drawing focused entirely on the enfolded model, capturing her head, breasts, and vulva in careful detail, as well as dissecting parts of her body—an eye, a hand, a nipple, her nose, her mouth and tongue—and scattering them in space.

In each of the remaining six sketches, Picasso drew the outline of a long, rectangular painting whose proportions were remarkably similar to the stretcher and canvas on which he began to paint Guernica four weeks later. It is fascinating to note that in terms of both composition and subject, the sketches began to foreshadow key elements of the painting. The town of Gernika still stood on April 18 and 19, yet already Picasso imagined a massive mural designed around a central compositional triangle; he was interested in placing a light at the apex of the triangle, and he imagined a staircase or ladder far to the right, as well as a partially open door. In the final sketch for the mural he thought perhaps he would call The Studio, Picasso even sketched the mural's placement in the covered courtyard of the Spanish pavilion—whose construction site he had visited by now. As he imagined the setting, placed at either end of the very long mural would be the two plaster busts of women mounted on stands that the artist already had sculpted and planned to contribute to the pavilion—busts that ultimately were exhibited a floor above the courtyard where Guernica was hung—themselves the curious precursors of the heads of anguished women that would anchor the final painting's left and right margins.

Although no record exists to prove it, it seems very likely that by April 19 Picasso had ordered a stretcher for the pavilion mural, and the stretched canvas may already have been waiting for him in his attic studio three blocks from the left bank of the Seine. Spain's renowned expatriate painter at last had truly committed himself to creating a major work for the Republican government's pavilion; by now he carefully had blocked out its composition and even imagined the company in which it would hang. And given Picasso's vaunted ability to marshal both energy and passion for his projects, it seems equally certain that The Studio would have been ready to greet eager visitors to the pavilion six weeks later had not the German Luftwaffe been so eager to see in the interim what blitzkrieg could bring to bear on an unsuspecting Spanish town.

The war in Spain at last had ended and Angel Vilalta was in his final year of high school in Franco's rigidly repressive Spain before he heard for the first time—in 1944—of a painter, exiled in Paris, who had joined the elite company of his country's master painters. A young, bright, and inspiring teacher had come to Lleida from Barcelona, and after class one day she had wanted to speak to the dark and intense young man who had seemed troubled by the state-mandated chauvinism he heard in a class called "Great Ideas of the Spanish Empire." Privately, secretly, she had wanted him to know that el imperio español es una vergüenza. "The Spanish empire is shameful. It is not, was not, something great. But we do have good things in Spain, you know. Spain has produced much that truly is great." Carmina Pleyan, in her mid-eighties and by now a lifelong friend of Angel's, had assured him on that long-ago afternoon that Lope de Vega, the prolific dramatist of Spain's sixteenth-century golden age, had been a national treasure and was the Spanish world's William Shakespeare. La Celestina, the fifteenth-century play by Fernando de Rojas, remained one of the first masterpieces of world literature, she explained, and was the most influential work of the early Renaissance. Miguel de Cervantes's great novel Don Quixote would be read round the world for all time, to be sure; and there were the great painters—Goya, El Greco, Velázquez—in which all Spaniards should take great pride. Even today, she wanted her pupil to know, Spain continued to produce great painters. A man who had been born in Málaga before the turn of the century, and who had grown up in nearby Barcelona, was the greatest painter alive, she believed. He lived in France and could not return to Spain following Franco's victory in the war, but he was Spanish in every way, and yes, of a man like Pablo Picasso her students comfortably and rightly should be very proud.

The work of Spain's painters and sculptors comprise the country's greatest artistic legacy simply because Spaniards are such visual people, Angel Vilalta suggested to me. "Our eyes are the most important sense to us, you know. We like to look at things. When I go to England, I see that everyone keeps their eyes down; people feel they mustn't look. But here, we look very much, very much. Sometimes foreign women complain because they are looked at so openly, but you know, we look not just at them. We look at everything."

Sitting in the library of his Barcelona apartment beneath a portrait of himself as a young man, one painted by his close friend, the renowned María Girona, Angel speculated that the Mediterranean climate, with its sunny skies, vivid light, and distant vistas, was foremost responsible for creating a culture of viewers. "It's through the eyes that we live in Spain, so of course, paintings are richly enjoyed, and it's very honorable here to be a painter, probably more than any other kind of artist.

"We have very few great composers, I think, because music is abstract and we don't care about abstraction. Even Picasso, you know, he never was an abstractionist. He always wanted to paint what he could see, to take it apart and then see it in a new way. And Velázquez, oh, he could see so many things. He saw so much. When Andy Warhol came to Spain and saw the paintings of Velázquez in El Prado, he said, 'this man had special eyes. He could see things other people cannot see.'

"We are not thinkers, los españoles, we don't stay at home and think like the Germans; that's why we have practically no philosophers. We like to be out where it's sunny and interesting, where we can see what's going on. When we go to other countries, the streets look empty to us. We think, where is everybody? Well, they're at home, thinking! But we don't think very much. Perhaps we should think a little more."

Although he was reluctant to do so, at last Angel named the men who he believed were Spain's foremost artists of all time: Velázquez, Zurbarán—and Picasso, but his exuberant mood shifted the moment he mentioned the third name. "You know, it is our shame that Picasso had to die abroad. It is our shame. But, of course, if he had lived here, Franco would have killed him. Franco hated him so much. Oh, politics have always been terrible in Spain, a tragedy really. You remember how it was with Franco in the 1960s; it was impossible to think, impossible to truly see and to paint." Then he brightened a bit and his face flashed his consuming smile. "But that has changed at last, and permanently I think. I hope so, of course. At last, before I die, I live in a democratic Spain where people are free to look, even to think if they can."

On the evening of April 19, 1937, Franco was bent on destroying Spain's mid-century democracy, and the country's democratic neighbor, France, seemed unconcerned. On the evening of April 19, Pablo Picasso was distressed to read on the front page of Paris-Soir—the city's largest-circulation newspaper and surely its most sensational—the account of a speech the day before in which French Foreign Minister Yvon Delbos strongly had urged the continuation of France's nonintervention policy in

Spain. "France, in its realistic desire to ensure peace and safeguard security, looks for an understanding with all and neglects no possibility of rapprochement," Delbos had declared. It was the same desire to appease that would result, three years later, in the Nazis' remarkably effortless invasion and occupation of France, of course, and it was a comment that also immediately enraged the artist. Over the photograph of Delbos and the article outlining his comments, he furiously drew a small figure with an enormous left arm thrust skyward, in his clenched fist a single-handled tool with a hammer at one end and a sickle at the other—the same gesturing arm and implement that he had included in his final drawing for The Studio a few hours before.

The crossed-handled hammer and sickle long and ubiquitously had been a Communist symbol, of course—and Picasso himself officially would join France's Communist Party soon after the Allied forces liberated France from the Nazis eight years later. But at the moment, the artist's scribbling of the charged motif onto his newspaper had far more to do with disgust than with ideology. Spain's democracy now was gravely at peril; Europe's other democracies were threatened as well, if only they would awaken and observe that ominous truth, but the honorary member of Spain's Republican government believed he could do little in response to the crisis but issue a private howl. And his mounting frustration at his helplessness is forcefully implicit in the fact that for twelve more days that spring, Picasso did no further work in preparation for the planned mural, days during which he must have puzzled at length over two interlocking questions: how could he square his artistic integrity and his fascination with his own interior myths and symbols with the need to create something truly meaningful—and valuable—on behalf of embattled Spain? How could The Studio save lives or even change minds?

Picasso had spent much of his life inside a succession of studios. He loved the visual chaos of painted canvases, collected objects, drawings pinned to walls; he loved the intoxicating smells of gesso, oil paints, and turpentine, loved the energy that hung in the air in those spaces, the creative possibility they inherently contained. It wasn't surprising, therefore, that the studio had captured his imagination as a subject for a grand mural, yet there was perhaps one more reason why it recently seemed so vital to him. In his three decades in Paris, Picasso had searched to find a perfect place in which to work and had never come as close to finding it as he had just a month before with the help of a young photographer named Dora Maar.

Since the end of World War I, Picasso had lived and painted on separate floors of a fine building on the rue La Boétie, a rather stylish street leading off from the Champs-Élysées. But beginning late in March, the painter began to commute to work across the Seine to a new block of rooms in an old seventeenth-century building in the rue des Grands-Augustins, an ancient, narrow, and cobbled street in the Latin Quarter reaching from the river toward the Boulevard Saint-Germain. The building, located just around the corner from Maar's own flat, had much to recommend it: the two upper floors the artist would occupy had vast open rooms with high, bare-raftered ceilings and red hexagonal-tiled floors. Huge windows looked out onto a gated courtyard, and the building's history seemed to offer excellent omens. Most recently, it had been a rehearsal hall for Maar's friend, the actor and director Jean-Louis Barrault, as well as the meeting space for a group of leftist intellectuals known as Contre-Attaque with whom she was acquainted and often allied. But better, and by a wonderful coincidence, it was No. 7 rue des Grands-Augustins that had been the setting for key scenes in Honoré de Balzac's The Unknown Masterpiece, published precisely a century before and one of Picasso's favorite novels, a 1931 edition of which he had illustrated with etchings and drawings. For the superstitious Picasso, that serendipity obviated the fact that the studio space was meant for him, and, as particular bonus, Maar, whose company he now regularly craved, lived only steps away and could be summoned to visit him at his whim.

Although women and the large subject of sexuality profoundly interested him throughout his life, passionate and libidinous Picasso had had only four enduring relationships by the time Dora Maar entered his life a year before. Soon after arriving in Paris in 1904, he met Fernande Olivier, an artist's model and fellow tenant in the bohemian lofts inhabited by painters and poets known as the Bateau Lavoir, and his relationship with her lasted seven years. As his relationship with big and often-brusque Fernande unraveled, Picasso shifted his amorous attention to Marcelle Humbert, the small and physically delicate lover of cubist painter Louis Marcoussis. Picasso called her "Eva" and treated her with unusual tenderness; she became the "Ma Jolie" who recurred in numerous paintings, but then had contracted tuberculosis, was hospitalized for long stretches, and died in December 1915, leaving Picasso heartsick and very much alone for a time.

In Rome in 1917—where he had gone to work on the sets and costumes for Parade—Picasso had met and immediately become entranced by Russian ballerina Olga Koklova, the daughter of a czarist military officer who danced with the touring Ballets Russes. From Rome he followed her to Madrid and Barcelona, then she had joined him Paris, and in July of the following year they married in a three-hour-long Russian Orthodox ceremony. Olga loved the arts but adored the haut-monde circle of patrons and socialites that surrounded them even more. She introduced her new husband to a life of receptions, dinners, and elaborate fetes, one of invitations and obligations that was entirely new to him, and for the first years of their marriage, the middle-class Spanish artist truly reveled in the high life to which his wife was so drawn. Yet that fascination waned with time. Picasso craved solitude, and, perhaps more than anything else, he loved to work, and already he had begun to tire of social demands by the time Olga gave birth to Paulo, their first child. Although he could be fascinated by the infant—if only for moments at a time—and although his paternal care and depth of connection flashed intensely on occasion, Picasso was not a good father, and the clash of his mercurial temperament with Olga's always strong and often fiery demeanor had increasingly made him a less-than-successful husband as well.

In early 1927, he met a seventeen-year-old Swiss girl in front
of the Paris department store Galeries Lafayette. "Mademoi-
selle, you have an interesting face. I would like to make your
portrait. I am Picasso," he said to her by way of introduction, but his name had meant nothing to her. Yet within
six months, he and Marie-Thérèse Walter had become secret
lovers, and her singular face and soft, round, and athletic
body had begun to appear often in his work. Simple and
unassuming Marie-Thérèse was as different from Olga as she
could be, and although his wife surely had some sense of the
girl's importance in Picasso's life, Olga tolerated her role—at
least what she knew of it—until, in the summer of 1935, she
learned that Marie-Thérèse was pregnant.

The news quickly had precipitated Olga's move, with
Paulo, from the flat in the rue la Boétie to the nearby Hôtel
California; Picasso sued for divorce, then dropped the action, probably when he learned from his lawyers that Olga
could claim and win fully half of everything he owned, including literally hundreds of unsold paintings. But regardless of the fact that they would never divorce—and that
Olga would remain deeply embittered for the rest of her
life—their marriage had ended in all but its legal contexts
in September of that year when Marie-Thérèse gave birth
to a daughter, Maria de la Concepción, whom Picasso had
adored from the outset, whom he sketched, painted, and
attended to with a devotion that he would never bring to his
other children.

Picasso's separation from Olga had initiated a period of
nearly two years in which his poetry—about which he was

always secretive—had been virtually his only creative endeavor. The dissolution of his marriage shattered him in
many ways, despite the fact that both Marie-Thérèse and
the daughter he liked to call Maya remained close at hand.
And he was not able to bring both interest and energy
back to his art again until he met Dora Maar—as antithet-
ical to Marie-Thérèse Walter as Marie-Thérèse had been to
Olga—and it began to seem wonderfully possible to Picasso
that he could, in fact, maintain simultaneous relationships
with two lovers. At the close of April 1937, Picasso lived
alone in the sprawling and increasingly squalid flat in the rue
la Boétie. Maya and Marie-Thérèse lived at art dealer Am-
broise Vollard's country house at Le Tremblay-sur-Mauldre
near Versailles, where, beginning the previous autumn, Picasso went for a few days each week to escape the attentions
of friends and sycophants and to paint a series of brilliant-
ly colored still lifes—of fish, fruit, flowers, plates, and cut-
lery—that were curiously distinct from his current work in
Paris. And now, Dora Maar had found and made possible
for him the kind of studio space he always had hoped for,
one so near her own flat that he might simply have whistled
whenever he needed or wanted her had telephones not been
a simpler means of communication.

Picasso had met Dora at the café Les Deux Magots in
the Boulevard Saint-Germain early in 1936. Seated with his
friend Paul Eluard, he had watched her rapidly driving the
blade of a penknife between her fingers and into the surface
of a nearby table, noting that when she sometimes cut herself, drops of blood would spread between the embroidered

roses on her gloves. Yes, Eluard knew the striking and unusual young woman, he replied when the painter inquired about her; and when Eluard introduced them, Dora had responded in Spanish to Picasso's greeting in French, thereby completing his instant infatuation. They left the café together and in the street he had begged for her gloves as a souvenir before they parted.

Although there had been an immediate and fiery attraction between them, the two didn't meet again for six months. In August, at the summer home in Saint-Tropez of surrealist writer Lise Deharme, they had been surprised to encounter each other, and went for a miles-long walk along the shore of the Riviera that forged the beginning of a relationship that would last a decade. The daughter of a Croatian architect and a Frenchwoman, Henriette Theodora Markovitch was born in Paris but spent her childhood in Buenos Aires with her parents. In 1926, at age nineteen, she left Argentina and returned to Paris to study art and photography. Although she continued both to paint and take photographs ten years later, it had been her surrealist-influenced photographs that had earned her a swelling reputation by the mid-1920s. At age twenty-nine, Theodora Markovitch had become the dark, dramatic, proud, and enigmatically beautiful "Dora Maar," and Picasso had been overwhelmed by her. "She was anything you wanted," he explained to her good friend James Lord, "a dog, a mouse, a bird, an idea, a thunderstorm. That's a great advantage when falling in love." Never before had Picasso had a lover who was his intellectual equal—or superior perhaps—nor one who was an artist as well. He painted and drew her with eager fascination; she photographed him at work, at ease, and at play, and together the two celebrated the power of their creative desires, a decidedly erotic intensity that by now enveloped them and bound them tightly together whether in bed, on the beach, or in the studio.

Because she visited them often before she met Picasso, Dora had been certain that the cavernous rooms in the building where Balzac had imagined his obsessive painter Frenhofer at work would perfectly suit the obsessive painter with whom she now was very much in love, and she was willing to accept the unyielding rule that the space was solely his. She was welcome only when summoned by him, and within a month after moving in, Picasso already had unmistakably personalized the space, quickly stuffing it with a painter's myriad accoutrements and the thirty years of acquired objects with which he simply couldn't part. In his rooms in the rue des Grands-Augustins, according to his friend the poet Jean Cocteau were

> *piles of booty, consisting of his own work and pictures by Matisse, Braque, Gris, the Douanier Rousseau, Modigliani and hundreds of others. The tables and chairs were littered with an amazing variety of objects: Negro masks, twisted pieces of glass picked up in Martinique in the lava that engulfed Saint-Pierre, ancient bronzes, plaster casts, peculiar hats, deluxe books, reams of Holland paper and rice paper, piles*

of reviews, and unopened packets. Picasso kept
everything he was given bottles of eau de Cologne,
bars of chocolate, loaves of bread, packets of cig-
arettes and boxes of matches, and even his old
shoes, which were lined up under the table.... He
had never thrown anything away, even hoard-
ing useless household utensils, the old oil-lamp
which lit the canvases of the Blue Period, a bro-
ken coffee-grinder ... He considered that any-
thing that had come into his hands formed part
of himself, contained a portion of himself, and
that parting from it was the equivalent to cut-
ting off a pound of flesh.

In its totality, Cocteau observed, the studio possessed "a
regal disorder, a regal emptiness—haunted by the monsters
he invents, who compose his universe." The poet surely
understood something profound and elemental about his
often-difficult and multifaceted friend when he added, "Picasso is a man and a woman deeply entwined. Like in his
paintings. He's a living ménage. The Picasso ménage. Dora
is a concubine with whom he is unfaithful to himself. From
this ménage marvelous monsters are born." The painter's libidinous but caring minotaurs likely were the specific monsters to which Cocteau referred, and already Picasso had
executed in colored pencil a lush and intricately detailed
drawing in which a beatific and compliant Dora was sexually
overwhelmed by the half-bull, half-man. And it would not
be long before more minotaurs emerged in those cluttered

attic rooms on the Left Bank of the Seine, before the bull and horse of the corrida again took shape beneath his brushes, before Picasso would find a way to depict the horrible handiwork of monsters then in Spain.

A week after Gernika was bombed, flames no longer rose from the ruins of the town, but piles of rubble still smoldered and the air remained thick with smoke and the stench of the fires. No longer did human bodies lie exposed to the elements, but the carcasses of dead animals still lay in the market plaza, and throughout the town, the air carried the stink of their rotting as well. Virtually everyone who had survived the attack by now had gone elsewhere—who knew when, or if, Gernika might be rebuilt?—and its sole inhabitants were the luckless rebel soldiers who were assigned to guard the massive destruction. It had been the vicious Reds who had dynamited and burned the town to the ground, the soldiers had been told, and it chilled them to think how truly horrible Communists could be—that they would destroy a place rather than allow it to become part of the glorious and godly Spain that Generalisimo Franco was re-creating. Rebel planes regularly flew over the town, as if to check to be certain that Gernika, in fact, was gone, and from the air reconnaissance pilots now could see clearly that the central core of the town, about fifteen square blocks, was entirely destroyed. A few walls still stood, but not a single roof remained. Trees had been burned to stumps, and cars that had been catapulted by exploding bombs lay overturned on top of the rubble.

On the outskirts, however, roughly twenty-five percent of the town survived. The hallowed Basque assembly building was undamaged, as was the ancient oak, and on the nearby slopes that led toward the village of Lumo, churches, convents, and a few grand homes stood strangely undamaged. Across town, the Astra-Unceta factory—where pistols, machine guns, and bombs ironically had been manufactured until the week before—also remained unharmed, as was the stone bridge over the Mundaka that had been identified before the bombing as the Nazis' key target.

Cemetery custodian Pedro Calzada and the men who volunteered to assist him had dug graves for hundreds of victims of the attack by now—some of them necessarily mass graves—but they had to work quickly, and no one knew precisely how many people had been interred. No one knew how many bodies had been carried away by grieving survivors; and neither did anyone know how many bodies still lay undetected in forests and fields.

Father Alberto Onaindía, who had seen much of Monday's killing himself, made his way to Bilbao by Tuesday morning and reported what he had seen and experienced in Gernika to Basque President Aguirre. Stunned and profoundly outraged by what the Basque priest told him, Aguirre asked Onaindía to travel to Paris as quickly as possible and relate his story to journalists, politicians, and anyone who would listen. The priest arrived in Paris by train early on Thursday morning and had been met and surrounded at the Gare de Lyon by newspapermen eager to hear who, in fact, destroyed the town. By Friday, newspapers throughout Europe that were sympathetic with the cause of the Spanish Republic as well as those that were openly anti-Fascist carried front-page stories of the horrors of the attack as seen through the cleric's eyes. In Paris, Ce Soir, L'Humanité, and the Christian-Democratic journal L'Aube all printed detailed accounts, accepting Onaindía's story with shock and without suspicion, and George Bidault, editor of L'Aube, editorialized as well that "faithful to ourselves and above all to our duty, we associate our voice with those raised around the world against the assassins of Gernika. For three hours, the German air fleet bombed the defenseless town. For three hours, the German airplanes fired their machine-guns on the women and children in the streets and in the fields. All of this in the name of civilization. And even, for the crusade, as they say."

Yet not everyone wanted to hear the priest, of course—or to believe him. And the rebel government in Spain remained diligently at work promoting the version of Monday's event that insisted that Basque and Asturian Communists—"Red hordes," they obliquely labeled them—had been the perpetrators of the crimes. Foreign journalists had been escorted to Gernika on Friday by rebel army officers on General Mola's staff and shown various "proofs" of the Communists' plunder. Most had been persuaded, and on Monday, May 3, only a week after Gernika had been annihilated, Le Figaro—a newspaper Pablo Picasso regularly read despite its editorial disposition toward the war in Spain—carried a lengthy article from the French news agency Havas under the headline GERNIKA COULD NOT HAVE BEEN DESTROYED BY BOMBS FROM THE AIR. IT IS THE REDS WHO BURNED IT "BY HAND." "Nationalist officers have drawn the attention of journalists," the report explained, "to the fact that nowhere does one find signs of bomb splatter and that the absence of traces of projectiles, as well as the verifications made elsewhere, show that the town was deliberately set on fire.... In spite of meticulous searching, the journalists have found no bomb holes." The large craters that everywhere pockmarked the bleak streets of Gernika were caused by exploding mines, the article continued, and at least as far as Le Figaro was concerned, there likely had been few casualties in the Communist-fueled fires a week before because even Reds would have been unlikely to have torched themselves.

P icasso sketched the first five of his May Day studies in pencil on blue drawing paper, executing each one in only a minute or two. From the outset, images of the corrida flooded into his consciousness as he considered how to respond to the atrocity that occurred five days before. Even in the very first image that spilled from his fingers, a wounded horse and defiant bull were present, as were the head and arm of a woman leaning from a window and holding a lamp in her extended hand in order to light the scene. The horse and bull would be modified many times before the studies were translated onto canvas and the painting was complete in early June—their positions, depictions, and attitudes changing often as the work inexorably assumed creative weight. But the observing woman, her profile once more an unmistakable likeness of Marie-Thérèse, immediately assumed such vital symbolic and compositional importance for the artist that she only very subtly would change throughout dozens of subsequent sketches and in the several states the final painting would assume as well.

Although he, like most Parisians, by now had heard many conflicting details about the incident in Gernika, not once did Picasso experiment with images of airplanes, bombs, or exploding buildings on that first day or any other. It was his ongoing interest in the surrealistic linking of the conscious and unconscious that immediately turned him away from a documentary response to what had transpired. Also, he had not been truly interested in any sort of visual documentation since before the turn of the century, regardless of its subject. Perhaps more importantly, from those first days in May, Picasso found himself interested not so much in what the bombing and destruction of Gernika meant politically or even in humanitarian terms, but rather what they meant in metaphor. He wanted to address emotionally the destruction of his beloved homeland that was taking place both from within and without, and he already possessed a personal visual language with which to do so, one anchored in the violence, suffering, and passion of the corrida and its centuries-old tradition of making viudas, widows, out of the wives of the men who played out its pageantry. The civil war itself was a ghastly and gruesome pageant, it appeared to

Picasso from France, one in which death appeared as terribly foreordained as it was inside the bullring.

In the second drawing of that Saturday, a small Pegasus appeared—similar to the fanciful winged horses Picasso remembered from the Spanish circus—mounted on the back of a confident bull. In the third, three fantastic monsters that echoed his horrific depictions of Franco some months before made a single appearance before they were discarded. The fourth sketch was a primitive drawing solely of a standing horse—a child's image, as it were, that seemed designed to test how best to represent the equine figure—followed on a subsequent sheet of blue paper by a highly realistic sketch of a fallen horse, this one an illusion of a flesh-and-blood animal whose predicament was dynamically conveyed in its struggle to stand and whose pain was telegraphed by a terrified eye and gaping mouth.

At the end of the day of sketching, the artist abandoned blue paper for a gessoed board, but he continued to use a pencil to sketch the several elements of the unified work he now envisioned—the commanding bull executed in full profile; the stricken horse, out of whose gaping abdominal wound flew a tiny Pegasus, which appeared for the final time; the woman, given breasts now, reaching far out from the window with her lamp; and across the whole of the foreground, the addition of a supine soldier, depicted only this once as a helmeted classical warrior clutching his lance in death. It was impressive progress in only a few hours of sketching. Already the horse, its head reared skyward, and the horizontal warrior together formed the strong compositional triangle that would anchor the finished work. Already the key figure of the observing and illuminating woman was permanently linked to the scene, her lamp at the apex of the triangle, just as Picasso similarly had imagined a triangular, lamp-lit composition for his now-abandoned The Studio. And the haughty and enigmatic bull—did it represent Franco's rebels, the Nazis, the whole of Spain itself?—already demanded focal attention. An image of a proud bull would, without question, become central to his treatment of the destruction of Gernika, a town ironically as far removed from the sunbaked soil of the corrida as was Picasso's Paris.

The artist worked feverishly on Sunday, May 2, as well, and just as he had the day before, he ended a series of new sketches with a second drawing on a prepared board of the evolving composition in its entirety. In the three studies that had preceded it that morning, Picasso had focused his attention solely on the head of the anguished horse, giving the animal a sharpened, spear like tongue each time and experimenting with the placement of its teeth. But when he was ready again to combine the several visual elements at the end of the day, this time he sketched the horse with its head and gaping mouth bending toward the ground. Unlike the final drawing of the day before, in which the several subjects were presented rather statically, the scene was full of action now. This time, the bull leapt into the air as if to escape calamity; the observing woman's face had grown full of alarm; two soldiers now lay on the foreground, their faces more certainly evidencing death than sleep, and—with its head touching the chest of the central soldier—the horse appeared to be falling into its death posture as well.

The boards on which Picasso executed his two end-of-day sketches were almost square, whereas the canvas on which he would begin to paint in nine days would be a dramatically elongated rectangle. But much of the mural's final composition already had been determined: the bull would dominant the upper-left quadrant; the woman and the window out of which she reached would command the upper right, and a triangular scene of anguish and death would rise out of the lower half of the composition. None of the images bore a direct link to the bombing of Gernika; none echoed attributes of the town or even Basque culture; none represented the literal realities of the war that then raged in Spain. Yet the images already were very much alive in Picasso's oeuvre; they were metaphors to which he long since had become wedded emotionally as well as visually. To him they—more than any others—spoke eloquently of Spain, of violence and death.

Given the great strides he at last had made on the mural during those first two days of May, it's curious that Picasso then abandoned the project entirely for a week. The reasons why he did remain a mystery: perhaps he traveled to Le Tremblay with Marie-Thérèse and Maya, where he continued his series of still lifes; perhaps the preparation of the mural's stretcher and canvas occupied much of his time during those subsequent days; or perhaps he and Dora, their relationship still new and deliciously consuming, may have focused that interim simply on themselves. Whatever the explanation for his hiatus, Picasso did turn his attention back to the mural on the following Saturday, May 8, and for the following three days, his sketching took a dramatically new turn.

During the preceding week, the reports arriving in Paris from embattled Spain had grown still more ominous. Basque resistance to the invading rebel army and its allied German and Italian forces had crumbled, in largest part due to the shock inflicted on all of the region by the horror of Gernika. Republican forces could not hold Bilbao much longer, it now was apparent, and British and French ships in the city's port had begun evacuating women and children in advance of the human carnage that seemed certain to follow its capture. Food was in terribly short supply, and for the old and infirm, death by starvation increasingly seemed as likely as death by aerial bombardment. In news reports sent round the world, reporters had begun to focus their stories less on the losing war effort and more on the plight of civilians and refugees, who were streaming onto roads throughout the Basque country en route—often on foot—anywhere that seemed to offer safety.

L'Humanité, the Communist Party-aligned newspaper Picasso read almost daily, published on Wednesday detailed and very disturbing accounts by survivors of the annihilation of their town, as well as recent photographs of frightened, perplexed, and now homeless refugees. On Friday, it published a wrenching image of homeless Basque children; on Saturday, the day Picasso returned to work on the mural, both the weekly picture magazine L'Illustration and Paris-Soir offered their readers pages of photographs of the

destroyed town and the now-desperate victims of the attack. While it is not certain that those stories and photos
were directly responsible for the new images with which
Picasso now began to experiment, it is sure that he saw and
was moved by them, and for the first time on Saturday, a
new composition study included—in addition to the images
with which he now had become conversant—the drawing
of a woman crawling on her knees with a dead infant in
her arm, her head bent skyward in supplication. The pencil
study that momentarily followed it focused solely on the
stricken horse and the woman again, her child's chest and
her own breast now drenched with blood. On Sunday, the
tormented woman returned three more times, first in a detailed ink study that reflected Picasso's ongoing fascination
with etching and engraving, and which poignantly depicted
the woman's agony and her terrible plight. In a subsequent
pencil sketch, Picasso moved the woman and child from the
ground to a fragile ladder, as if in attempt to add to her
torment, and in a pencil composition study also completed
that day, the woman and child now crawled onto the belly
of the fallen horse.

On his two most recent days of work, Picasso had begun
to draw on white paper that, when positioned horizontally,
was twice as wide as it was high. The change simply may have
been convenient, but it seems more likely that it was initiated
by a visit to the Spanish pavilion, now nearing completion
at the world's fair site. The painter was interested in the
prefabricated building and had visited the construction site
before; by now he would have been quite familiar with the

long courtyard wall on which his mural would be hung. Although there is no record of the date when the stretcher and canvas were ready for painting, surely they at least were under construction by that weekend, and it seems obvious that Picasso now would want his composition sketches to begin to mirror the proportions of the final painting.

This was his fourth composition study so far, and it was much more detailed and highly developed than the previous three. Never before had all the subjects appeared interrelated spatially; there were a depth of field and density of images that were new, and for the first time too Picasso began to focus his attention on contrasting darkness and light. The setting was unmistakably nighttime now, the subjects lit both by the high central lamp in the observing woman's hand and by bright fires that flared in the background. The bull remained focal, its attitude still ambiguous, but its head was intriguingly humanlike now, and suddenly it faced the viewer directly. The fallen horse's head continued to bend to the earth; four human corpses—including the body of the child—occupied the chaotic foreground space, and, in addition to the observing woman, who had been present from the start, Picasso sketched two more female survivors, as well as four disembodied arms and fists raised in the Communist salute, which had become a universal symbol in opposition to the Fascist war in Spain.

Picasso opted not to execute another composition sketch on Monday, May 10—a fortnight following the bombing and the first time he had worked on the mural on a weekday. Instead, he completed five more sketches of individual horses, suffering women, and a bull that by now had become very human. Unlike the minotaur—essentially a man whose bull's head implied his animalistic passions—this horned, spike-eared, and supremely powerful bull who possessed a classically beautiful human face seemed to be both primitive and comprehending, both base and somehow wise. With his addition of suffering people to the tableau that had included only the animals from the bullring in the beginning, the otherwise sharp distinctions between man and beast, between perceiving and feeling, between passion and compassion had begun to blur as the mural planning continued. And although it remained doubtful that he understood precisely what his bull-made-man "meant" in symbolic terms, it seems impossible to have escaped the artist's notice that the wide and insistent eyes of the bull now looked increasingly like his own.

T he canvas on which Picasso began to paint on the morning of Tuesday, May 11, was more than twice his own height and nearly eight meters wide, so large that the stretcher on which it now was mounted had had to come up the building's rickety circular stairway in pieces, then had been reassembled before the cotton canvas was stretched onto it, tacked, and gessoed. The studio's high ceiling rafters were suspended a bit more than three meters above the tiled floor, but the readied canvas measured three and a half meters, so it had to be tilted against the room's long wall, its top pressing hard against the rafters, the bottom held out from the wall with wooden shims.

For two successive weekends, the painter had foregone his habit of spending time in the country with Marie-Thérèse and their daughter Maya and worked diligently on the series of studies that readied him to paint. Work on the canvas—simply a vast white sea at the moment—now would begin to occupy his deep and transfixed attention every day for roughly a month. Dora would be with him constantly during that time, attending to his needs, discussing the painting's progress with him—something he otherwise always had loathed, his studio normally closed to visitors—as well as photographing the painting at numerous stages of its development. For decades, Picasso had been careful to date virtually every scrap of paper on which he drew as well as the back of every canvas—a means of anchoring his work in time and documenting its progressions and perambulations. Never before had he or anyone else photographed a painting of his while it was in progress, yet the idea greatly appealed to the artist. With Dora's photographs, he would possess a visual record of the mural's gestation, and historians might be interested as well—an issue to which he paid close attention. It seemed to make sense therefore that Dora would capture the canvas even at the close of Picasso's first day of painting, and he telephoned her at her nearby flat late on Tuesday afternoon to tell her to come at once to Grands-Augustins and to bring her beloved Rolleiflex with her—because the canvas no longer stood bare.

Using a narrow brush and black paint, Picasso had lightly sketched the outlines of all the characters with which he had become conversant during the previous six days of drawing, but although the canvas clearly reflected the final composition study he had completed Sunday afternoon, there were key changes as well. The bull, who had turned toward the viewer on Sunday, once more was depicted solely in profile, his eyes cast away from the rest of the scene. The wailing woman whose dead child lay in her arms had been moved from the composition's right margin to its left, where, it now was suggested, the bull offered her a bit of protection. And the right half of the composition, defined by the outline of a tile-roofed house, now included the figures of three more women in addition to the observer holding aloft the lamp, whose position as always remained unchanged. Akin to a drawing made on Sunday, one of the new female figures descended a faintly suggested ladder to escape the fire that threatened the building; a second woman was caught in mid-stride as she fled toward the mural's center; and a third lay lifeless in the foreground, her expression strangely serene. The dead soldier still anchored the composition's base as he had before, his clenched fist still thrust upward in salute, and the twisted, writhing body of the horse still filled much of the painting's middle ground. Picasso had painted for only a few hours that Tuesday, but already he had populated more than twenty-seven square meters of canvas with the characters he believed were his most compelling, the majority of whom would retain their current positions and collective importance as the canvas grew heavy with paint during the coming days.

In addition to the ten photographs Dora Maar made of the entire canvas as it evolved, she photographed her companion at work as well—squatting on his haunches to paint the bottom edge of the mural, working from high atop a precarious ladder, using a low rung of the ladder for a makeshift seat, standing upright with brushes strapped to bamboo sticks in his hands—and almost always with a cigarette pressed between two fingers or dangling from pursed lips. In virtually every image, cigarette butts and spent paint tubes littered the floor, as did the small cardboard buckets and thin stacks of newspaper that served as his ready palettes. In some of the photographs, daylight streamed in from the building's commanding windows; in others, round studio lights mounted on stands illuminated the gigantic canvas at night. For four weeks, Picasso did little but smoke and paint and occasionally stand back briefly from the canvas to consider what he had wrought. He left the studio in the rue des Grands-Augustins only to eat and sleep, Dora herself his sole assistant during those days, the war in Spain and the destruction of an innocent town now his principal muse.

It was a measure of the many sides of the complex man that he presided one day during his obsessive work on the mural over an ugly quarrel between Dora and Marie-Thérèse, a fight he apparently was happy to fuel. Marie-Thérèse had come to Grands-Augustins from the country and had been disturbed to find Dora in the huge studio, clearly rather at home in the cluttered and cavernous space. "I have a child by this man. It's my place to be here with him. You can leave right now," Marie-Thérèse instructed the dark, severe, and unhappy "visitor," but Dora was undaunted by the demand. "I have as much reason as you have to be here. I haven't borne him a child, but I don't see what difference that makes," she responded.

The two women continued to argue, according to an account written by Françoise Gilot—who, in six years' time, would become the next woman to feature in the painter's life, the story related rather gleefully to her by Picasso himself—until Marie-Thérèse turned to him and insisted, "Make up your mind. Which of us goes?" It had been a hard decision, he explained to Françoise. "I liked them both, for different reasons: Marie-Thérèse because she was sweet and gentle and did whatever I wanted her to do, and Dora because she was intelligent." So he simply suggested they settle the matter themselves. A bit of a catfight would amuse him while he painted, and, he swore to Françoise , the two women did indeed push each other about as they quarreled, and the painter took great pleasure in being the object of their struggle. He might be capable of exhibiting on canvas great compassion for women who suffered from war, but the agonies of these two women who loved him meant nothing to him, it appeared, and the incident remained "one my choicest memories," he later told Françoise.

But entertainment—whether dueling mistresses or something decidedly more conventional—was rare during those weeks, and Picasso was consumed with creative energy in a way Dora had not seen in the time she had known him.

He had begun to work out the visual structure of the great painting back in mid-April, prior to the bombing and while he still planned a mural replete with images of a painter's studio. He had begun to grapple with symbolic, then literal images with which to address the subject of Gernika's annihilation virtually as soon it had occurred, and by now he had amassed more than three dozen studies—there would be forty-five by the time the mural was finished—drawings that focused, then refined his visual vocabulary. Now he was rapt in the heady process of bringing his vision to bear on a huge, two-dimensional surface, and was doing so with the wonderful fluidity and malleability of oil. He was painting, and nothing, certainly not the two women who were devoted to him, could deter his artistic fascination or his focus on the truest of his life's many pleasures.

When Dora photographed the canvas again a week later, it had begun to assume a visual weight commensurate with its size. Large and irregular background areas now were black, and in contrast, the white and light-gray figures of both human victims and animals appeared to leap from the surface, the entire scene now lit by a bright disc of the sun that Picasso had placed at the focal upper center. The jumble of foreground bodies had been reduced to only the head of a female victim and the large corpse of the single soldier, his form turned entirely around so that his head now was near the left, positioned below the bull and the woman mourning her dead child. The warrior clutched a broken sword in one hand, and the other lay stretched beyond his head. His defiant salute also had disappeared, the painter concluding that the image that worked so well on propaganda posters appeared somehow hackneyed on canvas.

The next photograph in the series, likely taken about April 28, or perhaps a bit later—none of Maar's work was dated—showed the mural having reached a state in which, for the first time, its final visual and emotional forms were evident. It also recorded two dramatic changes: without altering the position of the bull's head, Picasso had reoriented his body, moving it to the far left edge of the canvas, so that the bull's head now was turned toward his uplifted tail. One eye, however, now was positioned below an ear, so that both of his piercing and intelligent eyes seemed to stare intently, and even with some supplication, out toward the viewer, the bull becoming the only character in the tableau who appeared to solicit direct communication. In the space where the bull's body previously had been, the horse's head now rose in screaming pain, his nostrils flared, a spear like tongue jutting from between his teeth, his body impaled by a lance. Instead of the bent and defeated animal of recent sketches, the horse now suggested defiance despite his deep wound—one caused, rather curiously, by the same weapon that is brought to bear in the corrida only on the bull.

When Dora captured the painting in progress again a few days later something brand new had occurred: Picasso had attached two separate pieces of colored wallpaper over the figure of the fleeing woman. A piece of red-checked paper covered the back of her head as if it were a scarf, and a bright strip with a floral pattern now hung from her shoulder, covering a previously exposed breast. The painter was uncertain, however, about whether he had achieved the effect he was hoping for. He soon removed the collages, then, on one of the first days of June, attached them again, as well as two more pieces: a rectangle of ornate purple-and-gold paper now covered much of the torso of the mother whose dead child lay in her lap, and a swath of checked paper reminiscent of a restaurant tablecloth, placed on a diagonal, now suggested a skirt worn by the woman falling from the building at the far right. The collages were attached only to female characters and may have been meant to suggest the reality of walls, tables, and personal possessions torn to bits by the bombs, or the extent to which victims now were bereft of even their clothes. Yet the artist also simply may have continued to experiment with the totality of his design, testing to see whether those specific areas of the canvas needed more activity, more detail or perhaps less. Whatever their intended purpose, the collages also directed attention to the surface of the canvas itself: it was a flat, two-dimensional plane—a conventional mural, of course—and it was obvious now that Picasso had simplified the many forms it contained over the course of the past weeks. He had created a massive picture, one replete in every part with action, drama, and even deep emotion, yet its shapes, forms, and depictions he purposefully had rendered quite simply.

Dora Maar's ninth and penultimate photograph, taken around June 5, recorded the painting very near its completion—and it was absent collages again. The dead soldier had a new, crudely drawn head now, his face turned upward, his two vacant eyes open and aimed at the viewer in a line directly below the expressive eyes of the bull. His head also had been severed from his body, but the break at the neck was a clean edge rather than a wound, one revealing that the inside of the soldier was hollow. He had become a plaster cast, a sculpture, only a fragile replica of a soldier in the last days, his meaning decidedly more ambiguous and less menacing now. The supine woman had disappeared entirely, her head painted over with a wash of gray, the only remnant of her the blossom she had held in her hand. The falling woman far on the right possessed only an upper torso now, but her skirt—darkened and striped by Picasso after he had pulled the paper away—remained on fire, her plight pronounced by the darkening of her uplifted arms in a way that suggested heat and smoke and the burning of flesh. A dim, dark, and simply-drawn table now stood between the heads of the horse and bull, and atop it a crudely sketched bird suddenly screamed at the sky. Nearby, the agonized horse had become, unmistakably, the tableau's central motif; his head presented in a kind of cubist detail that was unique among the many characters, his tortured face now lit by an incandescent bulb.

The round sun long since had been flattened into an oval, but for nearly two weeks, Picasso plainly had left it and the area around it unpainted—uncertain how best to complete it. His latest, and final, decision was to transform the oval sun into the shade of a suspended lamp, underneath which he sketched the lightbulb, sealing in the process the final ambiguity of whether the scene took place indoors or out. Walls, windows, and the tiled roof of the building suggested an outdoor scene, but tiled floors, the table, and now the electric light argued that the terror unfolded inside an enclosed place. It was an uncertainty that seemed to complement the overall chaos in the end, and a reference as well to the literal reality that in Gernika, the force of exploding bombs had thrown the inside of virtually every house into the open air.

There was little more Picasso was compelled to change, although he admitted in a call to pavilion architect Josep Lluis Sert that he really didn't know whether the mural was finished. By now he had devoted perhaps two hundred hours to the canvas, and likely a hundred more to the nearly fifty studies that had preceded it. Yet the mural finally would be done, he supposed, only when Sert came to collect it. He adjusted the tone of the background color in two locations; he added gray washes in others, and with Dora's assistance—the first time she, or likely anyone, ever had applied paint to one of Picasso's canvases—they worked together to stipple the horse's body with hundreds of short, vertical brush strokes that suggested hair, or perhaps the newsprint on which word of the atrocity had spread, or perhaps the tallying of the dead.

One of his final touches to the painting was the addition of an obscure and partially open door to the extreme right edge of the canvas, almost as if the painter had needed a way to extricate himself from the scene, a way to walk away from it and be done. And with that, it now made sense to him to see what some others opined, although Picasso understood, of course, that praise and congratulation were far more likely to flow from friends and colleagues than were suggestions on how the mural might be improved.

Although its date doesn't survive, and the accounts of the afternoon trip to the studio vary with each of the several visitors who described it, it is certain that more than a dozen people came to see the completed mural about June 6, even though Picasso continued to make minor changes to the canvas in the days thereafter. Close friends of the painter periodically had seen the mural's progress during the preceding weeks, but this was the first time a large group had been gathered together. Although the painting was far too big to be cloaked in a sheet prior to the guests' arrival, the occasion did have the dramatic air of an unveiling about it. Spanish friends such as the poet José Bergamín and scholar Juan Larrea—both employed at the time at the Paris embassy of the besieged Spanish Republic—and Italian sculptor Alberto Giacometti, German painter Max Ernst, French poets Paul Eluard and André Breton, as well as British painter and art historian Roland Penrose and the sculptor Henry Moore and his wife Irina followed a festive lunch with an excursion to Grands-Augustins. There they were greeted by the painter, whose mood was ebullient, his spirits high with the completion of the project, and it seems probable that Dora Maar was there to welcome the group as well.

Some, particularly those who were seeing the canvas for the first time, were quite stunned the moment they entered the enormous room. The large group immediately fell into a reverential silence, and all paid the work deep attention for some time. In an attempt to add a bit of theatricality to the occasion, Picasso had returned the several strips of wallpaper to the canvas, as well a bit of toilet paper attached to the hand of the fleeing woman and bits of bright-red paper that formed tears of blood flowing from the eyes of two women and the bull, whose direct gaze at the visitors clearly demanded their concentration. As the group stood motionless, still very moved by the massive work, Picasso approached the canvas repeatedly, each time removing another of the attachments, until at last only a final drop of red blood was anchored to the body of the dead child. As the painter moved to the painting and peeled it away—the canvas now bereft of any colors but black, white, and gray, Guernica now complete in every essential way—the group burst into poignant applause.

A lively celebration began not long thereafter, one that lasted well into the afternoon. Picasso smoked and drank with gusto; he accepted individual congratulations from his friends, and he spoke casually about the challenges of the project and his hope that the mural would be an important addition to the pavilion. When fellow Spaniard José Bergamín wondered privately whether one or more of the red tears might well belong in the painting's final form, Picasso embraced him, then quickly had a suggestion for his dear friend: why didn't the two of them save a single tear in a little box, then go to the world's fair every Friday and briefly place it again beneath an eye of the Spanish bull?

THE SORROW OF ARCHAEOLOGY

An excerpt from the novel

away from the surrounding ground

S craping earth away from the short gray femur, expos-
ing it to the air with a bamboo tool after seven hundred years of entombment, I can't help but keep thinking:
these canyons and crop-striped mesas mothered us both.
This child and I are siblings surely, sisters of stone and bone
and the curious accident of birth. Although I still can't see
enough of her pelvis to be sure, I've imagined she was a girl
during the two days since I first probed the midden's ashen
soil with a trowel and unexpectedly bumped it against her
skull. And in that time, it's seemed certain to me that she
was as rooted here as I am, strangely captive at the lips of
these sandstone bluffs. Perhaps she lived long enough to be
desperate to get away, much like I often have been, determined to see if life could be better lived in other landscapes,
to fasten herself to fresher country, or even to become a kind
of nomad, mercifully free from belonging somewhere.

In the dry early summer of 1992, I nominally remain a physician, but I dig in the dirt these days instead of taking stock of my patients' bodies, attending only to bones stripped of muscle, blood, and brain for almost a millennium by now. I sit in the shade of a juniper tree near the cliff-carved head of Tse Canyon in far southwestern Colorado on a blistering afternoon near the end of June, and part of a human skeleton is exposed in a meter-square hole beside me. Fragments of what once was a turkey-feather blanket lie among the vertebrae and finger bones, a tooth-tiered mandible and the small and delicate ribs. Beside them, and just now coming into view as I pick at the hard red soil with the blunted point of my trowel, is the dome of an overturned gray bowl, an intricate geometric pattern painted in black on its underside.

Working alone through the rising heat of the morning, then the blanched and baking hours of the afternoon, I expose the bowl, photograph it, and at last lift it and the mound of earth inside it away from the surrounding ground, then work to bare more bones to the light and the late twentieth century until I encounter something arresting: this second femur is much smaller than the first, seemingly stunted, and the tibia to which it once was attached also is atrophied, the child undoubtedly crippled by the misshapen leg. The defect must have been congenital, and it is easy to imagine that it also could have caused her death: the girl might have fallen from a rocky ledge, might have stumbled and struck her head. I'm eager to examine the skull as well now, but before I dislodge it I want Harry, my husband, and his crew to have a look at the remains of this poor Puebloan child, to ensure that my initial excavation doesn't destroy important information, to hear what they separately will make of a prehistoric girl who surely had to struggle to walk, who died in Tse Canyon and was buried beside this bowl.

"Me too," I mumble out loud, speaking to no one but the twisted skeleton as I labor to get to my feet, bracing myself with my cane as I stand, waiting before I start to be sure I have my balance, then walking with wide and measured steps along the powdered-dirt path to the place nearby where Harry too is digging into my homeland.

rabbit hunters on chestnut street

When I was almost as old as this skeletal child must have been at the time she died, it seemed to me to be particularly good fortune to have been born right in the center of things—an ocean on either side of us; the twisting spine of the Rockies sending rivers both east and west; four separate state capitals—each one so big that *buses* plied its streets—only a long day's drive away. Over a bare brown hill from the bank of the San Juan River, you could stand on a cement slab and touch four states at once: Colorado, New Mexico, Utah, and Arizona. The slow-witted tourists assumed you had to stick an appendage into each state to perform the feat, but we shrewder locals realized that all you had to do to truly center yourself was to plant an instep right where the incised lines intersected. The Colorado history text opened with the story of the people who first began to inhabit Montezuma County back when Jesus was growing up in similarly arid circumstances, and it ended with a brief mention of the oil boom of the early fifties that had turned little Cortez into a tacky version of modern times. It was hard for a twelve-year old to imagine that any other place could matter more.

We lived on the north end of Chestnut Street, my parents and my sister Barbara and me, right where an unnamed arroyo curled into Hartman Canyon, the shallow, sage-filled little depression encompassing all the magic of the wild West as far as the kids in the neighborhood were concerned. Unlike my father, who was vice-principal of the high school, or my mother, who made mosaic-tile serving trays and appliquéd barbecue aprons and who dreamed of a far bigger life, my grandparents actually seemed connected to the country—in part because they raised hay and red-hided cattle and canned food from their garden for the winter, in part because their last name, Lewis, was the same as the name of the farming community in which they lived, twelve miles north of town—both names supplied by my great-grandfather, who in 1897 had abandoned his Kansas City hardware store for "space," his appellation for the empty expanse of land that spread northwest from the settlements in Montezuma Valley toward scattered Mormon outposts in southeastern Utah. The fact that Hiram W. Lewis had established the still-extant post office called Lewis, Colorado, seemed to me to be further proof that I belonged to a line of people who were right in the thick of things. By the time I was in junior-high, the region's earliest settlers—whom my grandparents had always called *Moquis*—began to be referred to as *Anasazi*, a Navajo word the archaeologists took a liking to for a time, one that was supposed to mean "the Ancient Ones," but which actually meant something more like "old strangers who were our enemies" according to Benson Yazzie, a Navajo kid in my science class.

All I really knew about the Ancient Puebloan people in those days was that they were the reason a national park now covered much of Mesa Verde, a high and canyon-cut island of land that rose just south of Cortez, a place that somehow never lost its exotic luster, even after a lifetime of Memorial Day-weekend excursions—my father always delighting in the way the masonry ruins seemed exquisitely at home in the cool and arching sandstone overhangs, my younger sister never quite so enthusiastic, sometimes so bored she would stay in the Corvair with *Meet the Beatles* or another favorite book rather than trek with us into secreted, spellbinding Balcony House, suspended in a shallow cave hundreds of feet above the canyon floor. For my father, the Mesa Verde architecture was everything—the precisely shaped stones, walls as straight and true as transits and T-squares could have made them, balconies cantilevered on bark-stripped juniper beams, circular kivas dug into the hard-packed earth. My mother, it wasn't surprising, took far more interest in the hand-crafts—beautiful baskets, some woven so tightly they held water, sandals and satchels, bracelets and beaded necklaces, fine pottery seemingly painted by twentieth-century abstractionists.

I was a dozen years away from entering medical school, and bones still seemed creepy, but I remember being fascinated, even then, by the remains of the people themselves—skeletons of short and stocky people who were prone to suffer from bad teeth, bad backs, and osteoarthritis; the hard cradle-boards that flattened the backs of children's skulls; primitive menstrual pads made of woven barks and fibers; mummified bodies brazenly displayed in glass cases, the leathered skin on their faces drawn into expressions of quiet anguish. Yet more than anything else, I think I was intrigued by the Puebloans' surprising numbers: on Mesa Verde and throughout the tilting valley to the north, as many as thirty thousand people once had been at home here, three times the number who lived here now—early farmers tending land at Lewis, potters shaping clay from the banks of Hartman Creek, rabbit hunters on Chestnut Street, kids in breech cloths at play in the arroyo that later was ours.

extraordinary acts

My husband Harry wears a cowboy hat so bent into submission, so sweat- and soil-stained and indispensably part of his everyday field apparel that it has achieved true notoriety by now. His jeans are torn in the knees and crotch; the steel toes of his work shoes shine through holes in the leather, his forearms and broad, expressive, face so sun-darkened they nearly match the shoes. He is sifting soil through a frame-mounted screen—stopping occasionally to examine pebbles and ceramic shards that are caught by the wire mesh—when he sees me walking toward him through the trees.

"Well," he asks, vigorously shaking the last of the earth through the screen before laying it aside, the disarming smile he always uses to such easy advantage spreading across his face, "did you get her out?"

"She *is* a female, I'm pretty sure," I say. "I've got the pelvis now, and the sciatic notches sure look female to me. But I want you to come look. The right leg is deformed, stunted. I'm a little surprised she lived as long as she did."

"How old?"

"Ten or twelve maybe. I want to check the skull for signs of trauma, but you'd better lift it out. I don't want to screw anything up. Can you come now?"

"Okay," Harry surrenders. "Let me touch base with Alice and Charlie and then I'll be right behind you. You love it when I'm behind you."

This time I manage half a smile, pleased that, given the circumstances, Harry still can make a sexual jest, aware too that the love-making that for years so often confounded us with a kind of aching disconnection and Harry's pouting disappointment now is little more than memory. "I'll be the one stumbling down the trail," I tell him.

Henry David Donagan MacLeish, forty years old come the first of July and fully six years younger me, was raised in Cherry Hills, an affluent Denver suburb, his father an esteemed anesthesiologist who had made himself genuinely wealthy, his mother a lawyer who specialized in contentious divorces. Gregarious, engaging, his intellect quick and effortless, Harry first was captivated by the obscure science of archaeology during a summer in his teens when a group of students from Denver Country Day School lived in tents for ten weeks, at work on Tom John Brown's long-term excavation of the large Puebloan settlement called Cow Canyon Ruin in northwestern Montezuma County.

Something about the slow and measured methodology of this academic digging in the dirt attracted the kid who otherwise couldn't sit still; something about the rooting for information in stones and bones, in scraps of material that till now had escaped decay, seemed to challenge him, to goad his curiosity. And there was something even about the feel of the land in this dirt-poor, rock-crested corner of Colorado that had an indefinable kind of appeal. Rough roads and scattered ramshackle towns, dryland farms that seemed to cling to the back of the neck of the world, ranches where the fences were eternally falling down—all seemed oddly compelling during the long, sweltering, sun-drenched days of that summer.

When—in Boulder, nearly a decade later—I met him as he passed me a joint at a mutual friend's annual May Day party, he had seemed astonished to discover that the family-practice resident who didn't know quite how to take him had grown up in Cortez—the town and the country surrounding it still possessing a compelling kind of magic as far as he was concerned. "What a wonderful place to be a kid in," Harry had said, seemingly eager to sustain our conversation, infatuated by my hometown, I presumed, and certainly not by a rather unassuming looking woman who clearly was several years his senior.

"And a great place to get away from," I had assured him. "By the time you're a teenager, you're absolutely desperate for someplace hip."

The child buried at the head of Tse Canyon probably didn't live far into her teens, Harry agrees as he and I compare the leg bones. Then he takes my bamboo pick and begins to free the skull from the dirt packed tightly around it. "Look at this," he says before long. The girl had suffered a severe blow; the skull's arching parietal dome is marred by a ragged hole.

"She must have fallen quite a distance," I say as Harry helps me get down on my knees for a closer examination.

"But look at the hole. If she fell, she must have fallen on something hard and pointed. Maybe this happened when something hit her."

"Like . . . ?"

"Like an ax. A rock held in somebody's hand . . ."

"She was killed?"

"Could have been. You'd think that if she had fallen, the skull would be crushed. This looks like the blow was limited to the area where the hole is."

"Would they have . . . ? No. No one would have killed her because . . ." I can feel the blood drain from my face.

"The people in the lab will be able to do a better job of describing what penetrated the skull, but that won't explain anybody's motivation."

"Sometimes I wonder what all your collected minutia is worth when it doesn't end up explaining anything," I say, my mood suddenly soured by his too-brief explanation.

"What other fields do you know where they answer everything to everyone's satisfaction?" It's Harry's classic kind of response, an attempt to remind me that life isn't perfect anywhere. But then there's a shift in him, and now his attention to me seems laced with concern. "You okay? I should get back, but I could come finish this at the end of the day if you want to head home." He tips my hat forward into my face and massages the nape of my neck, and in doing so announces that it's far too hot for a fight.

"No. I'm okay." I reach into the hole and rub at the skull's brown-stained bone with my thumb. "This is my little project. She is." And as I go back to work, scraping, photographing, mapping the square, separating the last of the bones from the soil, wrapping each one in paper and laying each bone in a box, my thoughts drift away from my swelling miscommunications with Harry and back to the circumstances of this child's death—to what, or who, brought her short life to a stop. Surely her deformity was responsible, but how so? Was her death someone's horrible and brutal responsibility, a father's or mother's awful decision meant to save her from more suffering? I can imagine that: I have no children of my own, but I have been a physician long enough to know that simply staying alive isn't always—not every time—worth the terrible trial. And in the year since my own limbs have begun to betray me, I have discovered what this child too must have understood—that effortless movement is magic, sleight of hand or foot or thigh, proof, if we need it, that each one of us performs extraordinary acts a thousand times a day.

noms de cowboy

I was Gene Autrey for a time, racing across the lawn on Center Street with a stick-horse between my legs, making the middle years of the fifties safe for decent folk with the help of Bobby Magneson, my next-door neighbor, Roy Rogers by appellation, the two of us insisting on the *noms de cowboy* despite my mother's growing dismay at the specter of raising a tomboy. I owned a red felt hat with a drawstring, which I could wear flipped onto my back à la Annie Oakley when I was feeling feminine; I had a fringed jacket and a six-shooter on each hip, and for reasons I really don't understand, I was absolutely enthralled by that shoot-'em-up myth making until at ten or so I finally fell in love. With a horse.

Bill was a bay gelding with hoofs the size of pie pans and a commensurately sizable penis. I know I was put off that strange and slightly disgusting appendage of his on the occasions when I saw it fully extended, and I simply don't accept the psychologizing that suggests that horse cocks are the reasons for most girls' equine infatuations. I loved Bill—a sedate, seventeen-year-old cow horse my grandfather had bought with a nod of his head and a fifty-dollar bill at the Cortez Livestock Auction—simply because Bill seemed to be a gentleman. I could scrape his teeth inserting a curb bit, poke him in the eye as I struggled to lift the bridle over his ear, send the saddle spinning between his legs when I forgot to tighten the cinch, and still Bill was a model of measured composure. I would ride him for hours, round and round in the south pasture where he otherwise would be grazing, and he never gave the slightest signal that ferrying me wasn't a fine way to spend the day.

My grandfather, Win Lewis—the source of my red hair and an inveterate teller of tales—had tried to convince me that Bill once had worked at a racetrack in California, that he had run in huge ovals so much in his younger days that walking in similar fashion was simply second nature for him. But Granddad was careful to make it clear that Bill was his horse, that he didn't belong to Barbara or me or our cousins from Colorado Springs, who rode him (mercilessly it seemed to me) for a week each year in early August. We were merely Bill's "partners," as my grandfather put it, and I remember him telling me, just before a pneumonia sent him to the hospital and kept him there till he died, "Sarah, old Bill's a better person than most people are. Horses like him don't come around too often."

Mourners said similar kinds of things about Winton Albert Lewis on the blustery April day he was buried, and I like to think that their comments were genuine. True, he had disappeared on week-long drinking binges a half-dozen times in his married life; he could scold you so severely on occasion that you were sure you could never again look him in the eye; but he loved his own patch of ground with a sweet pastoral passion, and for forty-eight years he loved my grandmother with something akin to a schoolboy's crush. He revered FDR as a kind of secular saint and occasionally

would aver that Ike should have stuck to soldiering. He complained continually—sometimes cussing a blue streak as he
did so—about the stupidity of domestic cattle, yet on cold
spring nights he would readily surrender his sleep to help
bring new and bawling calves safely into the world. He told
me once, offhandedly, that I could do anything I wanted to
with my life, and that assurance, however subtle, supported
me like a stanchion in the years after they laid his body in
the small community cemetery a half-mile east of the house
where he had been born.

I don't think Oma cried on the day of my grandfather's
funeral. What I noticed on her face instead of tears was that
beatific expression that has always seemed to substantiate
her rare and precious wisdom, my grandmother greeting her
neighbors and kin that day with an unspoken acknowledg-
ment that all of them were sharing something elemental—a
death that indeed was hard to bear but that somehow had
to be. Oma worked in the kitchen in the early afternoon,
helping ready the casseroles that women from nearby farms
and ranches had dropped off a few hours earlier, cutting the
ham, heating the fat green King's Banquet beans she canned
with bacon and onion each autumn, and which long had
been her signature dish, working with a daughter, daugh-
ters-in-law, and friends to prepare the luncheon that has always seemed to me to be the only burial ritual that really has
much meaning. She hugged everyone in her house as, group
by group, people got up to go home late in the afternoon,
assuring them that she would let them know if she needed
anything, thanking them for something she left specifically

undescribed. She hugged me too when I told her I'd be back in a little while, a fourteen-year-old with her grandfather's hair explaining that it seemed like a good idea to go curry his horse.

a life like that

I'm boiling pasta when my mother calls from Santa Fe wanting to know how I'm feeling, eager to warn me again that working in the sun all day is something I shouldn't be doing.

"We've talked about this before, you know," I say into the telephone as I walk out onto the porch to wave Harry in to dinner. "I appreciate your concern . . . Yes . . . I know . . . But I'm not going to stay home and make myself crazy. Thank you for reading up on this, and yes, I know heat can make symptoms worse. It makes mine worse. But I haven't had an exacerbation in six months. I feel good. I'm happy, and I'm going to pretend I'm an archaeologist for as long as I can. I'm sure it does me more good than harm."

Harry mimes a cheer as he comes onto the porch, hearing my half of the conversation, assuming he knows to whom I'm speaking by the familiar filial strain in my voice. My mother and I long have tended to argue about which one has the clearer understanding of dozens of topics, far from the least of which is my struggle with disease and my mother's ongoing concern. As I listen to her, I motion for Harry to attend to the pasta, and I'm still silent when he opens the screen door again and sits beside me on the railing.

"Mother! No, for Christ's sake," I say at last, shaking my head, then whispering to Harry that I'll be off the phone in a moment.

But Harry surely isn't surprised when he eats alone. Although I seldom see my mother these days, the two of us talk regularly, my mother calling simply to inquire about how I'm feeling, calling with the splendid good news that barley syrup or mud-bathing or cold-water enemas have just been proven—beyond any doubt—to be an effective treatment for multiple sclerosis. Mother calls to remind me that Wednesday is the summer solstice, to inquire about whether my cookware is that awful aluminum stuff, to share the blissful information that she has begun to date the dentist who is treating her TMJ.

My parents divorced when I was ten, my father leaving Cortez with an English teacher ten years his junior, my mother reeling in angry disbelief for a long time afterward and somehow blaming Barbara and me for his disappearance, it always seemed. None of the three of us understood how he could leave us. My mother hoped for too long that he would be back, and I did my best to fill in for him in ways that I thought she would welcome, not understanding that lawn-mowing and the regular trash detail weren't his contributions to our little family that she missed the most. Then, my junior year in high school, he did return—with Fran, the English teacher who was now his wife—and that event ultimately spurred my mother into leaving the town she never really had been at home in during nineteen years of residence, going first to Denver, where she grew up, then on to New Mexico when Santa Fe began to seem the place she was meant to be. And in Santa Fe, Louise Lewis became Luisa, a weaver and a woman of many metaphysical interests, a great believer in the medical efficacy of crystals and a smorgasbord of cathartic diets, a woman who has become equally sure that astrology uncannily explains the human condition. Although neither of her daughters seem to be similarly seeking enlightenment, both my sister Barbara and I have been pleased in recent years by how secure our mother has grown, the literal terror and sustained sadness that followed her divorce finally replaced by brimming self-confidence, if also by an adherence to what seem to us to be some formidably odd ideas.

"She says she's sure that if I came to Santa Fe for six months and had therapy from this friend of hers," I say when I come into the kitchen at the end of the long conversation, "I could throw my cane away, at the least, and probably get cured. She's full of all these miracle stories, but they just sound like remissions to me."

"You want to go?" Harry is opening the bottle of beer he plans to attend to while I begin to eat.

"You want to get rid of me?"

"You are kind of in the way of some major scandal I'm planning."

I try to remain lighthearted, but his joke has touched on a subject that's much on my mind. "That's going to happen." I look at him and offer a smile. "You're going to get tired of having less than major-league sex with somebody who can't feel anything, who's about as lithe as a baseball bat."

Harry doesn't respond for a moment, trying to find an easy way out of a conversation he does not want to have. "Then you better go get that cure, hadn't you? Your health is one thing, but when my sexual needs are on the line, well, we're talking about something serious here." Joking is always his first line of defense, his first choice for an ally when I want him to be open with me, when I seem to understand too well who he really is.

"Listen to me for a second," I say, reaching across the table for his hand. "I just . . . The worst thing would be to ignore it, or for us to pretend that it isn't a problem."

"Sarah . . . I can't talk about it as if . . . not now anyway."

"Okay."

"I'll try to figure out a way to say what I want to say."

"Do," I tell him.

At twilight, the two of us and the border collie we call Teddy walk through the grass pasture and down to the edge of the pond. I use my cane to maneuver across the uneven ground; as he walks, Harry repeatedly throws a stick for the insistent, jubilant dog. Beyond the tall cattails that ring the glassy surface of the water, a green and newly mowed meadow stretches away to the south, its fragrance sweet and wet and thick with the pleasures of a summer evening. In the distance, the high northern escarpment of Mesa Verde rises abruptly up, its sandstone cliffs still orange in the last of the light.

"I don't want to make plans," Harry says as we sit on the wooden pier that reaches out over the water, its surface now roiled by Teddy's determined paddles. "I'll try to talk about this now, but I don't want to assume we already know what's going to happen to the two of us."

"The Santa Fe shamans notwithstanding, I think we know I'm not going to get better."

"But maybe not any worse. And this idea that you're waiting for the day I walk out the door . . . "

Harry's wounded tone triggers my sympathy, triggers something in me that is quick to try to relieve his pain. "No. It's just . . . If you were in my position you'd . . . I want you to know that I understand that this isn't easy for you. Any of it."

"And don't you see? What makes me feel like such a fucking shit is talking about what *I* have to deal with when you're the one with . . ."

"With the legs that don't work."

Harry doesn't respond, can't respond except to throw Teddy's stick and watch for its distant splash. I reach down, dipping my cane in the pond, cutting the water, splashing Harry's feet as if to say never mind.

"It isn't just this, just the MS," I add after a time. "From the moment I realized all those years ago that somehow you were attracted to me, I've known too that I wouldn't always be enough for you." His face is blank when he turns to look at me. "It's always seemed to me that you could love me enormously if I could turn into someone else."

"I've wanted us *both* to be different people, to change every day—to remake ourselves a million times. I mean, why would anyone want inertia?" He emphasizes his question by heaving the stick far out into the water.

"I've never been . . . I don't know, complicated enough for you," I say. "You want a whore and a mommy and somebody who can drink even you under the table all rolled into one. You get this ridiculously easy-to-spot crush on about every woman you meet. But *me*, plain-Jane Sarah Lewis from little Scratch Ankle, Colorado . . . of all the zillion things you're passionate about, I'm not sure you've ever felt truly passionate about me."

"What I've felt . . . what I've hoped is that we both really let go, soar with our lives," Harry says, defensively, "to believe anything's possible and make exactly what we want out of them."

"But this *is* what I want. You are. A life with you. And that scares the shit out of you, doesn't it?"

"Jesus, Sarah," Harry says, but then he says nothing more.

"The skeleton. That girl," I finally say to end the silence. "What are the chances of coming up with something substantive about how she died?"

"You're curious about whether she was killed because of the deformity." Harry lightens. I can feel him begin to relax with the change of subject.

"I don't know. Yeah. I mean, if it wasn't an accident, why would someone have struck her?"

"At an abandonment-era site like that, I suppose it's possible that her people all were heading south, and she simply couldn't make the trip. But . . . depending on what we find, we might be able to tell whether the site was inhabited for very long after her death. Maybe somebody in the lab will come up with something interesting. Shall we hire some hotshot forensic pathologist?"

"Do you find things like this very often—evidence of violence, if that's what it is?"

"Yeah. Well, not every day, but . . . It couldn't have been an easy life in the best of circumstances. Maybe half the kids survived to ten years old. People got sick, broke their arms and legs; got infections, pneumonias; got arthritis early, and probably never had enough to eat. Death had to have been almost constant. At Tse Canyon we've found several skeletons with trauma that makes it look like they were just dumped, not buried. Your girl at least had a burial."

"They might have been desperate enough to leave that they killed her and left her behind?"

"I would guess she died a good while before that site was abandoned," Harry says, acquiescing to Teddy's demands, throwing the stick yet another time. "Maybe she did fall. I'll be honest, Sar. I doubt that we have much chance of ever telling you something conclusive."

"Imagine a life like that . . ." I say.

an ungenerous geography

In the years since the Puebloan people had become "The Ancient Ones," a tourist-tailored notion of a hearty and happy primitive culture, it increasingly had seemed to me that their society was held together far more by hardship and stingy landscape than by anything else, that witches and powers evil enough to create constant havoc must have seemed as real to them as moonlight. Spirits, deities, all kinds of unaccountable forces must have been held responsible for ruined corn crops, for killing frosts and droughts that refused to surrender, for infertility and the deformities that often-accompanied births. Gods must have been to blame when, in the end, their collective lives here seemed too difficult to bear any longer and the people wandered away.

The pamphlets at Mesa Verde and the feature stories in the travel magazines tended to focus on the great "mystery" of the Anasazi's disappearance. Where had the people gone? Had they simply vanished? But those questions ignored the available answers: At the end of the twelfth century, the Ancient Puebloan people had made their way toward places now called Zuni and Walpi and Acoma, to Frijoles Canyon, Pecos, and Santo Domingo, south into terrain that was warmer, if drier, than that encompassing and surrounding the Montezuma Valley, southeast into the more receptive region that flanked the Rio Grande. Since early in this century, archaeologists had understood that the contemporary Hopi and Pueblo peoples were the Puebloans' descendants, and that generational connection seemed anything but mysterious. What remained unexplained to Harry and his colleagues in tattered field clothes was the complex mix of reasons why the Puebloan culture had survived intact and in place for a thousand years, then had fallen apart. Still, no one could say conclusively why these arid uplands of the Colorado Plateau had been a good home for so long, then, very quickly it seemed, had become a place from which to flee—villages, possessions, a whole history abandoned.

I had known what it felt like to be certain you had to get away. Often in earlier years I had imagined driving over the crest of Mancos Hill and never returning, not even glancing in the mirror as the valley became a tangled memory. What I hadn't understood, and perhaps never would, was the decision to come here in the first place, to stay, to build shelters and clear fields and huddle by winter fires when so many other places must have seemed more hospitable. Why did those Old Strangers lay claim to such an ungenerous geography? What did Hiram Lewis encounter here that he felt was missing in Missouri? How did Oma endure here in her nineties?

THE ENDURANCE OF
TENDERNESS

*To be with Lawrence was a kind of adventure, a
voyage of discovery into newness and otherness...
. He looked at things with the eyes, so it seemed, of
a man who had been at the brink of death and
to whom, as he emerges from the darkness, the
world reveals itself as unfathomably beautiful
and mysterious.*   — Aldous Huxley

He would call his new novel *Tenderness*, and with it
he knew he was writing more boldly, truer somehow
than he had before about the primal harmony of body and
mind and the way in which sex—sex surrendered to the
elemental pulses of living, sex infused with a soul—was the
essential balancing act of the universe, a ritual recreation of
the union of sun and earth.

Sitting beneath a canopy of umbrella pines in the crisp,
emotive air of a Tuscan autumn, he had begun to write what
he imagined would be a simple story, one that would return

him briefly to the woods and dells of the English Midlands now soured by smoke and coal-dust. He had imagined in the beginning that this would be a brief story about the war between the massive mechanized collieries and that wounded island earth, and the war as well between the privileged owners of the mines and the poor sods with perpetually blackened faces whose lives they crushed, then discarded. But soon the story grew and remade itself, and now it was about a different war as well, one between a battle-paralyzed colliery owner and his cultured wife, a couple who were dead to sex and therefore dead to each other, who warred with polite contempt and whose lives were as cold and brittle as ice.

It was clear to him now that the words he scribbled had begun to echo his own marriage and the way in which his wretched health had destroyed its most vital rituals—rendering him forever absent the erections that once had helped make him a confident man, making Frieda feel something like the welcoming earth on whom the sun could no longer shine, leaving her desperate to open to warmth and to light. He knew now, too, that his story inevitably and necessarily would swell into the sort of novel that must make an entire world of itself, one that would range and sprawl and dig deeply, coming—if he was lucky—to a kind of wisdom in the end, a novel that ultimately might make a brave case for tenderness.

David Herbert Lawrence—"Bert" as a boy in the soot-stained Nottingham hamlet of Eastwood, "Lawrence" during the years in which he quickly and quite dramatically made a name for himself in the world of English letters, and now "Lorenzo" by affectation—always had been fascinated and deeply stirred by women. Yet he was captivated as well by the insistent life-force of the phallus, and it had been Frieda who had shown him how man and woman together sometimes can become a third and altogether transcendent being. It was Frieda—married to another man at the time and the mother of three children—who utterly had transformed and emboldened Lawrence's life beginning in the spring of 1912. And it was Frieda who continued to complete his life fourteen years later, to make it safe despite their separate desires and temperaments, despite her huge hunger for the proof sex gave her of her own existence, despite Lawrence's phallic failures.

Now, in the leaf-scattered fall of 1926, the writer's long-delicate lungs and windpipe—first made fragile by the same coal-dust that perpetually had masked his father's face—had reduced Lawrence, barely forty-one, to something of a frail old man. Last year a doctor in Mexico City had pronounced the culprit tuberculosis, but surely the chap was a quack. Tuberculosis was a disease that slowly killed its sufferers, after all, and Lorenzo had much to live for and write about still; surely he was a victim only of the "wretched bronchials" that many from the coalfields were, yet in his particular case the accompanying shortness of breath, weakness, and occasional hemorrhaging now somehow kept his penis perpetually wilted as well.

Even in the years when his health was still good, Frieda sometimes had sought out other men as well, and those assignations had confounded and deeply hurt him. He, in turn, had never gone to anyone other than his wife until those two nights only six months before when twice he had slipped into his friend Dorothy Brett's bed in Capri only to feel both times like an utter and perfectly impotent fool.

In the year since Lawrence and Frieda had returned to Italy—living first on the Ligurian coast and now in a village not far from Florence—in the hope that his health might improve a bit and that Italy might infuse them both with something of the gaiety and passion they had known there before, Frieda indeed had encountered passion, but only in the arms of another lover. She nearly had swooned on the afternoon she met Angelo Ravagli, owner of the house they rented on the Riviera and an officer in Mussolini's Bersaglieri regiment. He was short and a little stocky—a good bit smaller than she was, in fact—yet the ribbons, buttons, and plumes of his dress uniform had buckled her knees, and Lawrence had been injured as much by Frieda's ineffectual attempts to hide her subsequent rendezvous with Ravagli as he was by the certainty that she now reveled in the same sorts of stolen moments with the military man that she secretly had shared with him back when she was a jaded professor's wife in Nottingham and he was her young and spirited suitor.

Frieda gave life to him then, and he had returned it to her as well, and for so long something of heaven had seemed to flow out of their shared love. By now, however, words were all Lawrence had with which he could continue to delight her, and it struck him as he laid down his tale that with this new novel he might make love of a sort to Frieda once more. The deadened and desperate wife he had named Constance Chatterley would come alive again in the arms of the gamekeeper who lived on her husband's estate, and thereby Lawrence could communicate to Frieda his understanding—difficult though it had been for him to engender—of what she had done and continued to do, as well as his deep love for her.

But as the Tuscan autumn gave way to the first days of winter, and as he filled a stack of ruled notebooks with rapidly scribbled words, something strange and transforming occurred: Lawrence had drawn from his own life, of course, in his creation of Clifford Chatterley, the cerebral man still much in need of a mother, a patrician whose lower body had been paralyzed in the Great War. But there was much of him, too, in the self-possessed gamekeeper, a collier's son scarred by a loveless marriage who nonetheless remained alive to the blessed communion of sex. And it was stunning to realize too as the first fat draft of the novel came to a close before Christmastime that something of Lawrence himself now inhabited Connie Chatterley as well. She, like Lawrence, believed profoundly in fidelity, but she also knew that true steadfastness demanded the sublime ritual of mating in order to stay strong. And like Lawrence himself recognized all-too -well by now, Connie Chatterley knew that it was sex that stood in proud counterpoint to illness, that sex was the world's only sure antidote to death.

Revitalized by his fevered weeks of writing, and believing against more honest opinions that he would regain his robust health, Lawrence looked forward to having one of the boys in the village cut a small pine tree that he and Frieda could transform into a bright and festive Christmas tree. He looked forward to painting pictures once again, something he had not done since he was an adolescent. He wanted to paint scenes that depicted something of the honest, true, and essentially spiritual sex that he believed the world had to find its way back to; and too, he looked forward to returning to the novel. It might need repeated rewriting, he suspected, because much in it seemed to matter enormously by now. It was a poem in prose for Frieda, and perhaps for him as well, given his enveloping sadness. It was a novel that would be difficult to publish, he already understood—its graphic scenes and earth-sprouted language would scandalize those who didn't understand that true sex was the very thing with which we all could save our lives, if somehow we chose to. Even at this early, unpolished stage, Lawrence saw something in it that made him hope one day the novel would speak candidly, even eloquently to more than a few readers about the truth that most anything life threw at you could be made endurable by honoring the sun and earth and the seasons, and by offering those with whom you shared your life some tenderness.

B orn in the coalfields of the English Midlands in 1885, Lawrence was the fourth child of a hard-drinking, high-spirited, and nearly illiterate coal miner and his wife, a former schoolteacher and great lover of books who openly regretted her choice of a husband. Despite his lifelong respect for the difficulty of his father's work, "I was born hating my father," Lawrence wrote. Yet he was deeply devoted to, and even romantically in love with, his mother. It was she who insured that he excelled at school, and who instilled in him an appreciation for language and the arts, a sense of his being culturally above the crowd, as well as a deep yearning to be elsewhere, to be enlivened by the exotic. Lawrence's first novel, The White Peacock, was published in 1910 only weeks after he had helped his mother, who had become terminally ill, commit suicide by providing her an overdose of sleeping medication.

Two more novels, Sons and Lovers and The Rainbow, were published during the following five years—and a thousand copies of the latter were burned by order of a Nottingham magistrate, who found them obscene—a period during which the young writer formed friendships with literary lions Ford Maddox Ford, Aldous Huxley, E.M. Forster, Katherine Mansfield, and Bertrand Russell, among others. Working first as a factory clerk and then as a schoolteacher, Lawrence soon vowed that he would find a way to leave his native country, which he believed was being destroyed by its rapid industrialization and a kind of cloying cultural conservatism. Following a debilitating bout of pneumonia in 1911—the first of a series of chronic pulmonary attacks that would dramatically shape the rest of his life—Lawrence visited Nottingham University language instructor Ernest Weekley on a spring Sunday in 1912, hoping for advice about how he might successfully move to Germany to teach English as a means of supporting his writing while allowing him to see a bit of the wider world.

Before dining with the professor, Lawrence spent a half-hour talking with his wife, whom he had never met before, an immigrant from an aristocratic German family named Frieda von Richthofen who was six years Lawrence's senior, the mother of three children, and, like Lawrence's mother, someone who believed she had married the wrong man. Frieda, Lawrence immediately knew, was "the most wonderful woman in all England," and only six weeks later she abandoned her husband and children and eloped with Lawrence first to Germany, then Austria, and Italy, the two tramping together carefree and very much in love, often surviving on nothing more than black bread and eggs. Frieda was strong, commanding, free-willed and openly sensuous—someone who believed that "if only sex were 'free' the world would straightaway turn into a paradise"—and from her Lawrence received not only something of the sort of unconditional love his mother had given him but also the sense that openly celebrated sexual love, uncomplicated by cultural strictures and untethered from taboo, was the truest path to spiritual harmony and oneness with nature and God. Frieda became not only the writer's muse but also the epicenter of his universe. "Frieda and I are together," he wrote, "and the work is of me and her, and it is beautiful."

Lawrence and Frieda returned to England prior to the outbreak of World War I, then soon found themselves made captives by the war. Her cousin, Manfred von Richthofen, was the German flying ace known as the Red Baron whose exploits in the air resulted in the deaths of hundreds of British soldiers and airmen, and given those family ties as well as the fact that Lawrence had become the infamous author of "filthy books," it wasn't surprising that they were accused—falsely—of spying for Germany from the spare, cold cottage on the Cornish coast where they had sought refuge. The constancy of that harassment, together with the ongoing censorship and outright banning of Lawrence's books, convinced the couple to leave the country permanently in 1919, escaping forever what Lawrence called "the beastly, tight, Sunday feeling which is so blighting in England."

For the next stretch of years, the two lived intermittently in Italy, Ceylon, Australia, Mexico, New Mexico, Spain, and France—often on virtually no income and always with the help of patrons and friends like New York socialite Mabel Dodge Luhan, who in 1924 gave them a 160-acre ranch near Taos, New Mexico in return for Lawrence's original manuscript of Sons and Lovers. Lawrence and Frieda sought out during those years of virtually constant travel locales that were warm and dry in the hope that their climates would help alleviate the symptoms of the tuberculosis that now chronically plagued the writer. Lawrence himself refused to acknowledge his disease, insisting that he suffered nothing more than "wretched bronchials," and although he passionately loved the sun—"pulsing with marvelous blue, and alive, and streaming white fire from his edges"—he was also irresistibly drawn to places that so far had escaped the mechanization and ennui of the industrialized world. It was in Taos, New Mexico most particularly that Lawrence believed he had found a place where lives were led in honest and intimate connection with the earth and the seasons—a place where he successfully could escape the cultural decay that was labeled progress—and where he said he hoped to live out his days.

Yet although Lawrence loved the ranch and the Hispanic culture of northern New Mexico, he had come increasingly to dislike the United States as a whole, believing that its citizens had grown too materialistic and deadeningly far removed from the vital organic rituals of the passage from day to night and the changing of the seasons. The author's ever-worsening tuberculosis had made him a near-invalid by 1925, and, still refusing to surrender his hope for good health, he and Frieda determined that his strength might rebound and his "bronchials" might improve if they left the United States and returned to Europe. Lawrence, seriously ill but still determined to live as fully as he could, turned forty-years old on September 11, 1925, as the train on which he and Frieda were traveling lumbered across the American prairie toward New York, where a ship would transport them to England and the region in the east Midlands he called "the country of my heart."

Across the Atlantic again, Lawrence briefly visited England twice but spent most of his final years in Italy, the country in Europe where he felt the greatest personal ease, one that for him still echoed the "blood consciousness" of the Etruscans—Italy's contemporary culture, he believed, still essentially pagan, earth-linked, and vitally hedonistic, a place where people still felt the "rhythm of the daily sun and the inward rhythm of man and woman too." Living in two rented villas—first in Spotorno on the Italian Riviera, and then in the village of St. Polo Mosciano outside Florence—both country houses that lacked plumbing and any source of heat save a wood-fired kitchen stove, Lawrence continued to write prolifically despite the hacking cough and pulmonary hemorrhages that left him weak, wasted, and by now sexually impotent. Money always was hard to come by, yet words were his stock in trade, and despite continual crises of poor health, he wrote the short novels The Virgin and the Gipsy and The Escaped Cock, a book of travel essays titled Sketches of Etruscan Places, many dozens of short stories, reviews, poems, and essays, as well as three distinct versions of Lady Chatterley's Lover while he and Frieda lived on the Mediterranean coast and in the Tuscan countryside.

The way in which an openly ritualized and celebrated sexual bond between lovers is perhaps the surest path to spiritual fulfillment was a theme to which Lawrence had paid much attention during his fifteen-year writing career, and because of his insistence on writing with both explicitness and candor, his work had been regularly censored or banned in Britain by the time he began the new novel in Italy in 1926, one he privately worried might well be his last because of his worsening tuberculosis. But Lawrence's life was troubled by far more than failing health: the idyllic union with Frieda that initially had filled him with a profound sense of wholeness had deteriorated after fourteen years into a marriage in which bickering was constant and the threat of permanent separation was virtually always in the air.

Frieda nowadays longed for a life filled with friends, novelty, and revelry, while Lawrence increasingly enjoyed the company of only a few dear companions; Frieda wanted to travel widely still but Lawrence now longed to find a true retreat from the world; Frieda at last was eager to bring her children back into her life, yet Lawrence was jealous of her attentions to them. And perhaps most chillingly for the two of them, Frieda was sexually voracious and eager to continue the occasional liaisons with other men that she had demanded as her right from early in their relationship, while Lawrence—his Protestant English upbringing as much a part of him as was his sexual boldness on the printed page—needed and wanted only Frieda. His impotency—its physical reality, the emotional burden it carried, and its powerful symbolism of a kind of death, one that both of them shared—loomed as a constant reminder that their years of abandon and bliss had been short-lived and would never return.

L awrence had little choice but to acquiesce when Frieda began a discrete sexual relationship with Angelo Ravagli, a tenente in the Bersaglieri regiment of the Italian army, who, with his wife, owned the villa the Lawrence's rented in Spotorno. Frieda immediately had been fascinated by Ravagli, whom she met on a day when he by chance was wearing his dress uniform—"I am thrilled by his cockfeathers," she gushed in a letter to a friend, "and he is almost as nice as the feathers!"—and the two soon began a surreptitious affair, one which Lawrence nonetheless was quietly aware of from its outset.

The affair was, in fact, something of a reprise of events that had taken place fourteen years before—Frieda desperate to live a larger life than her husband could offer her, then finding herself attracted to a younger and still energetic man, sensing in him the kind of vibrancy she believed life inherently ought to have, her husband quietly acquiescing to, if also hating, the circumstances because he was unable to do anything about them. When Lawrence and Frieda moved from Ravagli's villa in Spotorno to the upper floor of a Spartan country house just outside Florence, the army officer remained a regular visitor, and Frieda continued to find ways to absent herself from her husband in order to rendezvous with her lover. What was astonishing in that regard was that when Lawrence at last was ready to take up a new novel in October 1926, he began to draft a story in which he indirectly informed Frieda that he fully understood her infidelities, one that seemed to celebrate them, in fact.

Lawrence's blossoming story of Constance Chatterley, the wife of a wealthy mine-owner in the British Midlands whose war injury has left him both paralyzed and impotent, and her empowering and physically enlivening and nurturing relationship with the gamekeeper employed on her husband's estate, drew directly from Lawrence's own cuckolded experience, yet instead of writing with great sympathy about the wounded and drastically diminished life of Sir Clifford Chatterley, it was Connie, Chatterley's errant and ardent wife, who became the book's heroine—a woman who comes vibrantly to life only via the carnal alchemy of sex. And the gamekeeper—who became over the course of three successive drafts of the novel increasingly educated, wise, and tender—emerged, far more than Chatterley, as the kind of man Lawrence both admired and longed once more to be. If Clifford Chatterley represented Lawrence's own fate—both men disabled and defeated—the gamekeeper Oliver Mellors, a well-educated collier's son as well as a veteran of the army himself, came to represent both the man Lawrence dreamed of becoming again as well as Ravagli, the sole man with whom Frieda now made love.

The growing novel also reflected Lawrence's belief that the dominant coal-mining industry in the English Midlands had ravaged and ruined his beloved Derbyshire and Nottinghamshire homeland, and the story increasingly made it clear that ongoing warfare among the classes in Britain threatened to destroy the soul of the nation's people as readily as the mines and mills had despoiled the sylvan countryside. What was desperately needed, the author appeared to believe ever more strongly, was simply some tenderness—tenderness toward the land and its subtle and sustaining gifts, tenderness that might touch both the rich and the poor with the understanding that their lives were inextricably entwined, tenderness between lovers that would allow the hunger for sexual satisfaction to grow into transcendent union.

With the second draft of the novel, the explicitness of the descriptions of the lovemaking between the gamekeeper and Lady Chatterley increased dramatically, as did Lawrence's liberal use of sexual epithets that remained utterly taboo in publishing in the English-speaking world, yet something about the book's subject matter seemed to bring it forth from its author's hand in a rush of narrative—and also surely sexual—emotion. Although walking even a short distance taxed him greatly, each morning for seven months Lawrence slowly had made his way to the base of a favorite tree in the umbrella-pine woods that surrounded the villa, accompanied almost always by a local dog he had dubbed John, and had not returned to the house until he had written two thousand words or more. But by the time the second draft of the long novel was done in March 1927, so was Lawrence it seemed, and he ignored the novel for virtually the rest of the year, discouraged by the way in which he felt he had failed to get its ending right, and convinced, too, that the novel's graphic sex and coarse language might make it impossible to publish in any case.

During the previous year, Lawrence had turned to painting, something he had taken true pleasure in as an adolescent but had ignored in the decades since. It had been a gift of four stretched but empty canvasses from visiting friends Aldous and Maria Huxley that spurred his return to brushes and paint, and the challenges offered by creating in a visual medium lifted his spirits dramatically for a time, his first finished canvas one he titled "The Unholy Family" before deciding that "Holy Family" was, in fact, a better name. A dreamily realistic image of a dark, mustachioed man whose arms are wrapped around the naked torso of a voluptuous blonde woman, their heads surrounded by nimbuses, or haloes, and standing beside a seated child, the back of his chair creating something of nimbus as well, the painting was intriguing in its illustration of figures who looked very much the way Lawrence had described Constance Chatterley and the swarthy gamekeeper. And the child? Curiously, Connie would not become pregnant with Oliver Mellors's child until Lawrence had rewritten the novel a third time.

By the time Lawrence was satisfied with the third and final version of Lady Chatterley's Lover in the winter of 1928, his health had worsened enough that walking to the woods to write had been impossible for some time, and on many mornings, he lacked the strength even to get out of bed. So it was surprising, given his waning health, that in the spring he chose to take on a new project, an enterprise that was utterly unknown to him and that would tax his fragile constitution every bit as much as writing now did. Lawrence was keenly aware that numerous graphic scenes in the final version of the novel, as well as his liberal use of words such as "fuck" and "cunt" would both shock and outrage many readers and also would ensure that his friends and publishers Martin Secker in London and Alfred Knopf in New York would reject it out of hand because of their fears of being arrested for publishing pornography. But rather than battle those whom he called "censor-morons" or purge the offensive material from the text to satisfy trade publishers, Lawrence opted to fund his own thousand-copy publication with the help of a Florentine printer and rare-book dealer named Giuseppe Orioli, who, when warned by the author of the novel's explosive content, replied, "O Ma! But we do those things every day!"

Despite the complications imposed by the fact that Orioli's typesetter understood no English—setting "dind't, didn't, dnid't, dind't, din'dt, didn't like a Bach fugue," Lawrence lamented—the handsome, thousand copy edition was ready to be shipped by mid-July, and within four months, it had sold out entirely, as had a 200-copy reprint. But when bootleg editions of the book began to appear with astonishing speed around the world, Lawrence had no means to block the piracy because he had neglected to copyright his creation: anyone anywhere was free to publish and sell the novel without having to direct a penny of the income to its author, and dozens did so. Although few people around world would admit to having both read and liked the book, a legion of critics were eager to lash out at it, describing Lady Chatterley's Lover as "a literary cesspool," "a landmark in evil," "the foulest book in English literature," and perhaps most painful to Lawrence, "the fruit of a poisoned genius." "The hatred my books have aroused comes back at me and gets me here," Lawrence told a friend, pointing to his heart, a few days before he and Frieda departed from Italy for the last time.

By early 1929, the stresses of self-publishing the novel, together with the emotional turmoil caused by Frieda's ongoing relationship with Angelo Ravagli and the rising tide of fascism in Mussolini's Italy, left Lawrence dispirited, heartsick, and ready to abandon his adopted country for the itinerant life once more. Yet his poor health couldn't withstand much more travel, and following sojourns in Switzerland, the French Côte d'Azur, and the Spanish island of Majorca—the writer well-monied enough and able to travel at ease at long last only because of his dramatic financial success in selling Lady Chatterley's Lover privately—Lawrence agreed in February 1930 to enter a sanatorium for tuberculosis sufferers in Vence, near Nice. After only a month—and against his doctors' orders—he checked himself out of the institution to join Frieda at a country house she had rented nearby. A day later, with his wife, her daughter Barbara, and the Huxleys by his side, he died, six months short of his forty-fifth birthday.

Two years later, Angelo Ravagli, whom Frieda later would marry and who had agreed to carry the writer's remains to his beloved ranch near Taos, discretely dumped Lawrence's ashes into the Mediterranean. Frieda and Ravagli eventually returned to New Mexico, where they lived out their lives, and Ravagli liked to tell visitors to the ranch that he had mixed the great writer's ashes into the concrete with which he created a memorial stone to honor his wife's late husband.

THE DRIVE

An excerpt from THE COLOR ORANGE

The wind had whipped Lake Erie into a roily sea on Saturday; the thick gray skies made the barges, the rusting cranes, and waterlogged docks down on the Cuyahoga appear all the more forlorn; and from the outside, Memorial Stadium looked like an abandoned tire factory, its yellow brick stained by soot and the lakeside weather, dramatic cracks in the mortar snaking up from sidewalks to roof.

It was a wonderful place. Built almost six decades before by the Works Progress Administration in hopes of luring the 1932 Olympics—just one of many dreams to go sour in this much-maligned city—it still seemed like the kind of stadium where football ought to be played, where the weather ought to be lousy, and where the players' jerseys ought to end up gloriously soaked with mud. With its two broad tiers of seats, covered high above by a steel latticework roof—support posts spoiling the view from at least a few seats in every section—it was an icon of an earlier NFL, one without imitation grass or temperature-controlled comfort. And although it was almost empty now, it was obvious that it was the place where all of northern Ohio planned to redeem its dreams on Sunday: Standing on a tall ladder in the west end zone, a stadium employee was coating the goalpost with furniture polish in an effort to make it so slick that celebrating fans would not be able to tear it down once the Browns had defeated the Broncos thirty hours hence. Waiting in the baseball dugout which led to the Broncos locker room, a photographer for the Cleveland *Plain Dealer* was explaining that she would be leaving for Pasadena on Friday—feeling no need to preface her plans with a maybe.

The Broncos—the Browns' unfortunate sacrificial horses— bundled in parkas and topcoats and gloves, ambled out of their locker room a little before noon and nosed around, getting the feel of this ponderous place. Tony Lilly peeking under the massive tarp to try to see if the field was as muddy as the soggy sidelines, Vance Johnson running a stride or two on the tarp, Louis Wright throwing his head back and laughing at his team's looming predicament, Karl Mecklenburg squinting his eyes and nervously pacing the mud.

This was Saturday practice, but the defensive players didn't bother with any volleyball; the offensive players didn't fiddle with any run-throughs; Dan Reeves didn't call out the special-teams squads, and Rich Karlis kept his shoe on. The weather was simply too cold, the drizzle too damp to fire the usual Saturday shenanigans. Nobody felt like doing much but milling, stepping carefully to keep the slop off their snakeskin boots.

Tom Jackson couldn't help but pan the empty seats that surrounded him, remembering the sections where he had sat as a boy, remembering the games he had watched with his father. "It's such a big place," he said, looking up to the roof, his voice like a soft, Lake Erie fog. "I remember when I was a kid it seemed bigger than life. My dad would bring me here to see the Brownies and to see Jim Brown, who was every kid's hero then. On third-and-two situations we never wondered what the Brownies would do. We *knew* they'd give the ball to J.B. Like every other kid, I grew up wanting to be a running back, to be like the great J.B. But I lasted about ten minutes as a running back in high school. I fumbled the ball a couple of times, and the coach put me over with the linebackers, and that was that."

Jackson grew up on Cleveland's southeast side and graduated from John Adams High School in 1969, lettering in football, baseball, and wrestling. Although his high school coaches praised his ability and were impressed by his unflagging desire, Jackson, at five-feet ten and a hundred and ninety pounds, was considered too small to have much of a shot at a collegiate football career. But the football staff at the University of Louisville decided to take a chance on him, and he became one of the school's all-time stars, twice being named Missouri Valley Conference Player of the Year.

The Denver Broncos knew they were taking a similar chance when they drafted Jackson in the fourth round in 1973, and Jackson himself was crushed by their selection. "Before the draft, my hope was either to be drafted by the Browns so I could go back to my hometown, or by some team in a warm-weather city," he told me in the players' lounge at the Broncos' practice facility a week before this trip. "When I got a call from the Broncos saying that they had drafted me, I looked on a map in my dorm room to see where Denver was. It looked like it was way up in the Rocky Mountains, and I remember saying to my roommate, 'What amazing bad luck. I've been drafted to the Rocky Mountains. It's going to be freezing and blizzarding for my whole career.' I was very displeased. But after I'd spent one season here, I moved out here permanently, and made it my home. Now, I don't think I've ever been anywhere where I'd rather live than Colorado."

Jackson became a defensive starter at the beginning of his rookie season and was part of the Broncos' mid-seventies line-backing corps which included Randy Gradishar, Joe Rizzo, and Bob Swenson, and which was widely considered the best in football, a group that succeeded with speed rather than size. "Unlike Dick Butkus or someone, I didn't ever run through a lot of people to get to the football," Jackson told me. "I tended to run around people. I'm sure that's one of the reasons I've been able to play as long as I have. My body hasn't had to take that kind of abuse—although any position in football takes a toll. And I definitely don't recover from games as fast as I did even three or four years ago."

Named as the Broncos' most valuable defensive player three times, Jackson was also selected to the AFC Pro Bowl squad in 1977, 1978, and 1979. Following the retirement of Barney Chavous at the start of this season, he became the longest-tenured player on the team, surviving to date for fourteen grueling seasons. Sunday's game would be his 193rd as a professional, more than any other player in Broncos history. "I hope that when my time comes to quit I can show as much class as Barney did," he said. "But there is only so long that you play this game. And my dad has always reminded me that I should make the very most of these years I have to play it, and play it as long as I possibly can, because after that it won't be an option anymore. He's right. Even though I know I'll retire before too long, it isn't something I look forward to."

Jackson suffered a knee injury—the first serious injury of his career—during the 1985 season's training camp and had to undergo arthroscopic surgery, missing four games at the start of the season. Although he eventually returned to the starting lineup, his knee plagued him throughout the season, and there was wide speculation that this oldest linebacker in the NFL was finished. "I heard a lot of talk last winter and last spring," he said, "people saying I couldn't play. I wanted to come back at least one more year and show myself that my problems last season had nothing to do with lost skills, but with the injury."

At the start of this season's camp, Jackson told Broncos linebacker coach Myrel Moore that he wanted to be treated like a rookie. "The last few years, Myrel had started giving me some afternoons off to make things a little easier on me. But this year, I didn't know how my leg was going to respond. What I wanted from Myrel was for him to make me work really hard. I didn't want him to give me anything. And he didn't."

"Myrel means a lot to you guys, doesn't he?" I asked.

"He's like a second father to all the 'backers. He's careful to know each of us as a person. He knows what keys you, as opposed to what keys another person, and he focuses on that. Yeah. I really love Myrel."

If Myrel Moore plays a paternal role for the Broncos' linebackers, Tom Jackson in turn has become a similar kind of figure for his fellow players—those who work on both sides of the ball. They have voted him the team's most inspirational player each year since that award was created, and virtually all of them would agree with their head coach when he says, "Shoot, Tom Jackson *is* the Denver Broncos." The inspiration Jackson offers his team is far more than an incessant kind of cheerleading, however. It is something he described to me as simply his being "into the game all the time, always into the game. We can be down by twenty, and in my mind I'm thinking of ways we can win. If you truly believe it, maybe one out of a hundred times something like that will happen, and then, of course, you say, 'Hey, I knew we'd win it all along.' But the award, no, it only really means something because it comes from the other players. They know that I'm more than just a rah-rah ball player. They know it's real."

Then I asked him again about retirement. Would he call it quits at the end of January? If it came to that, would he play his last game in the stadium where he had first watched Jim Brown? "If we win the Super Bowl, there's no doubt in my mind that I'll retire," he said. "But if we get real close, but not quite there, it will really throw a wrench in the way. You wouldn't want to retire thinking the team was just this far away from it. You wouldn't want to watch everybody else go the following year."

As he surveyed ancient Memorial Stadium on Saturday, I asked him, if indeed tomorrow was his last game, what aspects of his football career he would be most proud of in the end. He thought for a moment, then his dark, expressive face flashed the emotion that is such an integral part of him. "I'm just real proud of the way I've played this game," he said. "I feel like I've put a lot extra into it. Merlin Olsen gave me this thought when I asked him something similar once—he said that when you're through playing, it isn't the awards, or the records, or the championships that you remember. You're just thankful that you played the game and played it well. I think when I'm finished—whenever that is—the thing I'll be most proud of is that I went out every Sunday and played the game. Just that I played the game."

C lose behind Tom Jackson on the Broncos' longevity list is guard Paul Howard. Although Howard was drafted in 1973—one round before Jackson was acquired—and is the oldest player on the team, he missed the 1976 season with a back injury, and for that reason has played one fewer season than has his fellow old-timer. Howard had suffered only the second serious injury of his career—a torn anterior cruciate ligament in his left knee— near the end of the Patriots game a week before, and the grizzled, 260-pound lineman's absence seemed conspicuous there in cold and cavernous Memorial Stadium. He had had surgery on Tuesday and would have to watch tomorrow's game from his hospital bed in Denver. "It hurts us bad," Dan Reeves had said about Howard's loss. "But hopefully, the times we've played this year without Paul will be a benefit to us now." When it came time to suit up tomorrow, the players said, it would sure seem strange not to have the old man around.

Howard's roster position was officially filled Saturday morning when Dan Reeves informed league officials that the team was reactivating Clarence Kay, his four weeks of drug rehabilitation completed. Kay had returned to Denver on Tuesday and had begun practicing with the team again on Wednesday, following a private morning meeting in which he discussed his treatment and his current condition with his coaches and teammates. "I told them what I went through and what was going on," he told the reporters who were anxious to talk to the new-leaf Clarence Kay. "I think it was pretty much accepted. I was honest with them. I told them how Clarence Kay was and what I went through." When he was asked if returning to the team was a challenge, he smiled wanly and said, "Everything is in black and white. I've got to maintain and do what I'm supposed to do, that's all. Clarence Kay has got himself together."

Following three days of practice, Reeves and his assistant coaches had agreed that although Kay understandably was a little rusty, he seemed to be in shape, seemed to want to play football, and given Paul Howard's absence, they were certain that Kay's blocking ability, plus his rediscovered self-confidence, would be invaluable against the Dogs of Cleveland.

Cleveland had become a wild-eyed football town in the weeks since Christmas, since the Browns cornered the AFC Central title with the handiwork of a twenty-three-year-old, home-state quarterback named Bernie Kosar, a legendary tight end named Ozzie Newsome, a no-name backfield as uncelebrated as Denver's, and a corps of expert defensive backs who call themselves "the Dogs." The Browns had finished the season 12-4, trouncing interdivision rival Cincinnati 34-3 on the next-to-last Sunday of the season to clinch the crown, then disposing of San Diego a week later to secure the home-field advantage throughout the playoffs.

The swell of civic pride in the Browns crescendoed when the New York Jets arrived a week ago, but by the time that game— the Browns' heart-stopping, come-from-behind, double-overtime victory—was over, the city of Cleveland simply went over the psychic brink, and Ohio's north coast lapsed into perfect ecstasy. All of a sudden, the Cleveland Browns were synonymous with the city's and the region's renaissance; if the Browns were winners, then everyone else was a winner as well. The Cuyahoga hadn't caught fire in more than a decade; the bravest strains of fish were swimming in Lake Erie again; Cleveland would soon be home to the country's Rock and Roll Hall of Fame, and those Mistake-on-the-Lake jokes would have to be shelved forever, surely. To top off all the excitement, the long-suffering Browns were now bound for the Super Bowl. If the goddamn Jets couldn't stop them with a ten-point lead late in the fourth quarter, then no one could. The Browns, it seemed certain, would bowl over the Broncos, then smash hell out of whatever NFC team dared to show up for the Super Bowl, and all of America would at long last get off Cleveland's case. It was going to be beautiful.

By the time the Broncos arrived on Friday night, go browns signs covered every flat surface in town. The statues in front of the Federal Reserve Bank were wearing huge papier-mache Browns helmets; St. John's Cathedral was displaying a banner wishing Godspeed to Bernie Kosar; a U.S. district judge was telling a group of seventy newly naturalized citizens that "the Browns symbolize America"; Mayor George Voinovich was sporting a Browns jersey bearing Kosar's number 19; supermarkets were reporting that dog bones—unofficial souvenirs of the Dogs, or rather *Dawgs,* on the Browns' defense—were in very short supply; bridal salons were offering specials on burnt-orange and brown gowns; hair salons were specializing in hairdos highlighted by shaved patches in the shape of a dog bone or in letters that spelled out go browns; television anchors were outfitted in Browns colors for their newscasts—which dealt, of course, with little but the fervor surrounding the football game; and the Cleveland *Plain Dealer* was screaming from its brown-accented front page, color this wild town brown. Everyone was having a whale of a time, and it was hard not to get caught up in all the revelry—unless, say, you were a Denver Bronco, trying to get a little sleep on Friday and Saturday nights, but listening instead to the honking horns of the parade of cars that cruised all night through the streets surrounding the Stouffer's Inn on the Plaza downtown, listening maddeningly to the devoted fans who somehow stole past the hotel's security guards (Browns partisans themselves, perhaps) and ran up and down the corridors till dawn barking and baying like dogs—like *DAWGS!*

"I don't think this town can be made fun of again," said Ron Bilek, news director of WKYC, Channel 3, a station that had done an entire "Today in Cleveland" broadcast from the kitchen of Pat Schottenheimer, wife of the Browns' head coach. "Yes, the Browns mania doesn't solve poverty, but it certainly gets people revved up. It has nothing to do with trivialities. It's solidified the fact that Cleveland's on the rebound."

Plain Dealer sports columnist Bill Livingston had little trouble agreeing, asking his readers rhetorically, "Isn't it nice to hear Cleveland being mentioned in a positive light because of the Browns?" But as far as Livingston was concerned, he couldn't wait to get beyond the semi-pro attention that the AFC championship brought the city to the big time, bells and whistles, front and center attention that the city would receive with its team in the Super Bowl. Oh, the Browns would be in the Super Bowl, all right, expect browns' victory, Livingston's pre-game column was headlined. That much was plain, purported Livingston, and he dealt it out this way:

> I see Elway scrambling around, trying to buy
> time. I see the lingering effects of last week's

injury slowing him just enough to become de-
fensible. . ... I see Kosar taking that Denver defense and withering it with the sheer power of
the fellow's brain. . . . Perhaps most of all, I see a
Browns team that simply does not believe it can
be beaten. It was said during the Steelers' Super
Bowl years that they loved nothing more than
facing a team from some posh, trendy place like
Dallas or L.A. I think the Browns are like that. I
think the Dawgs can't wait to fasten their teeth
on Johnny E.'s cuffs.

And if you might be tempted to call Livingston a "homer"
for picking the Browns simply because they were so near
and dear to his heart (the poor man assuming the sheer
power of Kosar's brain could pull off things even Shirley
MacLaine can't yet accomplish), the *Plain Dealer* included
a list of the prognostications of twenty-nine sportswriters
from around the country—*twenty-two* of whom favored the
Browns. Michael Knisley of the *Denver Post* guessed it would
be Browns 23-20 in another double overtime; Steve Caulk
of the *Rocky Mountain News* called it Browns, 22-19; Mike
Spence of the Colorado Springs *Gazette-Telegraph* chose
Cleveland as well, 24-21—no homers in that crowd, for
heaven's sake. "The Broncos won't stand in the way of the
Dawgs of Destiny," opined Vic Carucci of the *Buffalo News.*
"The Browns are not to be denied. Browns, 21-17." And
Ed Beitiks of the *San Francisco Examiner* summed things
up succinctly for Livingston and his fellow fans: "Everyone

from Denver is a fake. Elway will throw three interceptions. Nobody, but nobody, wants to see Denver in the Super Bowl. Browns, 30-10."

Wasn't it something? The Browns were Pasadena-bound, Cleveland was suddenly Camelot, and the Cuyahoga was aflame with hope. "Hey, everybody needs a love affair," said the Browns' owner, Art Modell.

A rguably the only people in all of Cuyahoga County who didn't really care how the game came out were the 120 members of the NBC Sports crew (75 engineers and 45 production people) who were on hand to beam it back to the Rockies and from sea to shining sea—AFC and NFC championship games tending to do very well in the ratings, even if, as in NBC's case this year, the participating teams weren't exactly from cities at the epicenter of American life.

It would be CBS's turn to broadcast the Super Bowl two weeks hence, so the Cleveland-Denver contest would be NBC's final football game of the season, and executive producer Michael Weisman and his crew were pulling out all the stops. First-string announcers Dick Enberg and Merlin Olsen would call the game, of course, assisted with pre- and post- and mid-game gab by NBC's Bob Costas, Ahmad Rashad, Bob Griese, Paul McGuire, and Frank Deford, and with the special guest analyses of Miami Dolphins' coach Don Shula. The operation would require three production trucks instead of the usual one; twenty-one cameras would be aimed at the field instead of the everyday six or seven;

by game time, twelve miles of video cable would be strung through Memorial Stadium. "Now we just need a good game," Weisman commented on Saturday afternoon, standing near the lavish pre-game set his crew had constructed on the sidelines, pronouncing his network's preparations almost complete. And he was pleased by the forecast that called for cold weather, gray skies, possibly a snow shower or two tomorrow. "The gray skies give us sharper colors, and with the natural grass, the players will get dirty, mud will fly in the air, we'll see their breath. It'll be perfect. What we want is another Cleveland-Jets situation—double overtime. But we're not greedy. We'll settle for one overtime."

The bookies and betting services all week had been taking wagers on the Browns by three, but the spread might have shot up to ten or more had they heard the incessant car horns and the bellicose, barking fans at the Broncos' hotel on Saturday night. Then the Sunday weather—colder, windier, snowier even than Saturday had been—seemed to seal the Broncos' fate. The Clevelanders looked like roustabouts from Alaska's North Slope as they converged on the stadium in the spitting morning snow, their stocking-capped heads turned away from the lake-borne gale. But it was perfect weather for football, wasn't it?—for a win by the Browns that would send them to sunnier climes. this game is going to the dawgs, assured a banner that was hung from the rail of the upper deck, no more cleve. jokes, demanded another. "Elway sucks," was the chant that rang out of the stands as 79,915 delirious fans pelted the field with dog biscuits.

"Wonderful," thought Michael Weisman as he panned the color monitors in NBC's central production truck, watching the frozen ball sail off Rich Karlis's foot and into the sullen skies.

This was going to be a good football game, that much seemed certain by the time the Browns had taken a touchdown lead on a textbook 86-yard drive. And you had to wonder if it indeed might not be a great one when Broncos linebackers Ricky Hunley and Jim Ryan pulled two of Kosar's passes out of the air on two successive possessions. The Broncos got Karlis close enough for a field goal early in the second quarter, and the Browns responded by fumbling away the ball as soon as their offense returned to the field. The Broncos were right back in scoring position—the ball on the Cleveland 38—when John Elway, his ankle obviously surviving the strain, took the snap on first and ten, looked for his targeted receivers, then thought better of the plan and ran to the 3-yard line—precisely the kind of a scramble Browns' coach Marty Schottenheimer had seen in his sleep all week. But the horses had little more power, gaining only two yards in three plays before they faced a fourth and goal at the one, as well as a devilish kind of decision. Another field goal would leave them behind by a point, yet the yard for the touchdown seemed anything but a certainty. On the sidelines, Dan Reeves opted for the gamble and the chance for the lead, and Gerald Willhite, sweeping right, somehow stretched the ball across the goal line as he was tackled by Cleveland's Chris Rockins. Karlis's point-after was perfect and the Broncos led by three.

In the final seconds before half-time, Kosar completed a 42-yard strike to Clarence Weathers, and four plays later, the Browns similarly needed only inches of grass for a go-ahead touchdown. But on third and goal at the 2, Kosar—seeing nothing but looming trouble—intentionally grounded the ball and the penalty set the Browns back to the Broncos' twelve. The touchdown denied, Mark Moseley kicked a field goal to tie the score as the period expired. The first half was history; the score was tied; and Ohio State University's Marching Buckeyes did their best to grind the new onslaught of biscuits into the turf.

I watched most of the rest of the game from a cramped seat in the baseball press box—directly behind home plate, had this been the summer game, and just beyond the west end zone in frigid January. The third quarter was quiet, offering little to see from that vantage point except Karlis's 26-yard field goal, which split the polished uprights and sailed end-over-end toward me. As the Browns opened the fourth quarter, Mark Moseley lined up two yards away from the spot where Karlis had stood three minutes earlier, then booted a 24-yarder that was every bit as true. Browns 13, Broncos 13, the season still in doubt.

But with just six minutes to play, I watched it all come to a sobering end, watched as Bernie Kosar backpedaled from the Broncos' 48 and underthrew a long ball aimed for receiver Brian Brennan. Seeing that the football was short, Brennan checked his stride and came back for it, twisting Broncos Dennis Smith to the ground in panicked pursuit in the process, Brennan then cradling the ball between his numbers and doing a deft sidestep around the kneeling Smith, who could do little but beg for another chance. The Browns led by a touchdown; the fans still had enough body heat to begin a tumultuous celebration; and the old stadium seemed assured of seeing its first championship since 1964.

On the ensuing kickoff, Denver returner Ken Bell bobbled the ball at the 2, falling on it and controlling it an instant before it was stripped away, ending the Broncos' six-month quest with a rookie's glaring misjudgment, and I made my way down to the field, wanting to see how the Broncos who had hoped for so much now accepted their fate. Dennis Smith stood far back from the sideline, absently pacing, painfully aware of his role in the Denver defeat. A dozen players in blue ponchos with hoods that covered their helmets shouted vain encouragement onto the field. Tom Jackson, his career just minutes from ending, was anguished but somehow gallant as he glanced at the clock, its numbers briefly stopped at 5:32, the veteran linebacker unwilling yet to surrender. Pat Bowlen, draped in his long mink coat, his trousers stuffed into the tops of his boots to keep them out of the mud, stood at the end of the line of players who were pressing close to the field, the owner doing his futile best

to appear impassive. Dan Reeves, at the center of the long
blue and orange row, seemingly had yet to hear about the
impending defeat, unaware that his hope was lost. He sent
in a play, then put his hands on his knees, the better to direct,
by gum, what was about to happen.

In the huddle in the west end zone, the eleven Broncos
were deafened by the jubilant crowd for whom the stadium
was suddenly Oz. But they could see the 98 yards of mud,
grass, and crushed biscuits between the ball and the distant
goal line; they could see by the clock the few minutes that
remained to them; and they could see by the streamers on the
uprights the taunting wind that whipped in their direction.

"We got these guys right where we want 'em," observed
Keith Bishop in his slow, West Texas twang, and ten Broncos
began to titter. "We all just giggled when he said it," tackle
Dave Studdard remembered after the game. "I about fell out
of the huddle," added guard Mark Cooper, playing in Paul
Howard's stead. John Elway flashed a confident smile, then
went to work, throwing a 5-yard pass to Sammy Winder
to get the horses under way. Elway handed off to Winder
on the three successive plays, the small back churning for 3
yards, 2 yards, then 3 again before Elway rolled out of the
pocket and scrambled for 11 yards of his own. With a third
and one and little breathing room at the 26-yard line, Elway
fired a 22-yard pass to Steve Sewell up the middle, followed
it with a 12-yard toss to Steve Watson, and the crowd grew
markedly quiet. But their spirits waxed bright again when
the Denver quarterback turned cool at midfield, throwing
two incompletions and suffering an 8-yard sack.

It was third and eighteen from the Browns' 48, and the Broncos seemed at an impasse. But with his ankle holding up and his confidence cresting, his big number 7 smeared by mud, Elway dropped deep and launched a 20-yard rocket to Mark Jackson, who had cut free from "head Dawg" Hanford Dixon at the 28. The Browns' fans grew faint of heart again just as the Broncos' bench erupted. You could *feel* it now; suddenly there seemed to be little doubt about it—the Broncos were headed straight for the cheap seats in the east end zone, headed for the section that had dubbed itself the Dawg Pound, and there wasn't a way in the world to stop them.

The Broncos moved to the 14 with a second completion to Sewell, moved to the 5 when Elway scrambled and raced toward the sideline, then went in for the score as Jackson stretched out and contained a low Elway fastball, rolling with it onto the biscuit-strewn grass of the end zone. The Dawgs in the Pound did their best to distract Rich Karlis into muffing the extra point, but their shouts went flat and sour till next season as the ball sailed through the uprights and tumbled down toward them. Denver 20, Cleveland 20. Ninety-eight miraculous yards in fifteen inspired, impossible plays. Not a dog barked in all of ancient Memorial Stadium

The Browns had thirty-seven seconds left to try to win the game; failing that, they could still secure the win in overtime, but by now that was merely theoretical. A tangible, palpable kind of chill—the coldest yet of the day—seemed to convince the Clevelanders otherwise. Kosar and company went through the motions, endeavoring to do no more than hang on to the ball in the final seconds, then, winning the overtime coin toss, they took the ball again and moved it all of eight yards before they had to punt it back to the Broncos. Camelot was collapsing, the love affair turning cold and cruel, the Super Bowl slipping away on the winter winds.

This time it took the Broncos nine plays to gain the 60 yards that took them to the Cleveland 15, Winder running and Elway passing to pull them off in clumps with a kind of passion now. As Rich Karlis came onto the field to finish the day, NFL and NBC officials were frantically moving the championship trophy from the entrance to the Cleveland locker room, where it had been waiting since midway through the fourth quarter, to the Denver locker room, where it now appeared ready for a more permanent home. Michael Weisman had gotten his overtime game, but the winner wasn't going to end it by the script. Keith Bishop snapped the ball back to Gary Kubiak, who set it down. The Cleveland defenders desperately dove into the air to try to block it, but Karlis got it up quickly, the ball hooking just inside the left upright, close enough to it that 80,000 people held out a final, momentary, heartbroken hope before they got up from their seats in silence, their renaissance shattered by the Broncos' sudden offensive brilliance, their dreams destroyed by an arcing barefoot kick.

"Karlis's kick is up; it's good!" Bob Martin shouted into his microphone from the KOA booth atop the stadium. "The Broncos again are going to the Super Bowl! But it's no miracle this time. This time they earned it!"

Rich Karlis's primary concern in the seconds that ensued, he later told the crush of reporters, was that he would die of suffocation, his face pressed into the turf and held there by a pile of very large men in very bright orange jerseys. Memorial Stadium was strangely, deathly quiet except for that mound of jubilant Broncos, and Karlis's shouts that he couldn't breathe were muffled in the turf. "It felt great to have made the field goal," he said, "but a couple of seconds later, I thought I was going to die."

By the time Karlis escaped from beneath the pile, the trophy had made its way down the dank corridor to the Denver locker room and AFC President Lamar Hunt had presented it to the Broncos' owner, whose jaws quivered with emotion, and whose eyes betrayed an uncertainty that his team had truly done it. "I was standing there on the sidelines," Bowlen said, "expecting to go congratulate Art Modell in a minute. I was damn near sick to my stomach. You never want to doubt that it can happen but... well, it didn't look good for us there for a while." But then his team had miraculously tied the score, marched down the field a second time, and Rich Karlis was lining up to try for the winning field goal. "I couldn't watch Rich kick that field goal," Bowlen confessed. "Those moments are almost too excruciatingly painful. But I knew we must have made it because you could hear a pin drop in that place."

Dan Reeves could hardly contain himself in the tent outside the Broncos' locker room, where he addressed the swarming press. "It's the biggest thrill in my coaching career. It's almost like a Hollywood script—it comes out just like you want it to." What about The Drive, the reporters wanted to know—the 98-yard march to tie the game, already epic only minutes after it occurred. "Yeah, I was a little discouraged when we had to start there on the one- or two-yard line," he admitted. "It looked bleak, but we knew we had a chance. I've been around the game twenty-one years, and I've *never* seen a drive like that. But I'll tell you what. With the pressure on him, I'd rather have John Elway playing for me than anyone I know."

Opposite Reeves in the confines of the tent, Elway, stripped to a T-shirt and already wearing a Super Bowl cap, was doing his best to field the shouted questions. A reporter reminded him that on their two previous possessions in the fourth quarter, the Broncos hadn't been able to generate a first down. What was it that made their final offensive spurt possible? "For some reason, we seem to play better with our backs to the wall," Elway responded. "And right then, our backs were about as close to the wall as they could get."

"Hey, John, what's it feel like to be going to the Super Bowl?" someone shouted.

"It hasn't sunk in yet. I don't know," he replied. "I guess I'm going to have to slap myself."

Rich Karlis stood on the third podium, a dog biscuit tucked into the waist of his uniform pants. "It's a collector's item now," explained the Salem, Ohio, native, telling the reporters clustered around him that the extra point to tie the game worried him much more than the field goal. "On the field goal, I was totally relaxed. As hard as those guys had just worked, the last thing I could afford was to go out there and miss it." Fifty of Karlis's family and friends had driven up to the big city, to see the game, and as he spoke, his mother struggled her way to the podium and embraced her son, the football hero. With tears streaming down his face, Karlis introduced his mother, telling the reporters that she was his biggest fan. "I don't know if I can find the right words," he said. "There's no place I'd rather win it than here. I know our fans in Denver would have rather had the game there, but I just felt like it was my destiny to win it in Cleveland. I feel bad because this city has waited so long for a championship. Cleveland really has a lot of nice things in it. It's really a great place, but... I don't know. This is just wonderful."

In the streets outside the stadium, the fans finally felt the cold. Most said nothing as they walked away, but some were angry, not at the Browns, who so cruelly had let them down, but at the visitors, who had stolen the spotlight they had sought for so long. "Denver sucks!" a group of young men screamed into the media tent. "You suck, you bastards!" When police pulled them away, they surrendered their fight, and two of them started to cry.

NBC's coverage of the game had long since ended, but in the Broncos' tiny locker room, the camera lights of the Denver stations still blared. From a high wooden platform, Channel 4's Ron Zappolo was conducting a marathon of live interviews, his crew sending a succession of players in shoulder pads, players in street clothes, a few players only in towels to join him in the bright light. For forty-five minutes without a break, Zappolo asked how tough the Browns had been, whether the game had seemed truly lost, how The Drive was inspired, what this triumph meant to them. Karl Mecklenburg, Louis Wright, Steve Foley, David Studdard, Mark Jackson, Jim Ryan—one after one they did their best to describe what couldn't be put into words properly, and Zappolo did a remarkable job of eliciting their responses. In the celebratory excitement, everyone was loquacious, everyone was in love with his job and his fellow teammates, and everyone sent joyous greetings back to family and friends and the legions of fans in Denver. It was live television at its informal, emotional best, and you knew that back in the Queen City, few channels had been changed to that other game.

I n a corner of the locker room, a small television set was tuned to the CBS broadcast of the NFC championship game—the New York Giants shellacking the Washington Redskins. No one was very interested, save a reporter or two who seemed strangely glued to the blowout. "Hey, who we going to play?" Ricky Hunley asked as he sauntered near the set, his words aimed at Vance Johnson, who was fingering his moussed flattop into place. "Who gives a fuck about the Giants and the Redskins?" Johnson retorted. "Shit, baby, I just know this time we're going to be in the sun, man. Wear

Bermuda shorts instead of this shit. It's going to be great. What's the matter with your voice, anyway?"

"I'm hoarse from eating dog biscuits," Hunley dead-panned. "I can still bark. I just can't talk."

John Elway had finally made his way back to the locker room from the tent; he had spoken at length with Ron Zappolo and with all of the Colorado beat reporters, but still a few others trailed him, trying to get one last quote, another twist on the story he'd been telling repeatedly for the past hour and a half. Finally, Jim Saccomano intervened, stepping between the quarterback and the reporters, explaining that Elway had a plane to catch, Elway taking quick advantage of the interference and slipping away to the shower. Then seconds later he screamed— screamed at the top of his lungs as cold water poured down on him from the showerhead. "Jesus," he shouted, his head peering around the tiled wall. "Isn't there any hot water left?"

"Not for about half an hour," came the reply.

"I love this town," he said, flashing the same grin that had started The Drive.

At last free of the attentions of the six hundred reporters who had descended upon this championship game, Reeves, Elway, and the rest of the Broncos boarded four buses that would take them to the airport, where their chartered plane awaited them. But on bus number three, there seemed to be one last bit of business before the Broncos left the waterfront. "Let's go by the hotel and honk the goddamn horn," Dave Studdard hollered from the back of the bus. His idea was an instant hit, and, despite understandable Cleveland loyalties, the bus driver saw no reason not to comply. He gave the big air horn a few hard honks in front of the main doors of the Inn on the Plaza, the players stuck their heads out the windows and barked into the dusk, then the entourage left for the airport.

But it wasn't going to be that simple to get out of town. When the equipment crates were finally loaded in the underbelly of the DC-8 and everyone was on board, the captain announced that the United operations office in Cleveland had just received a bomb threat. A bomb had purportedly been placed aboard the plane, and although the likelihood of the call being a hoax was enormous, there was little choice but to take it seriously. In consultation with Bowlen and Reeves, the flight crew decided to remove everything from the baggage hold and send it on a separate plane tomorrow. The players, coaches, and media people were requested to search the overhead bins above them, then to relax. They would remain in Ohio at least another hour.

"Let's get *out* of this fucking town," Tom Jackson shouted in the midst of the wait, pacing the aisle, looking like a banker in his gray suit, smoking a post-game cigarette. "Man, if we'd have known this, we'd have beat them worse. I don't want anything to do with this damn place," he said, embarrassed for his hometown, embarrassed to think that some crank would want to further tarnish its image.

At 8:45, four and a half hours after the game had ended, Broncos One at last rolled down the runway en route to Colorado and to a welcoming party that was reported already to be 6-8,000 people strong and growing by a thousand people an hour. Then somewhere west of the Mississippi, 30,000 feet above the Iowa cornfields, it was finally time to celebrate. "Listen up, y'all," Reeves drawled into a flight attendant's microphone. "We've got some champagne on board, and there's no question that we've got something to celebrate. We're the AFC champs. But I want you to remember a few things. We've all got to drive home. I want you to make sure you can drive. And another thing, there are about 10,000 people waiting for us at the airport. Some of you are going to have to talk. So enjoy yourselves. You've earned it. But let's wait till the night after the Super Bowl, and then we'll have a real party."

Reeves needn't have worried; it was already too late, his players too tired to initiate anything raucous. Some champagne was consumed, and hugs and slaps on the back were liberally traded among the passengers, but it was a polite party at best, Reeves himself the center of attention as he paraded the aisle with the shiny new trophy in tow. When linebackers coach Myrel Moore wandered back from the first-class section, Tom Jackson, a bottle already in hand, found glasses and told his mentor it was time for a toast. "This is the guy I've got to toast," Jackson said of the man he had called his second father. "This is the guy that I owe it to."

But Moore insisted on proposing the toast himself. "Here's to what football's all about," he said as Jackson poured a swallow into his glass. "Here's to what coaching's all about—Tom Jackson." Tears suddenly streamed down Jackson's face, and he embraced his coach as warmly as he could, kissing his cheek, holding him tight for a long time. The two men—one white, one black, one a gruff and grizzled coach, the other just a guy who played the game—said nothing more before they finally sipped their champagne in triumph.

Tony LaMonica was on the radio again, doing a live report as the plane angled out of the sky: "We're traveling at a speed of about 150 knots now, landing east to west. The aircraft continues to settle on its approach, landing gear down, and . . . touchdown." The players cheered as they felt the tires lunge onto the tarmac, and as the DC-8 taxied toward the United hangar, they peered through their windows to try to see just how big this crowd really was.

Television crews recorded the players' descents down the stairways and their reunions with their waiting families, and searchlights lit the United service lift that had been moved alongside the high fence holding the crowd at bay—15,000 fans, 20,000, no one knew in the darkness. When Dan Reeves and Pat Bowlen joined Denver mayor Federico Peña and Colorado governor Roy Romer on top of the lift, the crowd surged into pandemonium. They had waited for three hours, some of them, and this, at last, was bliss. Bowlen told them they were the greatest fans in the world, Reeves told them he loved them. Then John Elway stepped to the microphone in the midst of a wild and tumultuous cheer. "Wow!

Wow! Wow!" he shouted into the sea of faces, entranced by the welcome, the crowd screaming with delight in response to his chant. "I'll tell you what," he said when he could finally be heard again, "it was a great win for us today. It not only exemplified our team, but all of Colorado." It was the first time in all the months since I had begun to observe him that he seemed to truly enjoy the fans who so adored him.

When it was Tom Jackson's turn to speak, he was soft-spoken and subdued in contrast to all the shouting. "There was a lot written this past week about my playing this game back at home," he told the quieting crowd. "Well, I just want to tell you that I'm *home* now. *This* is home. *This* is home," he said.

DAILY BREAD

An excerpt from the novella

The sky is the daily bread of the eyes. — Ralph
Waldo Emerson, journal entry, May 25, 1843

T he old showman seemed astonished by the size of the
crowd—fifty thousand Denver citizens, maybe more,
braving the frigid February weather to see this curious symbol of the new century attempt to climb into the sky. Dressed
in high black boots and a fringed leather duster, his long
white hair flowing from beneath his signature broad and
loose-brimmed beaver hat, Bill Cody was arguably the city's
most celebrated resident, surely its most stylish, and he made
no attempt at anonymity that day. It made sense, after all,
that storied Buffalo Bill would be on hand to see this aerial
show of shows.

Organizers of the three-day exposition in Overland Park
had secured a special viewing section for the city's social
elite, but the crowd on the first afternoon was far larger than
had been expected, and the single rope meant to separate

men like Cody and my father—as well as my brother and me—from the larger and less-distinguished populace long since had been trampled, Cody laughing good-naturedly, I remember, as he was jostled by the press of people, wishing out loud that folks were this eager to see *his* show, suggesting that he might have to hire this fool aviator himself.

A wire fence separated those of us in the crowd from the flat dirt strip where the flying machine waited—a bi-winged airplane whose skin was yellow linen, simply a big box kite with a propeller attached, or so it appeared from some distance, the huge crowd careful not to crush the fence and get *too* close to the thing that surely would fall from the sky like a stone if it ever were airborne.

Yet just two weeks before, Frenchman Louis Paul-han—the papers called him "the Birdman"—had flown repeatedly in this same contraption at the Los Angeles Aviation Meet, making his subsequent appearance in Denver the cause of such keen anticipation. Paulhan's Farman biplane, shipped to Denver by boxcar, would leave the ground at 2:00 p.m. on February 1, 1910, the exposition's organizers had announced in thousands of handbills, then head south for sixty miles, where the Birdman would circle lofty Pike's Peak before his return to the city. The idea was outlandish, of course—even people who knew a bit about the nascent science of aviation remained uncertain whether an airplane *could* fly in Denver's insubstantial mile-high air, let alone at twice that altitude, but Paulhan intended to try, or so his promoters maintained.

My brother, whom everyone in the family called Young Roger—as tall as my father already but at least a hundred pounds lighter—craned his neck to see as at last the yellow box began to shudder and to move. Not quite fourteen, and two years Young Roger's junior, I was too short to see above the mass of heads and hats, but Bill Cody offered me the folding stool he'd brought along, and standing precariously on its leather seat, Cody's massive hands around my middle, I could watch as the machine slowly turned toward us, then aimed itself straight down the dirt track.

I could hear its motor throttle up, the propeller spinning so fast it seemed to disappear, and then I and all the citizens of Denver held our breaths because—who knew?—even breathing might disturb the enormous bird as it struggled to claim the sky. Yet there was no striving, no leaping upward like a cat trying to capture a moth. Unlike every bird that ever flew, this machine's wings did not flap, did not cup air and push it away like a swimmer carving a stroke. The Birdman throttled his engine hard, then somehow set it loose, the yellow box lumbering down the track, gaining speed, *racing* across the ground until, unbelievably, the box began to lift into the sky, fifty thousand folks gasping in unison, it seemed, then cheering wildly as Paulhan's airplane cleared the electric lines at the far end of the field, cleared the houses and the leaf-stripped tops of the trees, soaring steadily, gracefully, seeming to shrink as it sailed up and away, the wild crowd believing it now because *there it was* to see, yet it was visible only a minute more before the miraculous machine simply flew away.

How long would it take the Birdman to reach Pike's Peak? Would he freeze to death if he climbed high enough to circle the mountain? When would this heroic man return to Denver and to earth? There were no immediate answers to the flood of questions that suddenly begged to be asked, but because the sight had seemed so impossible, so utterly unreal, half of the fifty thousand surely also asked the single question for which their fellows could offer a firm reply: Did you see? Did you see the Birdman fly away in his yellow box? Could you see it, Son?, Bill Cody asked in my direction.

I saw, I told him. You think he's coming back?

He'll have to if he wants to repeat the stunt tomorrow, my father said.

I wish Mum had come, Young Roger said. But she and Louisa Cody had met for tea instead of joining the mass descension on Overland Park, the two women announcing that they didn't have the stomachs for watching a man die in a fall from the sky.

Tell her she's a fool for missing it, Father said to Young Roger. Tell her she's a silly woman.

I'll bring her with me tomorrow, I offered brightly.

You won't miss school a second day, he assured me instead.

But...she *has* to see it, doesn't she? It's near a miracle, and she'd best see it with her own eyes.

There are plenty of miracles that women pay no heed to. Isn't that so, Bill?

Oh, I'm old enough, smart enough, never to discuss the subject of women, Cody said, his eyes twinkling. They're as mysterious, and *wonderful*, let's say, as that flying machine. Do you suppose I could get him to travel with the show?

Yes, and me and Young Roger along as his assistants, I pleaded.

Absolutely, Young Roger agreed.

Fine, then, said the showman, his white Vandyke framing his broad and beneficent smile. We'll link the last century with the new one, from open wilderness to machines that ride on the wind. But he won't come cheap, that's a certainty. I may have to go hat in hand to see my banker. Cody angled this comment at my father.

Your banker, as it happens, could probably be talked into financing such foolishness, my father told him. Although I can't imagine how these airplanes will ever amount to anything, the masses seem willing to squander their pennies to see them.

I'd pay all I had to go up in one, I vowed.

Oh, you would, would—Father stopped as a sudden rumor rushed through the animated crowd: He's coming back! See! The yellow dot. It's the Birdman, back already!

No one could be certain whether Louis Paulhan had flown to Pike's Peak in the half hour since he had disappeared. There hardly seemed to have been time, yet who knew how fast his machine could soar? Perhaps airplanes gained enormous speed as they climbed into the rarefied mountain air. But what *was* a bright yellow certainty now was the Birdman's triumphant return. His big box kite was heading home, aimed as directly, it seemed, at the mass of fifty thousand as at the flat dirt track beside them. People at the far end of the field even began to try to escape their proximity to the field, afraid that the airplane was intent on them, before at last it was clear that everyone was safe and that the machine would touch down right where it had left the ground, its rubber tires kicking up a quick cloud of dust as they skidded and bounced and then began to roll, the roar from the crowd tumultuous now, Louis Paulhan pulling himself from the cockpit and standing up high to wave, my brother and I dumbstruck with excitement yet buoyant, too, with delight, Bill Cody leaning into our father's ear to shout that yes, there was much to talk about.

It had been the most stupendous sight I'd ever seen, and I ached to think that my mother had missed it, that I might not see it once more tomorrow or the next day or ever again in my life. During dinner that evening, I had been unable to convince my mother to join Young Roger and me to go see the Birdman fly the following day, and neither had I made headway with either parent and my carefully articulated argument that the importance of school paled in comparison with the magic of the modern age. Mother simply was too afraid of what *might* go wrong with the Birdman's flying apparatus, she said. The danger surely was far too great. And she chose not to offer a counterpoint to Father's commandment, expressed again as we sat at the long dining table, that both Young Roger and I would be at Grayland School as usual on the next two afternoons, and nowhere near the yellow machine that waited near the river in lowland Overland Park.

Yet although Young Roger was grudgingly willing to acquiesce to our parents' demands, I simply could not. Ordinarily, I would have obeyed them without much bother, but in this instance they surely were mistaken about what mattered for a fellow's education, so I simply stole away from school at one o'clock on the following afternoon and negotiated the tramway routes that took me to the park. The crowd seemed every bit as big again that day, bigger even, and although the reserved section was better secured this time, I knew I wouldn't be admitted there alone, so I followed a group of boys who had crawled under a sheep-wire fence and had found their own privileged viewing position on the roof of an aging bandstand.

What a spot it was from which to watch the Birdman, a scarlet scarf draped round his neck today, the strap of his leather helmet left unclasped. One of the boys, a wiry little fellow with a thick thatch of curly hair whom his friends called Avi, evidently had seen the flight the day before, but the rest of the pack had not, and as Paulhan pressed himself into the cockpit and began to maneuver the airplane into position, Avi offered an animated account of what we were about to see. And for a second day, the yellow kite sped down the track, again it soared into the sky and a second time it disappeared. As it had the day before, the huge crowd exploded with wonder and delight, and the knot of boys—with me mated to them now—screamed and jumped and nearly brought the bandstand down in our excitement as the

Birdman's miracle unfolded and the airplane flew away, but then Avi bore the sobering news that the craft would not draw near Pike's Peak in the minutes of its absence. They say he turned around right about Sedalia yesterday, Avi announced. Anyway, the airplane would break to bits if he tried to fly as high as the mountain. They say the air has ice up there that would rip it to bitty shreds.

This fellow Avi seemed to be a fountain of information, and I was glad to have encountered him, happy as well as to have joined him and his pals on their perfect perch. I wondered how Avi could know so much about air and aviation, and I paid attention when—just as the Birdman reappeared in the southern sky—Avi announced that one day he would have an airplane himself and become Colorado's own aviator hero. But before I could ask how he planned to set his fine future in motion, Avi had bounded down from the bandstand, the other boys in his pursuit, and they were racing toward the end of the field where Paulhan was about to bring his flying box to a triumphant rest. I longed to follow them again, to see the flying machine up close and maybe see the set of the Birdman's eyes, but I *had* to get home, I knew, and I climbed down—thrilled and downcast in the same instant—pushing my way through thousands of sunny people who were enchanted by what they'd seen. And as I stood on the running board of an overflowing streetcar headed toward home, my face pressed into the head wind it engendered, I imagined myself as an intrepid aviator as well one day.

My brother wasn't home yet, I discovered when I burst into the house; my mother was attending a card party, my father was still at work at the bank on Seventeenth Street, and my secret was safe. But how could I keep it quiet? How could I resist telling them I'd seen the Birdman soar a *second* time and that I'd met a friendly boy bent on being an aviator too? Outside again, I crawled under the back hedge and into Cheesman Park, running now for little reason other than to spill my manic energy, my arms spread wide on the chance that they would lift me off the ground. Buoyant, euphoric, my running a little like flying, I was sure, I raced to the park's edge at Thirteenth Avenue, a horse in harness shying from me as it passed, the buggy's driver shouting something I couldn't hear. But then I did hear a sound I recognized—the churn and rasp and throaty gurgle of my father's Maxwell cabriolet, heading south down Humboldt Street toward home at a strangely early hour. He must have gone to see the Birdman again, I decided as I raced toward the sound—that had to explain why my father was early today—and as I saw the motorcar make its way toward me, I *knew* I could share my secret and I waved in celebration, catching Father's eye, eliciting from him something akin to a smile, stepping out of the Maxwell's path, then ably leaping onto its running board and grabbing hold, my father neither welcoming me aboard nor scowling at the stunt, shouting *hello* at him, shouting *I saw it, too,* in the second before my father swung the motorcar into the drive and I lost my grip in the sweep of the sudden turn, tumbling into the street, a back tire barely missing me as my father braked to a panicked stop and rushed around the rear of the Maxwell to the spot where I lay motionless, bleeding and unconscious from the impact of my head against the curb.

A lthough my head was pounding and everything I saw from the bed was bent and blurry, I recognized my room, my mother close beside me, and there stood Anne-Marie, our family's cook, when at last I stirred at half past six or so. Her face radiant and wet with tears, my mother kissed my cheek and whispered, Good evening, my little man, as she saw me come to life, and I tried to say hello in response but the word stuck in my mouth. Anne-Marie had brought me warm consommé in a cup, but neither could I drink, and my mother caressed my forehead with her delicate fingers and told me not to worry; I would be fine, and only rest was what I needed now.

In the sitting room downstairs, my father and Dr. Galen Locke sat smoking, and the news from Anne-Marie that I had roused was cause as well for brandy. Although I had been unconscious when Locke first examined me, I learned later from my mother that the doctor had been quick to assure his friends that the cut on their son's head was minor, that he would come round and be well as soon as his brain had some time to settle. The brain is a gelatinous substance, Dr. Locke had explained, and a blow like the one the boy took sets it quivering wildly. But as long as the skull isn't fractured, then it's quite safe and cannot be seriously injured.

Just as the doctor had said it would, my brain had stopped trembling by morning and my headache had disappeared, and although I did not see the Birdman fly high into the sky a third miraculous time, my mother's efforts to confine me to my bed failed entirely on the second morning after the accident. I arrived at the breakfast table as if the injury were old news, ready for school but willing—if that was what they thought was best—to stay home another day at my parents' insistence. But it seemed to my father that I was well enough, at least, to be scolded for my stunt, and he informed me that I would spend afternoons in my bedroom for a month, as well as clean the coal bin, if I *ever* did anything similarly idiotic again. When I realized that leaping onto the motorcar was the only crime for which I had to answer—that my father hadn't heard my shouted news of my return to Overland Park, and that my secret still was safe—I was quickly contrite and I assured them that I had learned an important lesson. Young Roger, also ignorant of my secret expedition, nonetheless could sense that my remorse was a trifle over the top, and he advised me that I'd best buy some work gloves because I'd be in the coal bin before the week was out.

For the moment, at least, I avoided further punishment from my father, but two days later my mother bore the brunt of his ready anger when she told him the accident had been his fault as much as mine. What had he been *thinking* when he let me ride the last block home? Our parents had adjourned from the dinner table and had gone up to their suite for the Sunday afternoon respite they called their private time when we heard the shouting begin. It reached a crescendo with the slamming of a bedroom door and our father's loud descent down the stairs and departure from the house, the Maxwell's engine cranking moments later, the house soon quiet again and the two of us returning to the checkerboard that occupied the rest of that snowy February afternoon, our mother coming down at last at six to join us for a bit of supper, the left half of her face red and swollen, an eye already darkening, neither of us daring to inquire whether she was all right because this was a circumstance that our family played out with regularity, Young Roger and I apprehending that our only role was to pretend not to notice anything awry, our mother in turn always rebounding with a kind of lighthearted, if nonetheless injured, ease.

It was the next time my father's temper exploded, the next time my mother felt the sting of his words and his hand, when I was felled by my first spell. The winter night was hushed and frozen two weeks later when Father responded with theatrical outrage as my mother noted that she'd surely need to reset the buttons of his waistcoats if he grew much broader. Although we had seen through the years the regular evidence our mother wore of slaps and punches, neither of us actually had ever seen our father strike her until that night. As my father's curse swelled into a scream and a sudden blow landed against my mother's head, she shrank back protectively against the loveseat where she'd been sitting. Lying on the Persian carpet that framed the sitting area, I suddenly lunged at my father's feet. Flying at him without thinking except—instinctively—to separate him from my mother, I clung to his trousers and tried to tackle him, but instead he spun and seized me by the belt and tossed me aside in a single motion, sending me skidding off the carpet and onto the hardwood floor. I struggled to my feet as my father stormed out of the room, but then collapsed, convulsing, my four limbs flailing wildly, as my mother later described it, my eyes turned back their sockets, my breaths a staccato spasm, my urine pooling on the polished floor.

Reaching me in an instant, terrified, I'm sure, by what in the world was besetting me, Mother tried to quiet me, tried to still my wild movements, but she could not calm me, my arms flailing at her as she attempted to smother the convulsions, my blanched face consumed by what she said was a horrifying kind of absence, Mother shouting to Young Roger to telephone for an ambulance, *quickly!*, my father reappearing in the room as enraged as when he'd left it, offering no assistance and apparently unconcerned, simply marching past the place on the floor where I and my mother lay, her skirts soaked with my pee and her terror total now because I was still in the grip of a thing she couldn't conceive of as my father slammed the foyer door behind him and disappeared into the frigid February night.

The physician who attended to me at St. Luke's Hospital had told my mother—no doubt still beside herself with worry despite the fact that my convulsions at last had ceased—that her son had suffered what he called an epileptic seizure. But two days later, when Dr. Locke returned at my father's request to the house on Humboldt Street to look me over again, he scoffed at the diagnosis.

These young bucks are so quick to spot disease these days, he loudly announced to my parents as they stood in the hallway outside my bedroom. They don't believe they're doing their business unless they pounce on something sinister. Epilepsy, in point of fact, is a congenital disorder, and if this were epilepsy, surely we'd have seen it emerge before age—what did you say?—thirteen? Dr. Locke's diagnosis, on the other hand, had a simpler but rather more delicate explanation, one that had to do with vapors and exuberant energy and the emergence into manhood, and he had asked to speak with my father privately to discuss it in more detail.

For my part, I felt fit and healthy enough again. I had a fresh scar on my forehead, but it would fade, and all I could make of the spell was that it had come and gone and evidently had left me no worse for wear. Yet it did seem odd to me when my father insisted that the two of us walk in Cheesman Park one evening late in the month as a hint of spring blew into the city on a southern breeze.

As we walked the oval pathway, my father was full of unusual talk about procreation and what he called the male's place in the mystery, informing me that healthy living demanded that seeds be sown solely where they were intended, then changing the subject, or so it seemed, to say that it was time I joined him and Young Roger for boxing at Becker's Gymnasium on Saturdays. There's nothing that beats the pugilistic arts, my father maintained, for the channeling of excess energy. He said, too, that he planned to hang a punching bag in the basement, one he and we could use as often as we liked, and I wished I could tell him that yes, it was surely a fine idea for *him* to have something new in the house to hit.

Although boxing didn't hold real appeal for me—especially on those weekend mornings when my father insisted that Young Roger and I spar headlong with each other, the result always that I was beaten and bleeding from the nose by the time my father whistled the fight to a merciful finish—I was game at least, taking punches to the belly and the head without a whimper, sometimes even landing a blow to my brother's jaw that would win my father's nod of approval, Father declaring, Yes, damnit, you're a fighter!, as I flailed away.

But when I had a second spell in March while battling inside the ring, he seemed at once incensed by its onset and unconcerned about my welfare, leaving me unattended as I thrashed and contorted and at last lay splayed on the canvas. I'm not going to have this!, he shouted as I finally lifted myself to an elbow. I won't have you abusing yourself and inciting this business! Your brother doesn't stoop to such filthy stuff, my father scolded, but I didn't know what the stuff was to which he referred, and neither did Young Roger seem to know when I asked him as our father showered.

Just the fits, I guess, Young Roger told me. I guess he thinks you don't have to have them.

Both times, I said, I could feel something peculiar, only for a second, before I blacked out. But I couldn't stop it, because it seemed like it just had to start.

I suffered another spell in Becker's boxing ring before my father announced that I didn't deserve to learn to fight if I was intent on reducing myself to the animal level. You're no better than a stud dog licking his private parts, he snarled, driving away soon thereafter in the Maxwell with only Young Roger in his company, Father suggesting to him that they enjoy a Saturday luncheon at the Brown Palace Hotel, leaving me, woozy and weak and still unsteady on my feet, to find my own way home.

My arrival home alone in the middle of the afternoon—my haggard countenance and the confession that I'd had another fit, which my father hadn't stomached—was enough to spark a new confrontation between Mother and my father when the two Rogers returned, Father leaving in the house in the noisy huff that was his habit when she implored him to consider the possibility that I was injured, asking him to consider why women suffered spells as well if Dr. Locke's theory was right, Father solely contending in response that he wouldn't claim a son who was a weakling or a sissy-boy or a pervert, pushing her away in a fury, sending her tumbling against an armoire when she clutched his lapels and begged him to stay and talk this out with her, Father hissing, It's him or me in this bloody house, before he flew out of the bedroom and she collapsed on their bed and tried to be quiet as she cried, although I'd heard it all.

Two spells in day-short April, three more in the month of May, then I was felled by another fit on the fifth of

June, my brother's sixteenth birthday, the garden crowded with guests, a brass band entertaining them from the gazebo, my father tapping his glass with a dinner knife to draw people's attention, ready to toast his namesake and eldest son just as I fell to the grass. I know that every muscle in my body must have seized, then trembled wildly; I vomited that time, and a friend of my mother who apparently had some experience in these circumstances scooped the stuff out of my mouth before it blocked my breathing. Urine stained my new white trousers, and I'm sure I must have lain on the lawn in a ghastly way that seemed to my father to ridicule our entire family, mocking him most particularly, all he had striven for, everything he ever had provided.

Young Roger told me that I was still convulsing when three waiters carried me inside, followed by Dr. Locke, who evidently made a great show of his willingness to be of service as he departed the garden. And I suppose my father did his best to revive the festivities, gathering the guests' attention again as soon as I was out of sight, assuring them of the certainty that his youngest son would be all right, thanking Dr. Locke, who was absent, then asking Young Roger to come stand beside him, reminding everyone of the reason for their celebration.

His charity had escaped him, however, by the time Father had said farewell to the last of the guests at dusk and climbed the stairway to the second floor where he found Mother seated on my bed, pressing a cold cloth to my forehead. Leave the little bugger alone!, he demanded as he marched into the room. He doesn't deserve one moment of your attention.

The boy deserves neither you nor me nor the home we have provided him. These fits are his foul handiwork and I've had the last of them! It's him or me in this house. Have your pick.

Dear, please, she implored him, going to him, taking his arm. He still has a horrible headache, and I *swear* to you that these aren't his fault. *Please*.

I've never been more embarrassed in my life, he fumed.

It doesn't matter. No one thought the—

It doesn't *matter*? Father was infuriated now. You stupid creature, it matters in every way imaginable! I have a name to protect, a reputation to sustain, and that little shithole does this to me?

He shares your name, she reminded him in the instant before he slapped her, his open hand striking her face hard, sending her reeling to the bed where I was struggling to rise, attempting to stand and defend my mother, lunging at my father before I, too, was hit, my father's hand folded into a fist this time, his fat knuckles finding my jaw and dropping me to the floor like a bantam fighter felled by a heavyweight, Father beating me in retribution for embarrassment, beating me because these fits now seemed to fill our days.

If it came down to me or my father, then I simply would steal away, I decided. I could make a go of it on my own; I was thirteen and a half, almost—and I was clever and could work. I had clothes enough, and there was a little money from my grandparents Hegarty that I had put away. I wasn't certain yet where I would live; maybe I'd be a vagabond, or perhaps I could work for Bill Cody and travel the world with his show; *maybe* I'd follow the Birdman from town to town. I didn't like to imagine my mother without me, the two Rogers her only household companions, but I would talk to my brother and make him swear that he'd defend her forever from our father's blows.

On the Sunday morning after the birthday party and my very public *faux paus*, I told my mother my head still hurt too much for me to go to church, and while my parents and my brother were attending the ten o'clock communion service at the Church of the Ascension—my Catholic parents had become Episcopalians when they married because they would meet and mix with better people, my father had insisted—I packed clothes and shoes, an overcoat, even galoshes and mittens despite the summer weather, my money, and the *Book of Common Prayer* my parents had given me at my confirmation into a tattered suitcase I found in the basement. I brushed my teeth and donned clean clothes and wore my favorite shoes; and I wrote a note that explained my departure, leaving it on my bed: *I am sorry about these fits. I don't know why I'm having them, but I wish I wasn't. Until they are over, I'd best leave you all some peace. I'll be fine, and I'll be in touch when I can. (Young Roger, you can use anything in here that you like.) Your Son, Thomas Dumont.*

Then I headed downtown, intending to walk to save my money, but boarding a streetcar on Colfax Avenue when my case grew too heavy, cognizant of who and what I was leaving but uncertain about my destination, unconcerned about it, in fact, until the moment when I first considered where I would sleep that night. I could get a bed in a rooming house, I realized, but I wasn't sure how much it would cost, and whatever the price, I'd probably better protect my funds, I decided, until I'd found some way to replenish them. And the weather was warm anyway; why not camp down on the river, maybe meet some bindle men, maybe learn how to hop the rails and wander far afield. But then again, perhaps it was a better plan to stay in Denver for a while, a place where I knew the territory and how to get around. I'd fend for myself for the summer, then surely Bill Cody would hire me on in the autumn and I could begin to travel far afield.

I stepped down from the tramway at Curtis Street—a wondrous stretch of blocks I knew well and normally delighted in, its rows of cinemas and theaters familiar to me from dozens of Saturday afternoons spent deep in their welcoming darkness, transfixed by the exotic images that danced on their screens and moved across their stages, their marquees and high facades lit with a million electric lights, or so people said, enough at least to dazzle Thomas Edison when he had come to town. Yet Curtis Street was all but deserted on that Sunday morning, the bright lights darkened and only world-weary sweepers and window-washers out on the littered sidewalks. I read the movie posters for a while—and I reckoned I might even spend a dime to see *Indian Massacre* some rainy day—then I wandered over to Market Street, where I asked a saloonkeeper in an apron who was leaning in the open doorway of his establishment if he had any work a fellow might do for pay.

Not on a Sunday morning with God and the governor watching, I don't, the bartender told him. You old enough to work, are you?

I'm seventeen tomorrow. I'm just a little short, is all, but I'm a good worker.

Where you traveling from? The man pointed to my suitcase.

Well...Kansas mostly. The prairies of Kansas, Sir. Would you know of an inexpensive place where I could board?

You mean cheap or are you looking for free of charge?

Well, Sir, free would be fine for now, I'd say.

Then pick out a doorway, Son. But leave your case in a locker at Union Station or some thief will separate it from you. Spend your pennies on a locker, and you can wash at the station too, then sleep anywhere you like. And come back here when I'm open and I'll buy you your first Denver beer.

I thanked the fellow for his suggestions, and said sure, I'd be back, you bet I would. And although I never returned, it was the saloon man's sage advice that set me on my way. Union Station proved to be the perfect headquarters for a fellow starting out on his own. I could rent a locker for a nickel a day; the toilets were clean and as big as ballrooms and the shoeshines who inhabited them didn't seem to mind frequent visitors, especially if you had them polish your shoes once in every while. The great hall was filled with row after row of high-backed benches that looked like enormous pews, and although the men who worked for the station-master would roust you if they found you, they didn't go on regular patrol and a bench made a fine sort of bed.

The summer nights were cool and the rush and gurgle of the water made camping at the river's edge a pleasure—lots of fellows gathering there, men of all ages and races, most of whom had been born someplace far away and had come to Denver seeking something better. There'd be a bonfire everywhere a group of four or five were camped, and the fire always attracted three or four more solitary fellows like me. Many of them were bindle men who made a habit of sojourning in Denver in the summertime; others were established residents—some for many years—who simply lacked the means to find more formal housing; a few were boys as young as I was, although they appeared to come from very different sorts of families. One boy I liked said he didn't believe he ever had a ma or pa; another fellow's father had been a miner, killed in an explosion, his mother now working the line—as he described her occupation—up in Central City, although he said he hadn't seen her in a couple of years and couldn't be sure where she was spreading her legs these days.

I was one of the few fellows at the river, young or old, who could read and write, and although my skills never made me money, they did garner me a small measure of esteem. Someone would find a discarded newspaper and insist that I read it aloud by the firelight—one foul-smelling fellow who never traveled anywhere, as far as I could tell, always determined to hear the departure schedules of the trains; a man missing a leg below one knee taking curious pleasure in hearing the obituaries, saying aloud that he liked the thought that the fancy people also had to die. On occasion, someone would find or even buy a dime novel, and on those nights at the edge of the Platte, I would seem to some of them to be capable of a kind of magic, reading aloud a tale of high adventure and intrigue, transfixing the fellows with the words I spoke, sometimes begging for sleep when I grew tired and bleary eyed, but always forced to finish the riveting story I had started.

What my comrades offered me in return was their survivors' wisdom, what they'd learned along the way that made the alley life a little easier: how the delivery men returning to the Beatrice Creamery in the afternoons would give away milk that had got too warm; how sometimes, too, you could get good day-work chopping ice at the creamery when the weather was stifling hot; the fact that Morey Mercantile sold thick packing blankets for a buck; the point of view that hat and coat racks and their contents could be considered public property; the way to bust inside a warehouse loading-door when the weather was cold and killing; how a fellow could get drunk on a nickel a day, and smoke for free, and find a girl for fifty cents if she didn't have to be pretty, although I hadn't yet been brave enough to try. Most of all, the men who slept in doorways, under the bridges that spanned the creek, and at the grassy riverside taught me a kind of confident resourcefulness, the sense that all a fellow had to do was put his mind to his immediate predicament, to his daily desires and his needs, the certainty that the only essential difference between one man and another was how fat or slim his wallet was.

My persistent spells did not abate once I was on my own, but neither did they grow more constant. Three weeks, even an entire month might pass before a fit would follow the one that preceded it, but two spells might come back to back during the worst of weeks. Although I still couldn't fathom their cause—except to be sure somehow that Dr. Locke's notion of vapors and energy and insistent desire could not account for them—I had grown able by now to sense when a fit was on its way. My mouth would begin to taste odd, as if were filled with metal, as though I'd been sucking on nickels like they were sunflower seeds. Sometimes, suddenly, my eyes would go haywire and the light would flicker and pulse and dance; rarely, strangely, I'd have the fleeting sense that I was bound to heaven in an airplane, clouds parting to allow my passage and angels waving their welcomes in the instant before the image vanished and the spell commenced.

Always, a spell would leave me utterly spent, my head throbbing unmercifully for hours, for days, my tongue bitten and bleeding oftentimes, my energy entirely drained; and many times it seemed to me that I no longer could think. In the dull and dreary aftermath of a fit, I would lie on my blankets beside the Platte and do no more than listen to the passing water, too groggy to read or talk. When the weather was wet or cold, when an early snow settled on the bustling city, I would find what shelter I could—the basement boiler rooms of hotels, warm and hospitably dark; the grain bins at the breweries, where heaps of hops and barley made agreeable beds; the hard and high-backed benches at the train depot always were an option, and occasionally I would even

land in a bona fide bed that smelled of sweat and perfume
when the matron at a women's hotel where I was scrubbing
floors and cleaning toilets would recognize that I was ill and
insist that I stop and sleep.

I often remembered my mother, and I was aware of how
much I missed her when someone like Tessa Randolph,
whom the fellows called Big Tess, would demand that I strip
out of my hideous clothes and bathe in the brass tub on the
third floor of her brothel, then tuck me between browning
sheets on the bed in the little room that was adjacent to
her own, telling me my work could wait until I felt some
better. I had written my mother twice in the half-year since
I'd walked away from home, knowing she always was the
first to see the mail and assuring her that I was fine and that
my spells hadn't worsened. And although I wasn't certain I
should have, I told her, too, that I was still in Denver—not a
runaway but just a fellow who'd left home sooner than some
boys did—and I wanted her to know that one day when I
was sure she'd be alone, I'd venture out to see her.

I knew my parents had tried hard for a while to find me.
I'd seen flyers pasted to lampposts, in fact, and an old fellow
named Harry with whom I often wiled away evenings down
at the river liked to joke that if he ever were desperate for five
dollars, he would tuck me under his arm and haul me home
to my nursemaid and my mansion, unfolding the tattered
flyer he kept in his coat as proof that he knew one or two of
my secrets. Once, a cop who had caught me coming out of a
window on Wazee Street demanded to know my name and
where I lived, and although a name had come to me readily

enough, I stammered awkwardly about my residence, and the stony cop inquired, You ain't that runaway rich kid, are you?

No, I told him. But I know who you mean, and I saw that kid. He's taller than me by a head and his hair is black as coal. He was poking through the bins in the alley behind the Windsor not an hour ago. I bet he's still there. Surely the cop imagined winning a handsome finder's fee if he were the one who returned the fancy man's son, and his interest in me therefore ended abruptly, the cop simply telling me to stay out of places I didn't belong before he marched off to snare the runaway and the extra pay.

There were times, of course, when I was tempted simply to escort myself back to the house on Humboldt Street, to reclaim my room, my books, my collection of postcards painted with scenes of faraway places, my place at the dinner table. But it was that specific memory that always soured me on the prospect of going home—the four of us at the formal table every evening, my father seldom speaking and his silence always forbidding, his barbs aimed foremost at my mother until the fits commenced, when I became the central object of his wrath. When I pressed myself on sleepless nights to be honest about where I most would like to be, I always could reassure myself that, by damn, Denver, Colorado at large was home enough for now.

THE END OF DAYS

"When we are born, we start to die, and the end begins at the beginning." — Boethius

Their remaining days were nearly countable now: those few women at that February morning's mass. Four gray heads, two shrouded in silk scarves, four faces etched with age and more of living than I could yet imagine. Four names I knew: Mattie, Marge, Helena, Lorraine, though really little else about them except the steadfastness of their presence at that hour before the larger world awoke. The day was Wednesday, Ash Wednesday, the first of forty days of Lenten fasting that commemorated Jesus's solitary season in the wilderness, the forty days of preparation, we were told, that preceded his certain and gruesome death.

The four women came twice to the chancel rail that day: They rose to take communion, of course, but first—and almost silently—they left their pews then knelt near us and the priest dipped his thumb into a pot of ashes and made the mark of a cross on each woman's forehead, and finally on mine as well. Father Cole's vestments shrouded all of him except his ruddy, freckled, many-angled face, and he spoke in little more than a whisper as he touched our several brows:

> Remember, O man, that dust thou art and unto dust shalt thou return. ... Remember, O man, that dust thou art and unto dust shalt thou return ...

Five times I heard the phrase, the soft admonishment, but for a fifteen-year old, it remained bewildering: If we were dust already, then how could we return to that condition? And if the ashes that followed life were identical to living, then why all the fearful fuss? I glimpsed the sooty forehead of each woman Father Cole passed and I tried to gauge from her face whether she was as puzzled as I was. But those four parishioners—kind and observant and caught in their private thoughts—were unimaginably old, I thought, and perhaps they were no longer troubled by such topics. It might be that as life grew very long and the dust of death inevitably approached, answers to those kinds of questions simply emerged somehow, like age spots.

Throughout that day I wore the mark of the cross on my forehead and at school I presumed it was proof that I was part of a mysterious process to which my classmates were surely oblivious: ashes to ashes, dust to dust, a boy's life lived and then no longer lived with a kind of seamless continuity, I tried to convince myself. But the truth was that I was unpersuaded as the anguish of algebra ended the school day, unpersuaded still as I washed the cross away that night, and three decades later I've made only minimal progress in coming to terms with the end of time, in understanding how—or whether—death is allied with the life that it brings to a ruthless close.

Four decades following that February Wednesday, each of the four women is dead; I am far older now than Father Cole was during those years when I served at his side, and for reasons I cannot entirely explain, I am no longer devout. Yet I still look for the clarifying logic, call it the thesis of death, on the aged and infirm faces I encounter. And the simpler question of why death insists on arriving too soon crosses my mind as well when a similarly aging face daily troubles me in the mirror.

This death drew an uncommon obituary, one that was odd not so much because of the sentiments it expressed but because the deceased—a loving mother and stalwart member of her community—was a Tanzanian chimpanzee. "Flo has contributed much to science," animal behaviorist Jane Goodall wrote in the London Sunday Times,

> But this should not be the final word. . . . even if no one had studied the chimpanzees at Gombe, Flo's life, rich and full of vigor and love, would still have had meaning and a significance in the pattern of things.

In the pattern of things, Flo lived and died and nothing more, but none of us can brag of bigger accomplishments, and it is Flo's death and one son's response to it that seem most compelling to me. Observed by Goodall and her colleagues for eleven years, Flo was known for her friendly demeanor and many children, for her ragged ears and bulbous nose and a kind of sexual fervor that would have branded her a floozy had she lived in a culture as constrained as ours. No one knew Flo's age at the end, but she was probably about fifty and it was old age rather than disease that slowed her, then finally spelled her demise.

On an August morning in 1972 one of Goodall's assistants found Flo's body lying face down at the edge of a shallow stream. The scientist herself sat a sorrowful vigil near the body that night, concerned that bush pigs might scavenge it, and she watched as eight-year old Flint was left alone to try to come to terms with his mother's passing. The young male was aware that something was very wrong when Flo would not move; he did not stray far from her body during the night and repeatedly went to it, tugging at his mother's hand as if to draw her out of sleep. By the second day he had grown listless, his eyes vacant, and he would not eat. "Never shall I forget watching," Goodall later described,

> as three days after Flo's death, Flint climbed slowly into a tall tree near the stream. He walked along one of the branches, then stopped and stood motionless, staring down at an empty nest. . . . The nest was one which

he and Flo had shared a short while before
Flo died.

At last Flint's spirits seemed to lift a bit, and he followed an older brother away from the stream and into
the dense forest. Yet once more the loss of his mother
seemed to overwhelm him, and after only a few days of
travel, Flint returned alone. By now Flo's body had been
removed by Goodall and her colleagues, yet this was the
place where Flint wanted to remain and he stayed there
alone for more than a week. He grew increasingly lethargic; he ate nothing. Finally, almost too weak to move,
Flint dragged himself to the exact place at the water's edge
where Flo's life had ended. He curled himself into a ball,
then he, too, died beside the stream.

"For the fate of men and animals is the same," wrote
Solomon, the Preacher, in Ecclesiastes;

> one dies as the other dies; all have one
> breath and the advantage of men over ani-
> mals amounts to nothing; all is uselessness.
> All go to one place; all are from the dust, and
> all return to dust again.

Employing other words, the assiduous Sancho Panza
affirms the same universality of our fates in Cervantes's
Don Quixote:

> Death eats up all things, both the young
> lamb and old sheep; and, I have heard our
> parson say, death values a prince no more
> than a clown; all's fish that comes to his net;
> he throws at all . . .

Dogs, dolphins, chimpanzees grieve for the loss of their fellows, their mates, their mothers. The grief that descends on them, as Flint so sadly demonstrated, can be as profound, as catastrophic, as any human's. Grief is the anguished response of the living to the blanched reality of death—the way in which it robs the earth of individuals whom others depend upon and care about in the manner we tend to call love—and the expression of that loss is elemental to many animals. Yet there is a key distinction between our species and all others: We, unlike the rest, are capable of imagining death, of shaping it into a malleable abstraction, of linking our physical fears with the potential outcome of trouble. We alone can consider death before it consumes us, and—unlike the horse who stands for weeks beside the rotting body of a field-mate—we can understand that the fate of one of us will be the fate of all.

Death belongs to everything that lives: a truth each of us can acknowledge. Yet we are inclined instead to imagine death as an interloper, some nefarious foreigner who remains external, separate, until at last it catches us in its enveloping jaws. "He's no mower that takes a nap at noon-day, but drives on, fair weather or foul, and cuts down the green grass as well as the ripe corn," expounds the portly squire Panza .

> He's neither squeamish nor queesy-stomach'd,
> for he swallows without chewing, and crams
> down all things into his ungracious maw; and
> tho' you can see no belly he has, he has a con-
> founded dropsy, and thirsts after men's lives,
> which he guggles down like mother's milk.

However we conceptualize it—death the internal process that begins at birth, or death the thing that comes from far away when we aren't wary—it is universal in a manner unmatched by any other physical process. Death is everywhere. Death is all the time.

They were big-boned, massively muscled, and a brow ridge jutted outward above their eyes, yet these people labeled Neanderthal had become something other than apes. Although they probably did not possess pliant language, they made use of fire and stone tools and they, too, mourned their dead.

An arching cave called Shanidar cuts into rock that rises above the Zab River, a tributary of the Tigris in far northern Iraq. Today, Kurdish tribespeople live at Shanidar and it is possible that the cave has been continuously populated for 100,000 years. During his excavations at Shanidar in the

1960s, archaeologist Ralph Solecki encountered the remains of a Neanderthal man buried between two boulders at the lip of the enormous overhang. Solecki excavated the skeleton, removed it, and took samples of soil surrounding the spot where it lay. Sometime later, when the soil was examined for pollen content—a procedure that can lend valuable information about the season and climate at the time of a burial—something arresting emerged: Unlike typical soil samples, which include only a few grains of pollen broadcast by the wind, these samples contained enormous numbers of grains of yarrow, yellow groundsel, grape hyacinth, rose mallow, hollyhock, and blue bachelor's button—each of these species still flowering at Shanidar today as summer subsumes the spring.

The pollen grains clearly could only be accounted for if they represented the remains of whole flowers rather than individual grains randomly borne by the breeze. And if blossoming flowers had been intentionally buried with the young man's body, then these people—perhaps still absent abstract speech—were nonetheless capable of ritual and symbolic activity and therefore of complex thought. They, like the Tanzanian chimpanzees, must have understood the void of death and they too surely felt the depression, even despair, brought on by the loss of loved ones. Yet something more was made obvious by the fact that this body was buried amid flowers 60,000 years ago. Not only were the survivors capable of mourning their loss, they surely were aware of death in the manner that is uniquely human. They were beings who must have struggled to make metaphoric sense of it, who responded to death with the consoling symbol we still choose today to remind us of life's beauty and its brevity. "No animal, merely as such, will ever know what it is to die," observed the 18th-century philosopher Jean Jacques Rousseau, "and the knowledge of death, and of its terrors, is one of the first acquisitions made by man." Before speech had fully flowered and as the first tools took rudimentary shape, humans began to think about death. As we continue to do today, they surely asked themselves why death had to happen. They, too, must have wanted to know what followed death, and their fears must have been as potent and futile as ours.

I n a town near my town, twin girls were born eight years ago, the two joined at the chest, sharing a three-chambered heart. Ruthie and Verena were healthy during infancy, but by the time they reached age five their separate pairs of lungs hadn't had room to grow commensurably with their bodies and their single heart had become severely taxed. In an effort to help them survive, their parents moved away from Colorado's high altitude and thin air to a sea-level town in Rhode Island. The girls understood that surgical separation wasn't possible and that their prognosis was poor.

Their mother remembers that the girls' distinct and competing personalities had emerged very early on. But out of profound necessity, they had learned to compromise, she explained, and they understood that their separate lives depended on their shared biology. They knew too that one would probably die while the other still lived, yet that one wouldn't be left alone for long. Seven-year old Ruthie was the first to die, her brain's myriad functions failing while the heart she shared still pumped. "This is the time we're going to be dying," Verena explained to her mother when it became clear to her that Ruthie was gone. Calmly, betraying scant evidence of fear, she asked her mother to go inform her father, who was in another room. She named the several people to whom she wanted flowers sent, then reminded her parents that neither she nor her sister wanted to be buried: Unlike the reality of their living, both wanted to be free in death, she said, not consigned to a slender box.

Throughout human history, contends ethicist Paul Ramsey, cultures that have emphasized, even celebrated, the uniqueness and importance of the individual also have tended to deny or rebel against death. And conversely, in essentially communal societies—their members envisioned as components of a larger whole—death commonly has been perceived as something acceptable, if not necessarily welcome. Throughout human history, Ramsey insists, when the group has been granted more intrinsic value than the individual, the weight of death has been easier to bear, its prospect less frightening, its outcome seldom deemed tragic, and I am reminded of that curious correlation when I consider Verena's response to her sister's death and her anticipation of her own. I'm struck by her immediacy of mind in those moments, by a developing sense of death that was at once candid and accepting, evidencing neither fear nor anger, not clinging in vain to life but neither assuming that life in some form would continue without interruption.

Verena, too, died within the hour, and although their cremated ashes later were commingled, her death and Ruthie's death that day were essentially separate, as distant as mine will be from yours. Their lives had been more intimately allied than we can imagine, and although each girl died alone, their conjoined deaths also were communal, shared, their ends accepted with a kind of wisdom that belied their years.

D eath is simply the deepest sleep: so some small children will tell you. For other youngsters, it is easier to imagine death as a kind of extended vacation, one from which grandparents and departed pets never quite return. Until age five or so, living is the only comprehensible condition and death is therefore life only . . . different. Yet as the very young try to make sense of death in this context of departure, the notion of required travel, undertaken alone and for the long term, can seem more than a little frightening.

Between ages five and ten, death becomes personified, an evolution that is nearly universal, according to psychologist Maria Nagy. Death is now a personality, a character, whether skeleton-man or reaper: "Death comes when somebody dies," one seven-year old explained to Nagy,

> and comes with a scythe, cuts him down and
> takes him away. When death goes away it leaves

footprints behind. When the footprints disappeared it came back and cut down more people. And then they wanted to catch it, and it disappeared.

Unlike the initial stage of awareness, during which physical death is virtually unimaginable, it becomes real yet remote in this second stage. It is definite and it is deplorable, but it only happens to those whom the death-man snatches.

As early as nine or ten, however, a more sober scenario emerges. Death begins to seem inescapable, no matter how you try to out-run it. And it isn't a person anymore so much as a process, something that occurs, in point of fact, because you are alive. "If somebody dies they bury him and he crumbles to dust in the earth . . . the skeleton remains altogether, the way it was. That is why death looks like a skeleton. Death is something that no one can escape." This ten-year old, already a symbolist, understands not only that death descends on everyone but also that most of us require metaphoric means to imagine it—whether we envision skeletons or heavens. Death is the end of corporal life, we already know by the time we're ten.

His job, one he shared sometimes with his brother, was to use a .22 pistol to dispatch each cow to a better place before his father began the messier jobs of beheading, skinning, dressing, and quartering them at their small slaughterhouse in Dolores. My friend Ricky was thirteen when his father suggested it was time for him to play a role in the family business, yet he was already well-versed in what went on there, and for as long as he could remember he had accompanied his father on working trips to farms and ranches, where a cow or hog or sheep was sent from field to freezer during the course of a bloody afternoon.

No particular emotion accompanied Ricky's tasks: The job of killing cows wasn't what you would call fun, but neither was it frightening or repelling. He simply pressed the pistol to the animal's head and pulled the trigger. He would rather be fishing downriver in the hole by Blind Joe's swinging bridge, yet this work was endurable. He spent no time thinking about whether human beings ought to remain carnivorous, nor did he suppose that death was a terribly tangled issue. People died, and they did so under circumstances that sometimes were fraught with complications. The animals at Mountain Packing died as well, but something about their demise seemed inherently simple, and the whole idea of death was one that seemed part and parcel of the world he was getting to know.

Adolescence is a period marked by a burgeoning ability to think abstractly, and a few teenagers, like Ricky was, are able to weave the idea of death rather seamlessly into the fabric of all they observe—at least at those moments when it consciously crosses their minds. In contrast, I remember presuming during those awkward years that the fact that death to me seemed both bewildering and harrowing surely foreshadowed the certainty that I would die before

I made my way to adulthood, before I saw the world or served mankind or did that other thing that lately I yearned very much to do. I was not a confident kind of teenager, and together with my tentative struggle for adulthood came a vexing sense of vulnerability, my realization that socially, materially, physically things weren't always going to go well, and for a few years I actually presumed I was doomed to die soon. I did try my best to bargain away that unfairest of fates, as I recall: I would become a priest and commit my life to service, I professed, if only I could live, if only I could become the adult I so much wanted to be.

Yet for every teenager for whom life seems about to end in tragedy, there are five more who presume they will be forever immune from death. Wrapped inside their own "personal fables," in the terminology of the developmental psychologists, these adolescents believe they will never be harmed by anything. To them, death seems to differ only by degree from the exasperated history teacher who talks tough but who never follows through on his threats. And like the taunts that they aim at that long-suffering instructor, these teens find myriad ways in which similarly to flirt with death, to test it, to expand the heroic stories they tell about themselves in an effort to keep them from growing stale.

Ricky readily could have been this latter kind of kid—he might have flaunted the power of his pistol and insisted that his buddies come watch him blow cows to Kingdom Come. But as far as I knew, Ricky never did try to turn death into entertainment, nor did it seem to worry him in the ways that it regularly terrified me, and the truth is that early in the

1960s he didn't belong with those of us at either sophomoric emotional extreme when it came to the question of dying. Unlike the rest of us, Ricky actually knew a little something about the subject. At the end of every work day, before his dad drove him home then let him have a sip or two of his Schlitz, the two of them—father and son side by side at the steel utility sink—had to wash death off their hands.

I n the myths that survive from the Greeks, the ferryman whose small boat sails the shadowed waters of the River Styx is called Charon. He is old, crotchety, truly bad-tempered at times, yet he is strong and tenacious. The dead must cross the river in his ferry if they are to reach their destination in the underworld, but Charon assesses a fee for the crossing, and although he can be flexible about the amount, he insists in every case that a fare is paid. When Menippus, a philosopher recently deceased, demands free passage across the river, the ferryman inquires, "Didn't you know that you had to bring the fee?"

"I knew," replies the philosopher, "but I didn't have it. What was I to do? Not die?"

By way of offering a solution to the impasse, Menippus suggests that if he really cannot cross to the underworld without the payment, then Charon can bring him back to life instead. Grumbling that such charity would break an even more elemental rule, the ferryman relents and lets Menippus on board, but he complains during the crossing about the philosopher's good humor, asking him if he won't moan and wail a little like the other souls.

The fables that surround Charon and the crossing of the Styx underscore the concept of death as a journey, of course, a voyage one must undertake to pass from this life to the next. But it is the price of the passage, it seems to me, that keeps the story current. At the end of the twentieth century and in my middle age, I'm at ease with the idea that dying does exact its price. Add time to the primal stuff of matter and energy and some sort of transformation becomes a certainty. Among living beings as inclusive as protozoa and college professors, life yields to death and death to decay, rules as unbreakable as Charon's requirements. The evolution into death does cost us dearly in the end, and it's a toll we pay with the tick of days.

Days. The ordered gauge with which we mark our progress, our tarrying through time. Light to dark and dark to light again. Days the events that in my forties I'm learning to relish at last, now that it's likely that more of them lie behind me than wait impatiently ahead. And it's only from this perspective of middle age that death assumes new resonance, a kind of urgent reality it hasn't heretofore included. And it's from this temperate vantage point that many people like me begin to view death anew for the first time since the maudlin turmoil of their adolescence finally settled into the day-to-day we call adulthood.

For some, it is the wondrous birth of children that somehow awakens insistent questions about mortality, but for many of us it isn't until the decline and deaths of parents—our own status as children only truly ending at ages forty-five or fifty-two or sixty— that we can begin to sense viscerally that however long we live, it won't be long enough. Like it or not, we live in our parents' images, and despite the attendant discomfort, we know by middle age that we mirror them in everything from turns of phrase to nagging cholesterol counts. And when our parents prove no different from the masses—dying, in the end, just like ordinary human beings—that dolorous reality doesn't do much at all to boost our own prospects for permanence.

Newly awakened to the inevitability of death, the end of days a subject we now begin to take personally, middle age is a time of regret for some and of renewed resolve for others. Life's limitations and its host of disappointments—those myriad things that might have been—often become the prickling focus. Others in middle age seem actually invigorated by the clangorous ticking of the clock and the realization, even prior to menopause or the certain swelling of the paunch, that they are running out of time. We know dozens of people, each of us, for whom every birthday is a punishment. Yet I want to believe there are as many more for whom this terminal predicament, these fleeting days, are simply the fare the universe extracts for our eventual demise. And what else can we do but pay the price? Not die?

"I think life is a very sad piece of buffoonery," complained playwright Luigi Pirandello. "My art is full of bitter compassion for all those who fool themselves, but this compassion can't help but be succeeded by the ferocious derision of a destiny that condemns man to deception." Throughout his work, Pirandello repeatedly expressed his conviction that each of us lives inside cocoons of false reality, which we painstakingly and constantly spin round ourselves.

In his short play entitled "The Man With the Flower In His Mouth," Pirandello attends to our ready deceptions about growing old and dying. Late at night in a street café in Rome, his title character interrupts a stranded train commuter with whom he is conducting an impassioned conversation as a means of passing time. "Let me finish!" the man with the flower in his mouth insists,

> Wouldn't it be nice, my friend, if death were merely some sort of strange, disgusting insect someone might unexpectedly find on you. You're walking down the street and some passer-by suddenly stops you. Carefully, he extends just two fingers of one hand and he says, 'Excuse me, may I? You, my dear sir, have death on you!' And with those two fingers he plucks it off and flicks it away. That would be wonderful, wouldn't it? But death isn't like some horrible insect. Many of the people you see walking around happily and indifferently may be carrying it on them. No one notices it. And they are calmly and quietly planning what they'll do tomorrow and the day after.

Then, the man gets up and leads the commuter into the light of a nearby street lamp:

> Look, here, here, under the mustache. There, you see that pretty violet nodule? Know what it's called? Ah, such a soft word—softer than caramel—epithelioma, it's called. Pronounce it, you'll feel how soft it is. Epithelioma ... Death you understand? Death passed my way. It planted this flower in my mouth and said to me, "Keep it, my friend, I'll be back in eight or ten months."

As he explains his medical predicament to the commuter, it is the pleading of the man's wife and friends for him to stay home and keep peaceably to his bed while he waits for death to come for him that he finds particularly demeaning. If people could know in similar fashion that a calamity such as an earthquake soon would kill them, would they simply take to their comfortable beds?, he asks. It is an intriguing question, of course, and the curious answer is that, yes, some of them probably would.

By the time many people reach an age at which that most hideous of appellations—senior citizen—can be attached to them, I suspect they bear more in common than they care to acknowledge with the Man With the Flower In His Mouth, not because insidious flowers are necessarily growing in their own corporal nooks and crannies, but because steadily diminishing abilities and the mounting loss of friends surely begin to bring relentlessly home the issue of the amount of time remaining to them. But as Charles Dickens insists in Barnaby Rudge,

> Father Time is not always a hard parent, and, though he tarries for none of his children, he often lays his hand lightly upon those who have used him well; making them old men and women inexorably enough but leaving their hearts and spirits young and in full vigour.

So, old age could be imagined, at any rate, from Dickens's youthful perspective at twenty-nine, and no doubt he did define accurately enough a kind of elderly person for whom "every wrinkle [is] but a notch in the quiet calendar of a well-spent life." Yet for millions of others, the shrinking of life's final season induces not contentment but festering disgust instead, anger pitched not so much against the great unknown or what will be missed in one's absence but specifically against the utter inescapability of physical decline. "The tragedy of old age," understood Oscar Wilde, "is not that one is old, but that one is young." It was not the end of life that Wilde lamented but rather what he saw as the cruel and inexorable transformation of the old into weak, uncertain, incapable characters, as dependent as little children come the close of their days.

When I try to imagine how I will respond if one remote morning I awake and ascertain that I am eighty, it is hard to envision being simply satisfied—as Dickens would have it—with the life that lies in the weedy field of my memory. If I can no longer hike or swim or even sit atop a rusty tractor, if sports and sex and robust activity of every kind are lost to me, I don't suppose I'll find true solace in the fact that I took so much pleasure from them once upon a time. If somehow I succeed in reaching four-score years, I hope I'll feel some gratitude for my survival; with luck, I'll know I've learned a bit with each advancing day, yet I have a suspicion that I will also comprehend very viscerally what Simone de Beauvoir meant when she observed that "It is old age, rather than death, that is to be contrasted with life. Old age is life's parody." If the essence of living is possibility, opportunity, action, then she must be correct: The atrophy and, for some, even the boredom of old age surely offer mocking counterpoints to what has gone before. The elderly necessarily succumb to a state of disquieting inertia, to a point at which living literally lies behind them, and I cannot imagine drawing Dickensian vigor from that declining condition.

But it needs to be said that the old, all of them, are privileged in this curious, if singular respect: At least they have not died young. What we tend to call the injustice of death that comes too quickly—life ending before its lush bouquet of stages and experiences can be collected completely—is a fate from which only the old can be sure they have been entirely spared. It is not an enormous consolation, but it has some substance nonetheless: Collectively, we value survival nearly above all else, and the old—those who lead flourishing lives till the final tick of time as well as those whom Pirandello's character so despises for retreating to their beds—are our truest survivors, people who have lived thirty thousand days and therefore must inevitably pay this concluding price of decline.

Although he had become a pauper and his remarkable body of work was little appreciated when he died at thirty-five, the short life of Wolfgang Amadeus Mozart was as lush with experience and accomplishment as it might have been had he lived for nine decades. But mere longevity does not determine the excellence of a life, of course, and it was Mozart's recognition of his mortality, effected by his failing health, which foremost enriched his living, he was sure. In a 1787 letter to his dying father—whose death preceded his own by only four years—the son tried to persuade the sire that "death, when we come to consider it closely, is the true goal of our existence." That goal included Christian afterlife, as Mozart imagined it, an eternal continuum free from failure or pain or illness, a realm only accessible through dying. "I have formed during the last few years such close relations with this best and truest friend of mankind, that [its] image is not only no longer terrifying to me but is indeed very soothing and consoling! And I thank my God for graciously granting me the opportunity...of learning that death is the key which unlocks the door to our true happiness."

Death is humankind's "truest friend" because it ends the suffering and uncertainty of living and replaces them with the reward of perpetual bliss: It is this view of life as a rutted and difficult road that must be negotiated on the way to paradise that lies at the core of many religious traditions, and there is no surer means of mitigating the fear of dying than to believe that instead of oblivion, one's death will lead to life without end. Yet it is a view that is profoundly simplistic as well, one that not only denies death's reality but also steals from it the meaning it lends to living. If this life is nothing more than a span of temporal trouble that has to be muddled through in order to reach the good life, then our living is reduced to little more than a capricious kind of practice, a waiting game en route to the time when time disappears and true happiness is launched at last.

Even during my early and adolescent years, when religious observance grounded my days and securely marked the seasons, the notion of heaven—or an afterlife of any construction—never held real resonance for me. Assurances about the hereafter seemed even then like elaborate kinds of craving, and decades later I come closer to an alliance with the contention of American essayist and novelist Paul Theroux that "Death is an endless night so awful to contemplate that it can make us love life and value it with such passion that it may be the ultimate cause of all joy and all art." I suspect that death indeed is what imbues life with its richest qualities, that absent the knowledge of death we would be as uncreative as animals. Without death, ethics, aesthetics, and even the longing to love would lack conviction. Life would have little urgency, and questions about how best to live would never demand to be asked.

Yet death itself does not seem to me to be "too awful to contemplate." Surely there is an accessible mid-range between the denial of death grounded in the glib assumption of afterlife and an utter abhorrence of death seated in the suspicion and the breathtaking fear that these immediate days are all we can ever know. During the days that I still live, I want to search that largely uncharted middle ground, to map its complex terrain, to probe whether it is possible to accept and even revere the drab reality of dying cognizant of the prospect that death is the utter end of things. And I want as well to anchor myself to evidence that the process of death actually has much to offer us: a door perhaps...perhaps...but maybe solely an endpoint, one embued with the rich mystery of the universe at its sober terminus, one that not only punctuates the living that precedes it but that also offers it shape and art.

Too young still—or too naive—I can't yet agree with Simone de Beauvoir that old age is the antithesis of living. As I struggle to define this obscurity that is dying, I discover that I can truly grasp only its opposites, what it palpably is not, and solely this seems certain: Death is the opposite of living. Death is the end of days.

Death is not laughing, is not pain. Not a baby's smile nor a rapturous sunset, nor is it snowy blindness. Neither splendid sex nor ceaseless work. Death is not animus—not dancing, not lying still. Death brings an end to growth and to growing old; it stops the beating of hearts and the flashing of synapses in the brain, stops the ceaseless brushing of teeth, stops taxes.

It is not enough, I know, to label death "omega." The end is simply not enough of an answer, not an answer of any sort for people intent on the bliss of eternal life or those determined to return to this life as soaring birds or celebrated ballerinas. Even if you presume that you join nothing more than an unfathomable oblivion at the instant you depart—that you simply cease to be—still there is an insistent desire to better define death in the context of the wondrous living it brings to a close. If death is what lends life its luster and its meaning, then nothing ultimately matters more than dying and our complex anticipation of the moment when it commences. We awkwardly navigate our way to the day of our demise; we move blindly, some of us, and the course for everyone is often obscure, to be sure. Perhaps it isn't possible truly to define the destination, but at least we can scribble maps that help mark the relentless route. We can draw tentative lines on scraps of paper, if little more, watch for hands that wave us in truer directions, listen for the enlivened voices that occasionally say "this way."

There was a time when death seemed indistinguishable from ceremony to me. While I was still a faithful acolyte, I would feel the stirring proof of my importance on those occasions when Father Cole would knock at my classroom door and inform my teacher that I had been excused to assist him at a funeral. I'd jump officiously up from my desk and dart out of the room with an air intended to display my puny prestige, and, especially since those occasions meant being away from school without being sick, it was rare when my attendance at a funeral didn't seem like a piece of luck.

Requiem masses at St. Barnabas's; the more generic sorts of services at the local funeral home, often featuring the "Lord's Prayer" sung by tenors in aging suits; processions to cemeteries led by police cars with flashing lights; graveside rites that sometimes featured foolish-looking men attired in top-hats and aprons—I enjoyed them all, in part, of course, because I seldom had an emotional connection to the departed person, but partly as well because rituals of every kind appealed to me. I enjoyed the ancient liturgies of the church, the tacky pageantry of local parades, and even the overweening pomp and circumstance of high-school graduations, which nowadays make me wince. Yet the several rituals that surrounded death held a particular ceremonial allure and I'm still not sure I entirely understand why. Perhaps it was because there was something secretive, unspoken, hence inherently interesting, about death. Maybe I somehow got the point that the transition being observed was the major event that it turns out it actually is. I do know that even the death of my grandfather—the first time I had to deal with the loss of someone truly close to me—was something I responded to ritually rather than with much latent emotion.

Eighty-years-old when he suddenly collapsed on the kitchen floor of his farmhouse, my maternal grandfather's death was a mournful but far from tragic event. He had not been what you would term religious, yet the Methodist minister who conducted his funeral told everyone in attendance that he was sure he would have liked him had he known him. My grandfather's memory was further demeaned at the small country cemetery near his home when the men in top-hats and aprons took charge and the grand muckety-muck didn't know his lines and had to be prompted continually as the rest of us stood there and ached. When that travesty at last was over, people simply wandered away from the grave, the coffin still suspended above it, the gentlemen in suits from the funeral home making theatrical gestures to usher us on our way.

But my cousins Mark and Matt—teenagers, as I was—lingered a while beside the green carpeting that covered the mound of dirt, and it was Mark's idea that we set things straight as best we could by burying our grandfather ourselves. The mortuary men thought the request was a little unseemly, but they knew us and they acquiesced, and soon our coats and ties were off and the wheels were cranked that lowered the coffin into the hole. A lid had to be fitted on the fiberglass vault that contained the polished wooden box, and then we were free to shovel.

It felt absolutely fitting and fine, of course, to sweat in the mid-day heat, and our ad hoc shoveling ceremony did for the three of us what rituals are meant to do: It marked our grandfather's passing in a way that was meaningful to us. It washed that Masonic effrontery out of our mouths, and it was a way to say a final farewell to a workingman that seemed precisely appropriate.

Years later, my experiences of death are far broader, and my several perspectives are more complex. Death can be messy, even gruesome, I now know. Tragedy is sometimes its attendant and sometimes death is surrounded only by a void. I am no longer drawn to ritual in the way I once was, yet rites of every sort, I'm sure, play constant and critical roles in preparing the dying for their deaths and in providing solace and closure for those the dead leave unguardedly behind.

We were adults by the time my grandmother died, and we shoveled earth this second time in largest part because we had done the same for him—buried only inches away—back when the world was a more innocent place. This time Matt's and Mark's brother Tony was old enough to join us, and I remember that while we worked it seemed appropriate to Tony to regale us with dirty jokes. At the time, it seemed like the worst kind of taste to me, but I said nothing, and I'm glad now that I did not. Laughing and grieving are closer kin than I realized then. Surely there was some sort of necessary ceremony for Tony bound up in his light-heartedness, and now I make no claim to know the right ritual way for anyone to respond to the waylay of death.

Sir Thomas Browne, the seventeenth-century Anglican theologian and physician, offered this concise explanation for why we react so awkwardly both to the deaths that occur in our midst as well as to the plain reality that our own deaths soon will follow: "The long habit of living indisposeth us to dying." Three hundred years later, another physician, this one the essayist Lewis Thomas, noted that nowadays "the habit has become an addiction: we are hooked on living; the tenacity of its grip on us, and ours on it, grows in intensity. We cannot think of giving it up, even when living loses it zest—even when we have lost the zest for zest."

> At the very center of the problem is the naked cold deadness of one's own self, the only reality in nature of which we can have absolute certainty, and it is unmentionable, unthinkable. We may be even less willing to face the issue at first hand than our predecessors because of a secret new hope that maybe it will go away. We like to think, hiding the thought, that with all the marvelous ways in which we seem now to lead nature around by the nose, perhaps we can avoid the central problem if we just become, next year, say, a bit smarter.

The ten leading statistical causes of death in the United States, ranked first to tenth by the Centers for Disease Control and Prevention according to the total number of lives each claims, are these: heart disease, cancer, stroke, lung disease, accidents, influenzas, diabetes, AIDS, suicide, and homicide. Each of us possesses close acquaintance with these maladies—they intricately lace our lives; they are our common currency. Yet despite the constant company we keep, we still cannot prevent their occurrences, nor are we very adept at accepting their obdurate outcomes. Four hundred years ago, although Browne knew next to nothing about the biological mechanisms that induce these or any other species of dying, he nonetheless grasped something elemental about the stubbornness of living, a drive to survive that always will be with us.

Coded into the genes of every living entity is a wish, a desire, a longing to live. We live out of habit because something in our physical construction utterly compels us to preserve this animated condition as best we can. As humans, conscious of our lives, this is our unique and acute conundrum: Death is the endpoint we move toward each moment, yet it is a direction we inherently fear, a destiny toward which we are utterly indisposed.

"I n horror of death, I took to the mountains; again and again I meditated on the uncertainty of the hour of death," wrote Milarepa, the Tibetan Buddhist poet and saint who lived in the twelfth century. As a young man, Milarepa had been a sorcerer and had induced the deaths of many foes with his potent black magic. Yet it was the terrible fear of his own death that at last set in motion his journey toward enlightenment, and along the way he encountered a scrap of insight that did much to quell his constant anxiety: "This thing called 'corpse' we dread so much is living with us here and now," he began to understand.

This is the question I've carried with me like an acolyte's cross on a satin ribbon since the days when I first became acquainted with funereal affairs if not, in fact, with death itself: Does our inability to grow comfortable with this thing called corpse already dying inside us rob us of a means of enriching our private and public humanity and of more fully living our lives? Or does death so completely crush and counter life that the only affirmative and sane and sustaining response is to turn away from it, to deny it fundamentally?

It is a question that comes back to me on a flood tide when I look at a haunting photograph published in the San Francisco Chronicle—a group portrait of the 122 members of the San Francisco Gay Men's Chorus. Standing on six rows of risers that sweep up from a foreground grand piano, almost all of the men are dressed in black tuxedos, their faces unseen, their backs turned toward the camera. Only seven men, dressed in white dinner jackets, look forward. They are the sole members of the original chorus who have survived since 1989. The stark whiteness of their jackets and starched shirts is all that makes them visible in the midst of the massed black coats that symbolize the 115 chorus members who have been stricken and killed by AIDS.

We live in the midst of plague years, of course, and it seems unimaginable that these singers and others for whom this scourge is most terribly immediate have literally turned their backs on the subject of death in ways akin to the daily denial practiced by the rest of us. Certainly those seven survivors know death's grim terrain all too intimately, and as I look at the photograph I want to press my question to them. I want to know whether this by now ubiquitous disease and its fateful outcome have valuably instructed them about the end of days. I want to ask them: Are any of us capable of acquainting ourselves with the realities of death in ways that manifestly can assist us with our living? Or should we shout that we will not draw near to the ugly mystery of death, that we will live instead, at least for this moment and perhaps for the next? I want to know whether it makes some sense to them to think that all of us are dust—and that their brother choristers have turned to dust again.

THE URGENT TELLING OF A TALE

An excerpt from OUT OF SILENCE

"A nd then there was the bear," my maternal grandmother would remember, "but first you need to
know about the dogs." In fact, we already knew about the
dogs because we had heard this tale before— many times and
each time to our delight—but we would beg to hear it again,
of course, and so she would commence:

> Our dog, Bill, and a dog called John Ross,
> the herder's dog, just fought continually. They
> couldn't see each other without a fight. I don't
> know what was the matter, but that was the
> way they were. Anyway, one time we went
> up to sheep camp in the afternoon. Jim, the
> herder, was up the side of the mountain with
> the sheep, and Dad went on up. The sun was
> hot, so I went into Jim's tent because the flaps
> were up. I sat on his bed and started to read
> some old magazine he had lying around there.
> I didn't want to follow Dad up; the altitude

always gave me a headache. I didn't think of it until afterwards, but both dogs came in and lay down at my feet and never said a word to each other. They got just as close as they could get to me and put their heads at my feet, and I just went on reading. After an hour or so, I heard a little noise, and I looked up. There was old Jim with his eyes just bulging, his hands out like claws, coming right at me. He said, "My gun, my gun, my gun!" I didn't know what to think. I was so startled I couldn't think anything, but I'll never forget the look on his face. Then I thought maybe he was coming for me! I thought he might have gone mad. ell, Dad was right behind him, as it turned out, and right behind them, six feet behind the tent, was a *bear,* sound asleep. He'd been there in the sun all afternoon. And the dogs knew it, and that's why they were so afraid and came in quietly for protection from *me.* Imagine! When Jim rushed back out with his gun, that sleepy old bear got up and then just sauntered off across the meadow and up the rocks. I sure found out that day how much protection Bill and John Ross were, didn't I?

Yes, we invariably would agree, those dogs were fraidy-cats. But now—and since the subject was dogs—we wanted to hear once more about the mutt named Tip who loved to ride atop the high-stacked hay wagon, as proud as any king; and then too, there was the famous cat to be reminded of, the one she and her sister once had given fifteen names, the catalog of those names still clear as summer mornings in her memory.

The setting for these stories invariably was my grandmother's small sitting room inside the farmhouse where she had lived since her wedding day—pastures and lush hay fields spreading away from its windows toward the distant mountains. The tales she told from her rocking chair were her gifts to us, we knew, and each of her near two dozen grandchildren—then great-grandchildren whose numbers slowly but similarly grew large—understood that there was something wonderful in her words, some kind of magic in the soft and high-pitched melodies of her speech. Yet I think I realized only recently—several years now after her death—that it wasn't dogs or cats or bears that brought her stories to life; it wasn't how she had helped her father manage their tiny post office when she was a girl grown up beyond her years, or how my grandfather had loved to tease her when they were young and still childless and very much in love, that gave her stories substance. Rather, it was in the simple *telling* of her tales that those times and silly creatures and now-mythic events took on their meaning and assumed their special worth. We didn't long to live in those olden days she described; in fact, I think we tacitly understood that it was far richer, surely, just to hear her lilting recollections of how life once had been.

The creating and the witnessing of narratives are as essential to us as sleep. Stories in their many guises are as base and wonderful as sex, as delicious and irresistible as a cheeseburger ordered with everything. We tell our stories over countless cups of coffee in all the corners of the Earth; we unravel them on television in the minutes between commercials for detergent and disposable diapers. We call our stories the news; they commence as jokes or testimony offered under oath or this-crazy-thing-that-happened-yesterday, and sometimes we archly label them as literature. We project stories onto movie screens, and we print them on the pages of books, and we simply cannot help but do so.

"What would we talk about, sitting around the fire at night, if we didn't have language?" Melvin Konner asks in *The Tangled Wing*, remembering the rhetorical way in which his Brooklyn College mentor Dorothy Hammond would respond to the issue of the origin of language. We had to create language in order to shoot the fireside breeze, she surmised, only a little facetiously, and Konner can't help but agree with her. Among language's many tasks, it is the vehicle with which we tell our tales, and they—those tales in their simplicity and all their wonder—occupy the very heart of what it means to be human. Every story, even every sentence, Konner writes, "creates in the mind of the speaker as well as the hearer not merely a picture but a realm of intricate mental events encompassing all five sense modalities. Say what you will about nonhuman creatures—their admirable capacities, their behavior, their consciousness—there is not a thing like it in the whole of the animal world." We are the storytelling species, *Homo once-upon-a-tempus,* our brains built for seeking out relationships among things, for creating cerebral sorts of order, and for sensing the rudiments of narrative structure: how it was in the beginning, the middle, and at the end.

M edical investigation into the brain's role in human speech and language has been under way for little more than a century, spurred initially by a bold but largely unsubstantiated paper presented by French physician Ernest Auburtin to the Society of Anthropology in Paris in 1861. In speaking before his skeptical colleagues, Auburtin explained that damage to the frontal lobe of the brain of a young man under his care had resulted in the impairment of the patient's speech, from which slender evidence Auburtin was willing to assert that language function must be localized there—an idea that ran sharply counter to the then-prevailing notion that the brain did little more than energize the other organs of the body, playing an important but far from central role in their many functions.

Among those who listened to Auburtin that day was Paul Broca, the secretary of the society and a surgeon with a special interest in the brain. Intrigued by what he had heard, Broca invited Auburtin to visit one of his own patients, a mature man who was speechless and whose right arm and leg were chronically weak. As it happened, the patient died the day after their visit, and at the autopsy Broca discovered a lesion on the left frontal lobe of the patient's brain. Soon thereafter, Broca's autopsy on a similar speechless patient showed damage to much the same area of the left frontal lobe. When he later published his findings from these and other cases, Broca pointed out that these lesions of what later would become known as "Broca's convolution" or "Broca's area" seemed to affect only the articulation of speech. The comprehension of speech, and sometimes even the ability to write, tended to remain intact. Most patients still could make sounds, and with much effort some could produce a few intelligible words.

During the decade that followed, interested scientists and physicians argued with some vehemence whether the total of eight cases Broca had reported in which similar brain lesions resulted in similar aphasia (the loss or dysfunction of speech) were proof that there was a language "center" in the brain. Then, in 1874, a German medical student named Karl Wernicke complicated the question by demonstrating that damage to an area of the left temporal and parietal lobes of the cerebral cortex—damage that spared Broca's area, which lies above and farther forward—often resulted in a very different kind of speech loss. Unlike patients with Broca's area lesions, who could comprehend normally, patients with lesions in the region that now took on Wernicke's name tended to have great difficulty understanding what was said to them. And in contrast to the slow, frustrating efforts to speak that were common with Broca's aphasics, Wernicke's patients spoke smooth, rapid, even grammatical *nonsense.* Did these new findings mean that perhaps there were two language centers in the brain, one responsible for the production of speech, the other for the conveyance of meaning? Were these merely two of many centers? Or, in fact, was language so central—not only to speech but also to consciousness, cognition, and memory—that components of language function surely had to be located throughout the healthy brain?

In our time, these same questions—still unanswered satisfactorily—tend to be addressed in several, sometimes contradictory, ways, and the views of an American linguist by now have made as much impact on the debate as did those of the Europeans who began it. It was in 1957 that a young professor at the Massachusetts Institute of Technology published *Syntactic Structures,* a book that encompassed his life's work to that point, and an occasion of such import among the small and sometimes pettifogging fraternity of scientists of language that it became known simply as "The Event." Among the new and disputatious ideas espoused in that book by Noam Chomsky—perhaps the only linguist in the world whose name has become widely known outside his discipline's bounds—was the notion that all humans possess something he labeled a "language organ." Little interested in neuroanatomy, Chomsky made no attempt to specify this organ's location within the brain—there would be no Chomskian equivalent of Broca's or Wernicke's area. He was content simply to assert that there are "deep structures" within each human brain that are predisposed to the acquisition, even the invention, of language. In Chomsky's view, in fact, language's locus isn't in the throat or the left cerebral cortex so much as it is in the genes. And it is syntax, the set of "rules" that makes it possible to turn linguistic symbols into meaning, that our genes provide us. As Chomsky recently explained to documentary filmmaker Gene Searchinger,

> I'm enough of a materialist to think that language is in the brain. If you cut off someone's foot, he can still speak. In fact, it is useful to think of language as an organ of the mind. The brain is like every other system in the biological world: it has specialized structures with specialized functions, and language is one of these. But did we invent language because we were sentient? No more than we invented our circulatory system. What seems to be true about language is that its basic design is in the genes. The genes determine the structure and design of language.

In *Syntactic Structures,* Chomsky finds strong evidence for this genetic foundation: observing that every language's complex syntactic system can be reduced to a core group of rules and principles, which, curiously, it shares with *every other* language, he contends that languages aren't merely similar, one with any other; structurally, *syntactically,* they are identical—Japanese with Spanish, Navajo with Norwegian. And it seems most improbable to him that all languages might share their syntactic structures because they derive from a common ancestor—some protolanguage from some very long ago time. If that were the case, those earliest speakers of something that gave rise to language would have had to have created linguistic rules and patterns of astonishing sophistication for them to have survived unchanged till now. And that possibility, says Chomsky, is far less likely than what he instead sees as a certainty: our genes design us for language in the same way that they predispose us to walk.

But if Chomsky is correct—and an entire school of linguists known as "behaviorists," "environmentalists," "empiricists," or simply as "anti-Chomskians," are convinced that he is not, arguing that their colleague chooses to ignore ample and overwhelming evidence that children who grow up in bizarre kinds of isolation *do not* acquire language in the same way that they *do* discover how to walk—this question remains: Where and precisely how does the brain initiate and facilitate language? Put another way, what have our genes built into our brains that predisposes them to the luster and the utility of language?

A century and three decades after Auburtin, those queries still irritate and challenge scholars in disciplines that range from literature and linguistics to neurophysiology and molecular biology, who collectively are making important inroads into a basic understanding of how our three-pound brains perform this most complex of feats. Although their findings can't as yet, and indeed may never, prove or disprove Chomsky's genetic structures theory, they do point to the probability that the brain has *many* essential language centers— Broca's and Wernicke's areas important among them but far from the whole astonishing show.

Yet if language is located diffusely throughout the brain, contend several scientists who champion the Chomskian perspective, then surely the complex and capable brain should normally compensate when language areas are damaged, effectively relocating and relearning lost functions, which in fact is not the case. If language is *not* site-specific, they ask, why do minute brain lesions often wreak such havoc? And conversely, why do some seriously damaged or compromised brains remain adept at language?

Neil Smith, a linguist at University College, London, points to a twenty-nine-year-old man named Christopher in that regard. Socially inept, the kind of person who once would have been called "simple," Christopher cannot care for himself, cannot discuss abstract ideas or draw basic geometric shapes, his IQ having been scored as low as 65; yet Christopher speaks sixteen languages and can translate them effortlessly. His brain is abnormal, subnormal in most respects, Smith says, but his language abilities are unaffected, and indeed they are advanced beyond what most of us can imagine. Doesn't Christopher's case strongly suggest the presence of a discrete language organ, a part of the brain where language resides independent of other brain systems and functions?

No, says University of Washington neurosurgeon George Ojemann, whose "mapping" of neural circuits with the use of electrodes in the brains of patients undergoing surgery convinces him that not only is language seated in many areas of the brain—often including the *right* hemisphere—but that its location is highly individualized, as unique to each of us, perhaps, as our fingerprints. Publishing his findings in the *Journal of Neuroscience,* Ojemann argues that, yes, Broca's and Wernicke's areas are important language-producing and -processing centers for most people, but so are several additional sites on the temporal and parietal lobes of the left cerebral hemisphere, each one comprised of a dense cluster of nerve cells about the size of a grape, each governing a different aspect of language function—from verb recall to reading—each interconnected with the others. Many people also have at least *some* aspect of language function located in their right hemispheres, he contends. Curiously, men tend to have more of the "essential language areas" located in their left parietal lobes than do women. Equally intriguing, native languages tend to be compactly sited and organized, while second and multiple languages often are scattered diffusely, seemingly as if nerve cells devoted to their various functions must seek out available space in mature, language-barraged brains—a convincing counterpoint to the notion of one or two language sites or a single language organ.

But could both contentions be, in part at least, correct? Do we actually possess an integrated "language organ" whose components are located in many individualized sites? At the University of Iowa, researchers Antonio and Hannah Damasio believe the answer is a qualified perhaps, and their complex "convergence zone" theory has won plaudits as well as serious interest from both the Chomskian and the anti-Chomskian camps. The Damasios agree with Dr. Ojemann that the brain does indeed possess multiple language-processing sites, but they disagree that the entirety of any single language function—comprehension of spoken words, for example—can be located in any single area. Rather, those areas whose importance Ojemann has demonstrated with electric probes are "zones" in which information from several disparate sites is coalesced, mediated, and made sense of—neural data converging there in language-encoding activities such as speaking, as well as in the decoding processes involved, say, in listening to a story about a sleeping bear. This is how Antonio Damasio explained the concept to the *New York Times:*

> When I ask you to think about a cup, you do not go into a filing cabinet in your brain and come up with a ready-made picture of a cup. Instead, you compose an internal image of a cup drawn from its features. The cup is part of a cone, white, crushable, three inches high and can be manipulated. In reactivating the concept of this cup, you draw on distant clusters of neurons that separately store knowledge of cones, the color white, crushable objects, and manipulated objects. Those clusters are activated simultaneously by feedback firing from a convergence zone. You can attend to the revival of those components in your mind's eye and from an internal image of the whole object.

That same process is true of words. When I ask you to tell me what the object is, you do not go into a filing cabinet where the word "cup" is stored. Rather, you use a convergence zone for the word "cup" by activating distant clusters of neurons that store the phonemes c and *u* and p. You can perceive their momentary revival in your mind's ear or allow them to activate the motor system and vocalize the word "cup."

Yet if this convergence zone theory does indeed go some distance toward explaining the brain's basic language-processing system— and similar sorts of zones seem likely to be central to cognition and memory as well—how is it that widely distributed groups of neurons are able to fire simultaneously as required? Antonio Damasio believes that the convergence zones themselves are able to stimulate the disparate clusters, but he acknowledges that the actual initiating mechanism remains mysterious. But however the process commences, it does seem probable now that language convergence zones act as third-party mediators between words and concepts, between concepts and words. And from that perspective, it is the choate cerebral cortex, if not the brain in its entirety, that acts as a language organ—its convergence zones drawing data together, somehow sifting them, making momentary blends and blindingly quick interconnections, then issuing the fresh impulses that result in comprehension, in symbols scribbled onto paper or pecked onto a keyboard, in the uttering of a statement, the urgent telling of a tale.

L ike Ian, like Ian's long-suffering, caring, sometimes defiant mother, I was young in empty country. I too grew up in a kind of careworn pocket of Colorado that was scattered with cattle and sheep. Claudia and I and Carol (the youngest of the three of us, a mother as well now, and—doesn't it seem impossible?—escorting her older siblings into middle age) were born at mid-century to parents whose parents had seen a century turn, who long ago had ridden in horse-drawn wagons out to high, dry government land that was bare but for sagebrush, land they would "prove up" in time into pastures and crop-striped fields. The Martins to whom I'm inextricably attached long ago had emigrated from France across an ocean to Arkansas before a few of their descendants similarly struck out at the beginning of the twentieth century for far southwestern Colorado, where (it's hard from my perspective to imagine) farming conditions were storied to be better. The Rutherfords, my mother's family, came to Colorado nearly a hundred years ago as well, abandoning Red River lowland country that lay across the Arkansas border in Texas.

Like the Rutherfords, the Drummonds—Ian's father's clan— once were Borders Scots, and like the Martins, they too eventually wound their way to Arkansas. But unlike the others, the Drummonds then were home, anchoring themselves to the South over subsequent generations, Boyce growing up beside the wide Ouachita River in the grandly titled town of Arkadelphia in the years that followed World War II, his soft and lilting accent still a strong reminder of that sweltry southern place, those years when he was Ian's age.

My sister Claudia was named for my father, and of the three of us siblings, she is the one who most resembles him. She has his dark hair, his deep-set bright blue eyes, and in her face, like his, there is an ineffable sort of reference still to the villages and vegetable farms of Brittany despite his family's many generations on this continent. She shares my father's self-assurance and sometimes his stubborn resolve. Growing up in a dusty, backwater western town in the fifties and turbulent sixties, Claudia and her contemporaries in little Cortez missed much of the social and political turmoil that racked the nation in those days. She was a majorette in the marching band and salutatorian of her high school graduating class, and it wasn't until she spent two years in a remote corner of Costa Rica following college that she underwent the kind of sea change that marks—and makes—so many people whose formative years unfold in the midst of societal or cultural storm.

Claudia met Boyce in Gainesville, Florida, in the middle seventies. Both were married to other people, and among the illicit passions that bound them to each other was the promise of children; both were nurturers, it was obvious, and both were sure that it was within the context of parenthood that they wanted to spend their ensuing years. They married soon after the offer of a teaching position in the biology department at Illinois State University led Boyce to the Middle West, and before long Claudia was pregnant. Their first son, given the name Gareth in the first moments of a kind of anguish and overwhelming sorrow that I can only imagine, died as he was born.

Sarah, born healthy and vivacious and as blond as her father, followed in a year; and in only twenty-two more months, the similarly hearty, happy, likewise towheaded Ian Drummond came along, and the family seemed complete—years of tumult, pain, and disruption now behind them, it seemed. But when an offer arrived in 1984 for Boyce to direct a fledgling field station and research center on the rocky western shoulder of Pike's Peak, they could not help but give it serious consideration. It would be an opportunity for Claudia to return to Colorado, one that only the most callous native sons and daughters can turn away from; and the field station was in a setting rich with butterflies, which Boyce, a lepidopterist, found irresistible. So, they uprooted themselves again, Sarah subsequently growing up amid deep snow and the drama of summer thunderstorms, many miles from schools and playmates, Ian gamely learning to walk on the ruddy pea-gravel that sufficed for soil beneath giant ponderosas.

Claudia was teaching part-time in the nearby town of Woodland Park—working with gifted children, which by now has become her ironic specialty—when Ian began to grow strange, when he went mute, and terror overtook him. And surely that scholastic commitment, those other children for whom she was also responsible, kept her bafflement, her mounting grief, and her anger from completely consuming her as she tended to Ian's daily tantrums and did her best to protect the necessary precision of his schedule. She poured herself into her son with a thoroughly blended mix of motherly devotion and academic obsession; she vowed, despite the unique household in which her daughter lived, that Sarah would grow up feeling secure and entirely loved. Occasionally, she would recoil sharply against the well-meaning but less than sensitive people, like me, who tried to remind her that this was not the end of the world—because, dammit, it *was* the end of what the world might have offered Ian—and sometimes she simply would slump into a chair late in the evening after at last both children were asleep, pressing a cup of tea to her cheek and laughing or crying with some real release, wondering what else could come calamitously her way.

Sarah, a shy and delicate little girl who was quite verbal and clearly very bright—and who, I think, might have seemed achingly oversensitive in even the most ordinary household—had to contend now not merely with a younger brother who stole her parents' attention but with a sibling who virtually never acknowledged her, yet around whom every family activity and decision necessarily was centered, with a brother who seemed to be in incessant agony, and with parents who often must have seemed terribly distracted, if not utterly spent and unavailable. Instead of acting out in response to her plight, instead of deciding—as you can imagine she might have—to become as difficult as her brother was, Sarah retreated into fantasy. She listened voraciously to stories and her appetite for tales of elves and sprites and princesses seemed nearly boundless. She would become, quite completely, the characters in the stories she heard and saw, the characters in the stories she too began to tell—insisting that her bedroom was a forest or a fairyland or an enchanted castle, insisting that her name was Guinevere or Maid Marian or, more mundanely, Rainbow Brite—and her parents have reminded me that it was with the rich reality of narrative that Ian's sister Sarah somehow coped.

The relentless daily demands of the field station offered Boyce a commensurate if far less Active avenue of escape. On de facto twenty-four-hour call, he had to play the roles of scientist and registrar, planner and proctor, counselor and plumber, and his own ongoing research also took him on occasion to Central or South America. The distractions that riddled his days kept him at a kind of emotional remove from his son's autistic chaos early on, although Ian specifically demanded Boyce by his side several times each morning and night. Boyce's ready sense of humor and soft-spoken southern countenance—as well as his work—seemed to buffer, for a time at least, the otherwise harsh reality; and it was Boyce who once funneled his amalgam of reactions to his family's complex circumstances into this rhyming verse:

Wordless now, a troubled mute
It doesn't fit, he seems astute
Across his face expressions spread
But from his lips no word is said
Bizarre behavior, ritualistic
Yet loving, tactile—a rare statistic
Just past two, a boy so strong
But behind blue eyes, something's wrong
Autistic-like, schizophrenic?
More exams, another clinic?

Parades of doctors, questionnaires
Endless questions, ours and theirs
Answers scarce and unconvincing
Understanding slow commencing
The future vague, a vast unknown
Uncertain growth for the seed we've sown

Although it must have seemed at times as if the chaotic visits to the clinics wouldn't end, they necessarily slowed, then stopped, before many months elapsed because there was little more that physicians could tell them, no medical treatment they could offer Ian except to recommend—a few of them—that he be admitted to an institutional behavior-modification program, the tough-minded, traditional sort that blithely utilize canvas straitjackets, Tabasco sauce in screaming mouths, and similar kinds of aversion therapy in an effort to inhibit unacceptable behavior.

In a follow-up to Ian's catastrophic initial visit to Denver's Children's Hospital, an EEG had been performed in those final frigid days of 1985—but this time with the otherwise terrified patient under sedation. The results of the electrical brain wave test were read as entirely normal, and neither had a subsequent CAT scan of his brain evidenced any abnormalities. An amino acid test was normal; a white blood cell screen was normal; tests of mucopolysaccharides, muscle tissue, organic acids, and chromosomes all were normal: very quickly, a variety of known and sometimes identifiable causes of autistic symptoms had been ruled out, and as the doctors explained to Ian's parents, those results were not surprising. Only ten percent of all reported cases of autism as yet can be linked to organic abnormalities. Neither Claudia nor Boyce had asked that January whether a DPT immunization nine months earlier might have set Ian's symptoms in insidious motion; despite their efforts to find *some* explanation for their son's dramatic transformation, that connection remained elusive, as unimaginable still as if his cutting teeth might have been the culprit.

Although she could offer little in the way of optimism, pediatrician Pamela McBogg had prescribed chloral hydrate to help Ian sleep. She had suggested that his parents experiment with his diet—to the degree that this finicky noneater would allow—to investigate whether food allergies might be exacerbating his symptoms; and although studies of vitamin therapies for the treatment of children with autism had shown inconclusive results, the doctor had averred that daily megadoses of the brain-stimulating B complex would be worth a trial. And instead of referring Claudia and Boyce to the kind of behavior-modification program that already was anathema to them, Dr. McBogg had suggested that Ian be evaluated by the staff at the University of Colorado's JFK Speech and Language Center, where, she assured them, they would encounter attitudes kindred to their own, and where they would receive relevant assistance in developing an intensive home intervention strategy, the kind of relentless, highly structured, and emotionally supportive socializing and schooling program that *might*—very slowly, surely laboriously—reacquaint and then reconnect Ian with the world.

Among the many health professionals who by now had met Ian, JFK Center director Sally Rogers and her staff were perhaps the first to express an immediate kind of attraction to him, declaring how handsome he was, exhibiting their fascination with his rituals and repetitions, and praising his several special skills, and they seemed not at all bothered by the fact that he shrieked in utter terror of them. They knew children with autistic behaviors well, to be sure, and they *liked* them, and Ian's parents understandably were drawn to these people who realized—as they did, of course—that there was much to like and to love in this little boy for whom almost all of living seemed-so traumatic. "Ian is a 34-month tall, husky, attractive towhead with markedly deviant behavior," Sally Rogers straightforwardly began the lengthy write-up of the staff's assessment:

> He demonstrated catastrophic reactions, with crying, screaming, and agitated motor outbursts, to new situations and new people, which did not diminish over the three days of his evaluation. . . . Ian appears to demonstrate developmental delays in all areas. There is no evidence of symbolic play or symbolic thought processes occurring either in his play or in the descriptions of his behavior that his parents provided. He does appear to have mastered some sensorimotor skills, but there is no evidence yet of pre-operational thought. Thus, his cognitive development appears to be in the

12-24 month range, with object permanence skills at the upper end of it and symbolic, social, and language development at the lower end of that range. . . . Prognosis for children with autism is never optimistic, but autistic children vary considerably in the level of functioning which they ultimately achieve. Ian's responses to the intensive interventions which his parents provide in the next year or so will provide some indication of where in the range of abilities of autistic children Ian will fall.

And with the center staff's periodic support, as well as the help of others with some insight or expertise in autism who were scattered around the region—and with the daily devotion of Carla Crittendon, a recent college graduate in special education whom Boyce and Claudia had hired and housed at the research station for ten months, taking on Ian as a kind of gritty, postgraduate introduction to her difficult field—they did intensively intervene, spurred by the fear, as they did so, of what might befall him if they did not. They demanded much of Ian every day for the next thousand days, challenging his intellect and ever expanding his repertoire, encouraging him—carefully, cautiously—to reach outside himself, yet deferring as well to his singular wants, his ritual needs, his horrible fears, his parents each day desperately seeking meaning in his behavior, trying to understand who he was and why he acted as he did.

One good day often was followed by three days thick with chaos; a mood that had seemed fine in the busy morning might well explode in the otherwise languid afternoon. Without any means of understanding why, one stranger would be welcome—even in Ian's bedroom—while another, perhaps even someone he had known, couldn't enter the house without his awful objection. Overseeing Ian's daily schedule often seemed like one part parenthood to two parts rescue mission, a task for tightrope walkers as much as puzzled teachers—the meticulous journals Boyce, Claudia, and Carla kept during that time reflecting each day's uncertainties, the giddy gains, the losses. This is Carla's entry for June 11, 1987:

Bad day.

Claudia left early, just as Ian wanted to go out & he tantrumed until I took him out for a ride to Panoramas. He still fussed a lot though, & when we got back home he would not stop screaming until we went on another ride. One ride to Evergreen Station & a third to Panoramas later, he was still very fussy. Pooh Bear & tofu helped. Boyce put him down; he slept for 2 hrs. & wanted to go for another car ride about 5 min. after waking up. I tried to get him to play in the yard twice—both did not work. We came back inside screaming & thrashing. He finally calmed down with Pooh Bear (4th time today!) & I tried a worktime with just a few of his favorite books. He screamed & got furious all over again & almost ripped Busy Bear in half. He calmed back down with chips, then

Cl. & B came home & Cl. was able to get him to play in the yard after 10-15 minutes of crying.

Lots of teeth grinding today.

But on a Sunday three days later, Claudia reported much success:

AM: I forgot to move the car out of sight, but just one ride to Panoramas was OK. He got out & ran happily.

WORKTIME: 30 min. Very good.

Books: <u>A Sleepy Story, I Am A Bunny, Bialosky Goes Out, Ian's Birthday, My Horse, Busy Bear, Colors</u> Games: all x4—wiggled his own thumb. Too excited about "open/shut" to clap on his own

Toys: wood animals puzzle X 2—excellent! circus puzzle X 1— excellent.—flying flags;—button can;—button & chip can together, just 2 prompts;—block tower of 6, 2 X , no prompts

PM: 2 X going out to yard, swinging & playing on glider & slide (w/ my prompting)

Bedtime: Ian went to get his pajamas for Boyce. No crying but laughing all night long.

By the autumn of 1987, there were days that seemed little less than stellar breakthroughs, proof of Ian's progression toward some kind of normalcy. This is Boyce writing on November 9:

When I got home (6 pm) Ian "asked" for 1-2-3 game, removing and lining up the 3 couch cushions himself. After supper, I played with him in his room from 7:30 until 8:45—a new variant on the "stand behind seated Boyce, flap his hair, and get flipped over in a somersault" game. Variation was the addition of a billed cap, which Ian put on my head (I secured it, saying "put hat on"), then he would knock it off before flapping my hair and being flipped by me. He obviously loved it, keeping it up for over an hour.

Ian does a lot of imitative behavior with his movies now. Examples: In <u>Free to Be</u>, runs when Atalanta runs (has been doing this one for weeks). In <u>Secret of NIMH</u>, asks for bath water to be trickling when Nicodemus, Justin, and Mrs. Brisby are in the boat under the old mill and there is water dripping down. In <u>Goldilocks</u>, Ian opens our front door when, early in the movie, the bears open their door to go outside. Ian also turns off the lights in his room early in the movie when the poor quality of our print makes the scene dark. He "falls down" when Goldilocks sits in Baby Bear's chair and it collapses. Only one week later, however, Ian was refusing to watch *any* of his videos except for a cartoon version of *Robin Hood*, demanding that it be started again the moment that it ended, watching it ten, even twenty times in succession, flapping his fingers or other objects in front of his eyes as the television droned nearby.

On November 19, Claudia made this entry in the journal, her scrawled handwriting reflecting her mounting stress:

Ian is in <u>bad shape</u>. He sat in front of the TV w/ only snowy picture and flicked toy cars in front of his face for 30 min. after the movie ended. Then on his ride he fussed & would not run even though I carried him down into the trees. I even tried driving the car over to the fence & he still would not get out of the car. He stayed in the car for 30 min. alone w/ door open after the last ride & finally came in on his own. Pointed to movie—<u>Robin Hood</u> again. Awoke from his nap—watched <u>Robin Hood</u>, then sat on floor and flapped cars in front of his face for 2 $^{1/2}$ hours!! This breaks my heart. What regression!

Better days finally followed, days when Ian didn't need—what was it?—the stimulation or the security of his particular types of perseveration, the flapping of objects inches from his eyes, the same movie played time after time after time; days when he would smile at his sister and, for the briefest moment, would seem to pay attention to the ways in which she played; days when he actually didn't scream. There were wonderful, if only occasional, times when books truly could capture his attention; and there were others, equally encouraging, when his movies seemed to offer him something more than utter sameness, hour on maddening hour, times when they were bright and fascinating stories and Ian simply was a receptive, wide-eyed child.

There have been occasions when people whom I care about have commented to me with some concern, "Isn't it a shame that Ian is so fixated by television?" They've tended to be, it is true, the sorts of people from my own generation who see the cathode-ray tube as the flickering mesmerizer of the masses, the source of most everything that's wrong with the world—from rampant illiteracy to the hoary rise of Ronald Reagan—and who claim that the only TV they ever have watched has been "Masterpiece Theatre," on the rarest of occasions and on someone else's set.

I don't share their sentiments in general, and in Ian's context, I'm sure I've responded to them querulously, feigning uncertainty about just what they mean, then telling them, in effect, that I don't think they understand. You see, it isn't as though Ian were a classic kind of couch potato, and he *does* have some taste, after all; he doesn't watch Sally Jessy Raphael or "Rescue 911." In fact, he is entirely uninterested in anything that is broadcast—not Bert and Ernie or Bryant Gumbel on a daily basis, not the Super Bowl once a year. Instead, Ian is a movie buff—he keeps his own collection— and people who've seen *Casablanca* or *The Rocky Horror Picture Show* twenty or thirty times can't hold a candle to him. He has seen the animated *Charlotte's Web,* I would wager, fifteen *hundred* times; and his parents regularly have had to make new copies of it and other favorites because he literally wears them out.

Royce and Claudia shudder to think, I know, what their lives would have been like if Ian had come their way prior to the dawning of the age of the videocassette. While other families curse their VCRs for being so nearly unprogrammable, Royce instead has added VCR repair to his household repertoire, and he and Claudia have always hoarded hand-me-downs and closeout specials against the nearby day when Ian's current machine surely would die. In his early days of trauma and throughout his life, Ian seldom has been far from a videotape player and its companion television and their uncanny capacity to calm him—but what I mean, of course, is a given *movie's* ability to quell a raging tantrum, its knack for a time, at least, for setting things right by telling him a tale.

I've often wondered whether he as readily might have relied on, let's say, toasters—the ritual, dependable dropping of the bread into tandem slots, the building, rising heat, the coils glowing orange, the bread transformed at last and popping up with some completion—to anchor him throughout his day, to provide him with some solace. Could building forts from plastic blocks, or making mountains out of mattresses, or banging his head relentlessly against a bedroom wall, God forbid, have served him as successfully as his movies?

I'm convinced the answer is no. From an uncle's necessarily patchy perspective, it seems sure to me that Ian's movies have made all the difference, that they've given him far more than repetition, that they have *meant* much more than sameness. Even at ages two and three, it was clear that Ian truly watched and listened to what unraveled on his bedroom television. He would carefully, meticulously line toy cars across the carpet, his eyes never seeming interested in the screen; sometimes he would demand that favorite music play simultaneously with a movie, their combined sound tracks creating a cacophony he somehow seemed to need; yet he would scream in sudden anguish *if Dumbo* didn't begin at the beginning, and with his frightened cries he would plead with his parents for them to speed the tape through the portions of *The Return of the Black Stallion* and *Lady and the Tramp* that he found terrifying. He began early on, as Boyce noted, to mimic scenes from some of them, and dolls and toy representations of cartoon characters—the ensemble cast of *Winnie-the-Pooh* in particular—became his bedroom buddies, his fastest friends, vital allies against what lay beyond his bedroom door.

What Ian's movies offered him—it seems to me, most importantly—was the organizing, ordering, delineating aspect of narrative. With their bright colors, festive music, and busy animated action, they were, nonetheless, a comforting, *quiet* counterpoint to the sensory bombardment that otherwise beset his brain. They offered him, even couched inside cartoons, realities—limited, controlled, mercifully measured—that he couldn't manage, that he couldn't distill on his own. And every narrative, each one of even the simplest stories, is its own reality, of course, a realm unto itself, a world comfortably contained.

"To classify consciousness as the action of organic machinery," sociobiologist Edward O. Wilson wrote in *On Human Nature,*

> is in no way to underestimate its power. In Sir Charles Sherrington's splendid metaphor, the brain is an "enchanted loom where millions of flashing shuttles weave a dissolving pattern." Since the mind recreates reality from the abstractions of the sense impressions, it can equally well simulate reality by recall and fan-

tasy. The brain invents stories and runs imagined and remembered events back and forth
through time.

Millions of flashing shuttles, their pattern ever dissolving
it is a fine metaphor and it's reminiscent of the necessarily
more prosaic notion of the convergence zone—the momentary interweaving of disparate threads of neural data into
a fabric that becomes the word *cup,* the word *cow,* in the
milliseconds before another word is woven and a story is under way. In a normal brain, notes Wilson, the senses supply
the raw material out of which consciousness is shaped, and
"reality" is merely the ordered collection of those myriad bits
of information.

What happened in Ian's case, I conceive—and surely what
happens still—is that those convergence zones for language,
as well as for certain kinds of cognition perhaps, chronically
retrieve too much of one type of sensory information, too
little of another, integrating them poorly or perhaps not at
all—the intricate, momentary synchronizing demanded by
the linking of words into sounds and concepts rendered haywire, neural data converging, to be sure, but only in a kind
of utter disarray. If that indeed is this little boy's predicament, if neural information tends to run rampant in his
cerebrum instead of blending, fusing, harmonizing toward
some successful end, then is it any surprise that stories—tales
he knows so well that they effectively become his own—matter enormously to him? Doesn't it make some simple sense
that he finds musical melodies and rhyming verse equally

attractive—essential, *ordered* counterpoints as well to the tumult inside his skull?

It's true, of course, that some of his obsession with his movies can be accounted for by his demand for daily ritual—the desperate need for today to commence with *Pooh* because yesterday did, as did the day before—yet that need for sameness in his schedule is obviously also a desire for structure and a kind of order he otherwise can't impose. Stories on videotape simply offer him that much more—a world in which the toys of a boy named Christopher Robin come to life again every day, in which a bashful bear named Pooh is always hungrily obsessed with honey; or a similarly secure, dependable place where a young elephant turns his ridiculed ears into wings, where he soars *absolutely* each time the tape begins to turn and the story once again is told.

What narrative offers each of us is exegesis, a commentary on what we encounter in our lives, yet it may well be that the *process* of describing and explaining is far more important than any specific thing described, explained, or interpreted. It may be that narrative is a kind of mimicking of the way our brains successfully order and make sense of information. It may be that for Ian, narrative offers him the only order he knows.

There is a fundamental and, to my mind, fascinating question, one I can't begin to answer, a question even the cleverest scholars tend to shy away from or amble carefully around, and it is this: Is abstract thought possible without language? Put another way: Is language the sole medium through which we think?

It may be some years since you've done so, but think for a moment, for example, about Winnie-the-Pooh. Are you doing so with words? Or is it with wordless *images* that you bring him back to mind? Now name his playmates and re-create, as best you can, the place they inhabit. The names, of course, are linguistic symbols, but are you otherwise employing language? If your melon is much like mine, the truth is that you can't be sure. You simply begin to think about a bear—or your troubled bank account, or the brain-taxing business of Stephen Hawking's black hole evaporation theory—and the process is so sudden and encompassing that you can't describe or decipher it.

Albert Einstein reportedly was convinced that he thought in images absent words. Near the opposite end of the thinking spectrum, I suspect that my cognition is mostly word-based, and among my slim evidence is the fact that although I seldom can tell you the color of someone's eyes, I often can recall that person's peculiar turns of phrase, and song lyrics and advertising jingles stick with me for decades, to my discouragement and regret, perhaps because the "thinking" I've done about them has tended to focus on their words. Those two examples may say as much about my memory processes as my meager stabs at what neuroscientists call "higher cortical thinking," yet nonetheless, those are my suspicions. I believe I rely more readily on language than on pictures or far more ephemeral *concepts* to contain and organize my thinking.

Derek Bickerton, who envisions language as arising from our need to represent reality—a view that locates him in the vicinity of Chomsky's camp on the language organ question—believes that language and thinking are inextricably intertwined, and his argument in support of that perspective is simple and straightforward: The kind of cognition of which humans are capable clearly involves symbolic representation, and if thinking and language are *not* interrelated, then the brain necessarily has evolved two (or even more) distinct and separate representational systems, and that possibility would seem so uneconomical and impractical as to make it most unlikely. Bickerton does imagine, however, that a single and perhaps innate representational system could logically be as adept with images as it is with words. "It is quite conceivable," he writes,

> that thought processes conducted entirely in linguistic terms could, before arriving at conscious levels, be translated into imagery. Alternatively, images could simply take the place of words, but they would still have to be organized by syntactic mechanisms. In either case, if the elements of thought, whatever they might be, were not arranged in some type of formal structure in which their relations to one another were lawful and predictable, but instead they were just allowed to swirl around as they pleased, then no serious thought process could be carried through.

Thus, either some mysterious additional way of structuring thought is available, or syntax discharges that function.

Syntax again. Rules and regulations. Bickerton's contention, oversimplified, is that we employ rules, some sort of structure, to mediate and control thinking, much as language demands and is built from rules. And surely the complex cerebral symbol-making that evolved as human language began to flourish bears much in common, if indeed it doesn't share everything, with the symbolic processes at the core of abstract thought. It is a notion that answers the question of whether we can think without language by eclipsing it, by positing the possibility that one does not depend on the other. Rather, perhaps, language and thought are separate channels of the same representational river, its banks and its gradient shaped by syntax, its course unconstrained and limitless.

Considering that argument for a moment, Hannah and Antonio Damasio's theory of cerebral convergence zones comes back to mind. The Damasios argue—persuasively, it seems to me—that the cerebral cortex contains physical, identifiable, exceedingly sophisticated, and surely fragile zones that mediate the many components of thought in precisely the same way they coalesce and control language. Might syntax—whether it is genetically coded or the product of cultural imitation and experiment—have its neural locus in these zones? Is it possible, at least to some degree, to account for the wide range of intellectual and linguistic capabilities among our species by anatomical and neurochemical dissimilarities within convergence zones? I have said that Ian's cerebral disarray may be explainable, perhaps even in large part, by damage to one or more of them, but is it therefore syntax that Ian so seriously lacks?

"About the age of three," observes critic Peter Brooks in his book *Reading for the Plot,*

> a child begins to show the ability to put together a narrative in a coherent fashion and especially the capacity to recognize narratives, to judge their well-formedness. Children quickly become virtual Aristotelians, insisting upon any storyteller's observation of the "rules," upon proper beginnings, middles, and particularly ends. Narrative may be a special ability or competence that we learn, a certain subset of the general language code which, when mastered, allows us to summarize and retransmit narratives in other words and other languages, to transfer them into other media, while remaining recognizably faithful to the original narrative structure and message.

Every weary parent understands firsthand that early explosion of interest in stories to which Brooks refers—every child's need for an endless sequence of simple stories that explain when that time called tomorrow will at last commence, where Daddy is always going, or how and why he bakes a cake. Every enchanted parent knows how stories read at evening bedsides and shared cozily on sofas introduce wonder and worlds of possibility into their youngsters' lives. Even people like me who aren't parents can begin to apprehend children's desire and their utter demand for narrative rules. Stories must have characters—they must be *about* mothers or kids or cats or scary monsters. They must be located in time—once upon a time or perhaps that time we still remember—as well as place, and they must describe or attempt to re-create transitions, shifts, passages from one place to the next, from one condition to another—dogs must shy away from bears or a bear must get his head stuck in a hive—but something has to *happen,* a story has to have a plot.

In a file of family memorabilia that is actually just an overflowing cardboard box, my parents keep the first formal story I wrote, one I titled "Green Valley League," its short manuscript typed for me late in the 1950s by my father, the only copy still extant on long-since-yellowed onionskin. I probably was eight or nine when I wrote it, and I suppose I offer that as something of a mild defense; you'd think that after thirty years or so, you might grow a bit more sanguine about your work, but this case simply doesn't seem to warrant it:

There was going to be a little league in Green Valley, the town Bob lived in. Bob's team was called the Cubs. The coach was Mr. Dell. Bob wanted to play shortstop, but a boy twelve was going out for shortstop too. His name was Dan. He was very good. Bob thought he would have to work really hard to beat him. Bob saw that Dan's glove was new but his was getting old and worn out. Dan began making fun of it. "Look at your glove, Bob, where did you get it, in the trash can?" "No, my dad gave it to me two years ago," said Bob. "I don't think that there is anything wrong with it." Then the coach said, "Get out in the field and we will work our way up to bat." The first boy struck out, then Dan hit a fly ball, but another boy caught it. Bob was up next. He hit a ball out of the park. "That was a good hit, Bob," said the coach. The next day he told the boys where they would play. Bob just made it for shortstop. Dan played right field. "Thanks, Coach," said the boys. "We think we will have the <u>very best team</u>."

I underlined those last words for an effect that's now lost on me, and I can't help but cringe at the story's leaden tone, among other things, at its blatant moralizing, and a kind of hale and brave-hearted attitude that would have befitted Horatio Alger. It's curious to me from my present vantage point that the story seems more readily reflective of the kinds of boys' sports books we read in the 1950s than it is of anything I truly knew or was concerned with in my life—it's a story about baseball stories—yet it is a passingly adequate narrative, nonetheless. Its main character—its protagonist, in the lingo of the English department—is Bob, of course; the setting is summer in Green Valley, and the thing that happens is that with pluck and a level swing Bob does indeed make the team. Its attendant subplot, if you will—and the thing that makes its author seem far too prissy for comfort—is that despite the talent of the boy named Dan, surely it's his little taunt that results in the ridicule of right field.

Now, compare that narrative to a story called "To the Moon," written only the other day by my sister Carol's nine-year-old daughter, Laurel, its text composed in her still-awkward hand and accompanied by an illustration, bound with staples into a little book on sheets of orange paper:

> Once not long ago, a young man told himself that he had to do something in his life so it would not be wasted on junk food. So he went to the moon, where he met a moon girl. They got married that very day. And they had a moon kid and lived happily ever after, trying to understand each other.

Laurel's drawing shows a "moon girl" saying "Ooo hhhh do" in a bubble over her head, and the young man responding "What?" I laughed heartily when I first read it, and Laurel *is* a comic, yet even at age nine she surely understands the delightful double entendre of her story's final words. They describe the very literal problem of translation, yet they also represent a universal kind of conundrum— the fact that often you can't seem to figure out the very people to whom you're closest, or even more specifically, that happily-ever-after is a condition filled with pitfalls. Laurel has written a symbolic story—a tale about more than it seems to be on its surface; she too has obeyed narrative's rules, and never mind the fact that she's also subjected her poor uncle to fiction-writing shame.

My grandmother, Roxie Elizabeth Lewis Rutherford—"Dandy" to Laurel and me and almost everyone else—didn't consider herself a storyteller. She wasn't the sort of person who takes up folktales in lieu of arts and crafts, and *she* would have told you that it was her husband who had been the raconteur. For her, telling stories was simply a natural and congenial means of communicating, a lifelong entertainment, a languorous, word-lit way of connecting with the people whom she cared about until the winter day she died. "Well, sir," Dandy would say colloquially, and that was the certain cue that she was remembering a story. "Well, sir," she would add minutes later to signal the tale's turning point, its subtle epiphany, occasionally its crisis. Her stories weren't meant to moralize or to be blatantly instructive, and she seldom offered a commentary other than to exclaim, "Can you imagine?" *Can you imagine?* she would ask us as her stories closed, and it was as though she were asking,

"Isn't life the most amazing thing you've heard of?" It was as though she were inquiring whether the story itself had come alive.

Stories had shaped and delighted Dandy's eighty-eight years, and although she seldom, if ever, wrote one down or gave any conscious, calculating thought to a story's telling, she too knew the rules. She, like you and me, understood them intuitively, and it seems sure as I mention her that narrative must be, in Brooks's terminology, "a certain subset of the general language code." The fundamental elements of syntactic structure, common to every language, are subject and predicate—noun and verb. Each language's basal components for conveying meaning are simply and identically those two—a person, a concept, a *thing,* coupled with the action it undergoes or a statement of its condition—and they bear far more than a basic relationship to the fundamental elements of narrative: character and plot.

The bare structure of a story duplicates and surely is closely kindred to the simplest process of sentence structure—sensory, cognitive, syntactic, and lexicographic data momentarily merge in our cortices, and it is their sudden and inscrutable convergence that allows us to give breath to stories in very much the same way that it permits us, seemingly effortlessly, to link nouns with verbs. The rules are simple, and they are inescapably shared. The sentence *Ian cannot speak* is constructed of the same neural materials as is a tale about two mongrel dogs who can't muster much in the way of courage. The fanciful sentence *Ian speaks beautifully* is built in much the same manner as a story about a resolute, romantic man who ventures to the moon. Both sentences and stories are utterly constricted and contained by their consonant structures, yet those same structures allow *limitless* combinations of subject and predicate, of character and action. Our brains—those of almost all of us—are marvelously adept indeed at blending morphemes into meaning, at performing the kind of neurochemical alchemy that turns symbols into substantial sentences, then sentences into an infinite trove of tales.

I an was three years old when Dandy died. She lived long enough to know and to grieve in her own internalized way about the torment and the isolation he suffered. He was old enough at her end to have been able to visit her country house on a few occasions and to have run with real and visible relief beside the weathered fence surrounding it. She would remain wonderfully calm, almost beatific, as Ian screamed near the chair where she spent her days, and she always would mention to my sister what a beautiful boy he was.

In the weeks before Dandy died, my mother had discussed with her whether some of the money that she would derive from Dandy's small estate might go toward buying Ian a computer, and Dandy had responded with a kind of quiet pleasure. My grandmother had been born the year before the century turned—almost a decade before Orville and Wilbur Wright convinced the world that they had found a way to fly—and she had been fascinated seventy years later when some young men actually made it to the moon. She had never seen a personal computer, but despite her advanced years and her own isolation, she was intrigued by what she had read and heard about these small, surely magical machines that could store and retrieve and readily manipulate language. It seemed to her that, yes, one day a computer might just give Ian a surrogate sort of speech. It seemed to both of them that perhaps it could enable him to shape words into sentences in time, that it just might allow him to tell his stories in a way his brain alone could not. "Can you imagine?" she asked my mother in her small and soon silent voice.

ABOUT THE AUTHOR

Russell Martin's nonfiction book *Beethoven's Hair*, a United States bestseller and a *Washington Post* Book of the Year, has been published in twenty-one translated editions and is the subject of a Gemini-award-winning film of the same name. His highly acclaimed book *Picasso's War* has been published in seven international editions; *Out of Silence* was named by The Bloomsbury Review as one of the fifteen best books of its first fifteen years of publication, and *A Story That Stands Like a Dam: Glen Canyon and the Struggle for the Soul of the West* won the Caroline Bancroft History Prize.

He directed, produced, and wrote the documentary film *Beautiful Faces*, which won the Silver Palm Award of the Mexico International Film Festival. He produced and co-wrote the Monette Horwitz Prize-winning documentary film *Two Spirits*, and is an award-winning, internationally published author of two critically acclaimed novels, *The Sorrow of Archaeology* and *Beautiful Islands*, as well as many nonfiction books. He has written for *Time*, the *New York Times*, *New York Times Magazine*, and National Public Radio. His books and screenplays have been optioned by

Robert Redford's Wildwood Enterprises, the Denver Center Theatre Company, and New World Television, and he is a veteran script doctor and consultant.

He taught an annual creative nonfiction course at Colorado College for two decades and has served on the faculty at numerous writing conferences. When Colorado College awarded him an honorary doctorate, the citation read, in part, "Mr. Martin offers to general audiences precise and accurate, but highly readable, studies of extraordinarily complex issues. He does more: he sees beyond what is already known; he moves beyond synthesis to new insights. His work is disciplined, analytical, and creative. It is also profoundly humane."

He lives in Scottsdale, Arizona, USA.

www.ingramcontent.com/pod-product-compliance
Lightning Source LLC
Chambersburg PA
CBHW060807030726
47503CB00002B/379